D1547485

Reparations to Africa

PENNSYLVANIA STUDIES IN HUMAN RIGHTS
Bert B. Lockwood, Jr., Series Editor

A complete list of books in the series is available from the publisher.

Reparations to Africa

RHODA E. HOWARD-HASSMANN

with Anthony P. Lombardo

PENN

University of Pennsylvania Press
Philadelphia

Published by
University of Pennsylvania Press
Philadelphia, Pennsylvania 19104-4112

Printed in the United States of America on acid-free paper

10 9 8 7 6 5 4 3 2 1

Library of Congress Cataloging-in-Publication Data

Howard-Hassmann, Rhoda E., 1948–
Reparations to Africa / Rhoda E. Howard-Hassmann ; with Anthony P. Lombardo.
p. cm.—(Pennsylvania studies in human rights)
Includes bibliographical references and index.
ISBN 978-0-8122-4101-3 (alk. paper)
1. Reparations for historical injustices—Africa. 2. Africans—Reparations.
3. Economic assistance—Africa. 4. Slave trade—Africa. 5. Colonies—Africa.
I. Lombardo, Anthony P. II. Title.
K970.H69 2008
362.840096—dc22

2008012682

To the many Africans who gave their time and thoughts to this book,

and to my son, Patrick McCabe,
with thanks for the twenty-seven years of unbounded joy he has given me

Contents

Reparations to Africa

Chapter 1

Reparations to Africa

A New Kind of Justice

This book discusses the claim for reparations to Africa from the West for the slave trade, colonialism, and some postcolonial relations. By "Africa," I mean sub-Saharan Africa. I am a political sociologist, a specialist in international human rights with a background in African studies. This disciplinary and substantive background informs my views, although I also draw on philosophy, history, and law. I analyze the social movement for reparations to Africa, the arguments reparationists put forth, historical debates about the claims reparationists make, and some potential remedies for past wrongs against the continent.

In the popular view, reparations are associated with financial compensation, often to individuals. In actuality, however, financial compensation is often given to groups, for collective projects to remedy past ill-treatment. Moreover, reparations include other, more symbolic yet often very important actions, such as acknowledgment of past injuries, apologies for them, and access to the truth about past events.

I believe that the West—or certain Western entities—owes Africa acknowledgment of past wrongs, apology for them, and, as far as possible, the truth about the past. I support reparations to individual Africans for crimes against them in the recent past. I have no objection in principle, moreover, to financial reparations to Africa, or Africans as a collectivity, for damages their ancestors suffered in the distant past. If in the future some Western states decided to pay such reparations, or if international or national courts mandated them, I would support such decisions. The sections on the law as it currently stands, in subsequent chapters of this book, are not meant to suggest that the law should not change.

Nevertheless, as a legal, political, and practical matter, I believe that pursuit of financial reparations to Africa is not a good strategy, for reasons I explain throughout this volume. As a matter of principle, moreover, I believe that distributive justice for living Africans should take precedence over restorative justice for crimes committed against Africans long dead. I argue for distributive justice rooted in the international imperative to fulfill everyone's economic rights. I believe that the West is obliged to assist Africans to realize their economic rights now, in the present, regardless of who or what in the past caused the enormous suffering of so many of them. The international law of economic rights provides stronger backing for Western responsibility to Africa than a claim for reparations for injuries to Africans long dead. Western publics who vote on their governments' policies are more likely to be swayed by the needs of living Africans than by accounts of long-past historical wrongs.

Some readers may object to my use of the term "the West" because it homogenizes all Western history, experience, and thought. I have been engaged in scholarly debates about "Western" and non-Western views of human rights for a quarter century and have often objected to this homogenizing tendency. "The West" is the right term, however, in this book. The claim for reparations to Africa is part of a larger discussion in which many Africans contend that they are routinely oppressed by the West. To them, the West is the developed North Atlantic world of former slave-traders and colonialists. Therefore, many activists for reparations suggest that the West has particular obligations to remedy the destruction it has wrought on Africa. Nevertheless, although I use the term "the West," I do so with caution. Throughout, I note the responsibilities of non-Western actors, including Africans themselves, Muslim slave-traders, the former Soviet Union, and contemporary states such as China, for African suffering. "The West" is a useful heuristic term, but the West is not the only actor relevant to analysis of Africa.

This book is an introduction to the debate about reparations to Africa. It is not, and is not meant to be, a general theory of reparations. Finally, it does not reflect events that occurred after July 31, 2007.

Reparations and Recognition

Africans have been victims of the West, reparationists claim, since the Portuguese landed on their continent in 1443 in search of gold, slaves, and other valuables.[1] Not only the period of the slave trade but also the colonial period and, indeed, the postcolonial period were characterized by massive Western exploitation of Africa, in the view of reparationists. Such massive perceived exploitation, one might think, would impel strong calls for reparations. Yet the social movement for reparations to Africa is small and weak, as I document in Chapters 3 and 4, and does not presently influence international relations.

Reparations claims are a form of demand for social justice. Reparationists seek both material and symbolic compensation for past ill-treatment.

This sets reparations claims apart from demands for redistribution of wealth. Redistributive politics focus domestically on inequalities among social classes and internationally on inequalities among states or regions. There is some concern that reparations politics will remove attention from redistributive demands because the demand for social recognition takes rhetorical priority over the demand for redistribution of wealth.[2] Groups whose ancestors suffered injustices in the past now want that suffering recognized by their past abusers, even if none of the individuals who suffered is still alive. They also desire recognition as a collectivity with a particular history, a history that in part shapes their present identity.

The gold standard of reparations claims is the successful Jewish movement for reparations for the Holocaust (discussed in Chapter 4).[3] Jewish suffering during the Holocaust has long been recognized, and Jewish victims have received financial compensation and sometimes return of their property. Theirs is not, however, the only successful claim for reparations. Both Japanese Americans and Japanese Canadians—men, women, and children, citizens and noncitizens—were interned by their respective countries during World War II.[4] In the late 1980s, their respective governments apologized to them and gave them financial compensation.

Other groups have had different experiences obtaining recognition and compensation. It is estimated that during World War II the Japanese kidnapped about 200,000 women to work as sex slaves for Japanese soldiers. About three-quarters of these women died, many brutally murdered. Although they had been seeking reparations for several decades, as of early 2007 the few surviving women had not received what they considered to be an official apology from the Japanese government. Nor had they received any monetary reparations from the government of Japan, although a private compensation fund had been created.[5]

The social movement for reparations also derives in part from international discussions about how to reconcile previously antagonistic groups. In the mid-1990s, the South African government set up a Truth and Reconciliation Commission (TRC), whose objective was to ascertain the truth about human rights abuses in apartheid South Africa. Although it was not the world's first truth commission, others having previously been created in South America and elsewhere in Africa, the TRC set off an international discussion about reconciliation and the need for narrative truth. A narrative truth allows individuals to tell their stories; it also permits evolution of a new national history. The individual narratives of suffering are combined into a grand narrative that becomes the official national story of relations among groups within the country.

In the context of this discussion, it is not surprising that sub-Saharan Africans should also hope that their narrative truths would be recognized.

Aside from creation of a national narrative, recognition of past wrongs also requires atonement, acts of repentance, and guarantees of nonrepetition. The need for atonement appears to be a subtext in much of the African discussion of reparations. Hundreds of millions of Africans are overwhelmed by their suffering. Life expectancy at birth in sub-Saharan Africa in 2004 was only 46.1 years.[6] Largely as a consequence of AIDS, in most countries between a third and a half of children born between 2000 and 2005 will not live to age forty; in several countries the number was well over half.[7] In 2002, 44 percent of sub-Saharan Africans lived on less than $1.00 per day, and 75 percent on less than $2.00 per day.[8] Moreover, since achieving independence many countries have experienced civil wars, and some have experienced genocide. Much of this devastation, reparationists argue, can be traced to the slave trade, colonialism, and postcolonial relations with the West.

African reparationists ask for recognition of their suffering at the hands of the West, for public atonement in the form of an apology, and for financial compensation. One might consider this call for reparations merely rhetoric, or a "tactical political move,"[9] to demand more attention and aid. But it would seem that it is more than such a tactical move. There is a genuine desire for recognition not only of African suffering but also of African humanity.

Reparations in International Law

Unfortunately for the movement for reparations to Africa, international law does not mandate that retroactive reparations be paid for the slave trade, colonialism, or postcolonial relations. Although laws concerning reparations developed during the last decades of the twentieth century and continued to develop in the twenty-first, they referred for the most part to reparations between states for violations of treaty obligations or other agreements.[10] Many international and national principles and laws also mandate that individuals, or their immediate families, be granted reparations for gross human rights violations. Reparations are particularly required under international law for genocide, crimes against humanity, and war crimes. Generally speaking, there is no statute of limitation on punishments for such crimes, but in most cases the crimes must have been outlawed before they were committed.

These general principles render it unlikely, although not impossible, that African reparationists will succeed in legal claims against the

West for financial compensation for historic wrongs. As I discuss in Chapter 5, the slave trade was illegal only during the latter part of its existence, and colonialism was not formally declared illegal until 1960. Thus, reparations for these two periods would fall foul of the principle that crimes must be considered illegal at the time they are committed in order to mandate reparations.

Reparations law is also oriented toward individual victims of crimes such as extrajudicial execution, disappearance, and torture. Although sometimes victims' immediate heirs are also entitled to reparations, reparations to descendants several generations removed are almost unheard of, except for restoration of property, for example, to the great-grandchildren of victims of the Nazis. Reparations, in any case, are not oriented to national or continental groups. Thus, there is no precedent in reparations cases to compensate Africans for the loss of some of their ancestors in the transatlantic slave trade.

This short description does not mean, however, that there is no possibility of reparations to Africa. Law evolves as new claims for justice arise, as in the case of the United Nations Convention on the Prevention and Punishment of the Crime of Genocide (1948), which followed the Nuremberg trials of Nazi war criminals after World War II. Moreover, there is no legal ban on retroactive restorative rather than criminal justice.[11] The purpose of restorative justice is to repair damaged relations between different entities, even if no law was violated.

In 2002 the International Criminal Court (ICC) was formally established. The ICC defines reparations to encompass "restitution, compensation and rehabilitation."[12] However, this definition applies to reparations to individual victims by persons convicted by the ICC of perpetrating crimes against them. Moreover, the ICC's jurisdiction is over genocide, war crimes, and crimes against humanity, not over the entirety of human rights and humanitarian law. Its jurisdiction is also prospective, meaning that it cannot convict people of crimes committed before the court was established. As of early 2007, there were cases before the ICC involving Democratic Republic of Congo, Central African Republic, Uganda, and Sudan (Darfur). All of these cases, however, referred to intra-African relations, not relations between Africa and the West.

Despite these obstacles, there is a growing international consensus on the basic principles underlying reparations. In 2005 the Office of the (United Nations) High Commission for Human Rights (OHCHR) issued a resolution entitled *Basic Principles and Guidelines on the Right to a Remedy and Reparations for Victims of Gross Violations of International Human Rights Law and Serious Violations of International Humanitarian Law*, which summarizes previous reports and recommendations about the law of reparations.[13] In December of the same year, the United Nations General Assembly (UNGA) passed a resolution endorsing the OHCHR's basic principles.[14] This resolution is "soft," unenforceable law. For it to become "hard" law requires that states incorporate it into their domestic laws.

Nevertheless, the developing law provides some indication of what reparations might mean in the case of Africa. The *Basic Principles* cast a wider net than the ICC and refer to victims of violations of international human rights law and humanitarian law in general. The principles define victims as "persons who individually or collectively suffered harm . . . [and] where appropriate . . . the immediate family or dependants of the direct victim."[15] The principles provide for reparations to groups as well as individuals, defining "group" as "persons who are targeted collectively."[16] Victims, according to the *Basic Principles*, are entitled to "restitution, compensation, rehabilitation, satisfaction, and guarantees of nonrepetition."[17]

Restitution includes acts to "restore the victim to the original situation before the gross violations of international human rights law or serious violations of international humanitarian law occurred."[18] For Africa, this is impossible: even if it were retroactively ruled that the entire period of Western-African relations was one of gross violations of Africans' human rights, the original situation could not be restored. It would be impossible to determine what the situation was in the fifteenth century or at any later date taken as the appropriate one for restoration. Nor indeed, one assumes, would African reparationists wish to return to the fifteenth century. Their complaint is that the likely evolution of their continent toward a progressively higher standard of living was blocked by the transatlantic slave trade and colonialism.

Compensation, the second aspect of reparations, covers "any economically assessable damage" resulting from the wrongs, including physical or mental harm, lost opportunities or earnings, material damages, moral damages, costs for social services, and the like.[19] The focus of the African reparations movement is on compensation for almost six centuries of deprivation by the Western world, but the damage allegedly caused by the West is not economically assessable, in any practical sense (discussed in Chapters 5 through 9).

Rehabilitation, the third aspect of reparation, includes medical and psychological care and legal and social services.[20] These are not aspects of reparations commonly referred to in African claims, although one might argue that financial reparations would permit more African investment in health care and social welfare. Thus, in the African case, financial compensation would be a tool for rehabilitation.

Satisfaction is the fourth aspect of reparation. It includes cessation of current violations, verification of the facts, and "full and public disclosure of the truth." It also refers to public apology, "commemoration and tributes to the victims," and inclusion of an accurate account of the violations of international human rights law and international humanitarian law in educational material at all levels.[21] Those seeking reparations to Africa do seem to want satisfaction of this kind (discussed in Chapters 10 and 11), although that satisfaction is secondary to their desire for material reparations.

Finally, the *Basic Principles* mandates nonrepetition of harm. Nonrepetition might seem irrelevant to African reparationists because there is no longer a legal slave trade from Africa and colonialism is no longer practiced. However, some supporters of reparations do consider that postcolonial economic and political relations between the West and Africa constitute continued exploitation of that continent, for which guarantees of nonrepetition are required (discussed in Chapter 8).

Aside from the ICC laws and the *Basic Principles*, there is a developing national jurisprudence, especially in the United States, that might offer hope for reparations to Africa. These developments are in the area of civil law.

The United States' Alien Torts Claims Act (ATCA), passed in 1789, can be used by non-Americans to sue other non-Americans in U.S. civil courts for torts (wrongs) that occurred outside the United States, if the court concludes that a crime is so horrendous that it has universal jurisdiction over it, irrespective of where it occurred and who committed it. Generally speaking, such crimes are deemed to shock the conscience of humankind, and include piracy, the slave trade, attacks on or hijacking of aircraft, genocide, war crimes, and some acts of terrorism.[22] Increasingly, they also include gross violations of human rights, such as torture; the torturer is deemed to be *hostis humanis generis*, an enemy of all humankind.[23] Even though an American court can decide it has universal jurisdiction, however, ATCA requires the presence in the United States of both the complainant and the alleged perpetrator.

The first modern case tried in the United States under the ATCA was *Filartiga v. Peňa-Irala* (1980). Jose Filartiga was a teenaged boy tortured to death in Paraguay in 1976. After his death, his sister emigrated from Paraguay to the United States, where she discovered that her brother's murderer had also immigrated. She and her parents won a judgment against the torturer for $15 million in damages, although it was never collected.[24] In 1990 two Ethiopian women sued their Ethiopian torturer under ATCA after one of the women encountered the torturer at an Atlanta hotel where she and he both worked. The court ruled against the torturer and awarded the victims compensatory and punitive damages.[25] Both these cases, however, involved living individuals who sued other living individuals for crimes committed in the recent past. Thus, they are not a precedent for claims that states owe reparations to Africans for crimes committed in the distant past.

Another area of U.S. civil law that holds out some hope for African reparationists is the right of private citizens to file suit against other private citizens or against private entities, such as corporations. These suits are not filed under ATCA but under ordinary civil law. In the 1990s Jewish and non-Jewish victims of the Nazis sued Swiss banks, European insurance companies, and European manufacturing companies in the United States. They sued these entities for keeping prewar Jewish deposits rather than turning them over to the owners or their heirs after the Holocaust, for not paying claims on insurance taken out by Jews, and for employing Jewish and non-Jewish slave laborers during World War II. The claimants won large collective judgments, although each individual received a rather small amount.[26] Moreover, formal organizations such as the World Jewish Congress were recognized as legitimate representatives of Jewish victims, as was the state of Israel, suggesting that a similar formal organization—perhaps the African Union (AU)—representing all Africans might be considered a legitimate claimant for reparations to Africa in the future.

Another civil case reaches back ninety years. In 2003 a U.S. court permitted an Armenian group to sue New York Life Insurance Company for nonpayment of insurance policies purchased by Armenians in Turkey before the Turkish genocide of the Armenians during World War I.[27] The extension of this time limit to 1915 might be considered a legal precedent for attempts by the Herero people of Namibia to sue for reparations for the genocide against them by German forces from 1904 to 1908 (discussed in Chapter 7).[28]

Another possible precedent for reparations to Africa might be contemporary land claims by indigenous peoples in Canada, the United States, New Zealand, and Australia, who demand that treaties their ancestors signed with European invaders, sometimes more than two centuries ago, be honored.[29] Although treaties are legal documents and adherence to their terms is legal justice, not reparation, such distant precedents might work in favor of African reparations, especially if those reparations are for lands lost to European settlers in such countries as Zimbabwe, Kenya, Namibia, and South Africa.

These legal developments suggest that there might be some mechanisms, in the United States and elsewhere in the Western world, for some Africans to sue some Western (or indeed, non-Western) entities for discrete cases of injustice that occurred in Africa during the preceding half century, perhaps the preceding century. One principle that activists cite as justification for reparations to Africa is "unjust enrichment" (discussed in Chapter 5). This is a legal term acknowledged under American law. There are also legal cases that refer to violations of human rights laws by corporations cooperating with dictatorial political regimes. One often cited case is that of Burmese citizens who sued, under ATCA, the American company Unocal for violation of their rights in Burma, specifically for "forced labor, torture, and crimes against humanity arising out of the development of a natural gas pipeline."[30] This might be considered a precedent to sue American corporations collaborating with dictatorial postcolonial African regimes, but it would be more difficult to use it as a precedent to sue for reparations for corporate abuse in the more distant past. Such cases depend, furthermore, upon interest by American lawyers, who take them on a contingency basis: the plaintiffs do not pay the lawyers' fees, but the lawyers are entitled to a percentage of the financial settlement if they win the case.

American law with regard to extraterritorial offenses (offenses outside American borders) by American corporations against the human rights of non-Americans is weak. In general, American courts enforce extraterritorial legal rights of American corporations, such as trademark laws, but do not enforce the rights of foreign citizens against those same corporations.[31] Nevertheless, African activists may be able to refer to precedents such as the Unocal case when they believe that U.S.–based corporations have violated the rights of specific groups of Africans. One such possible case (discussed in Chapter 9) concerns the environmental damage inflicted on parts of southeastern Nigeria by the Shell Oil Company.

A further difficulty in suing foreign corporations in U.S. courts is that domestic African corporations may be let off the hook.[32] This is a problem in South Africa, where domestic corporations owned by white South Africans may have been more deeply implicated than foreign corporations in supporting the illegal (under international law) apartheid system. So also, suits against non-African, but not African, individuals may ignore African responsibilities. For example, an attempt to sue Zimbabwean President Robert Mugabe under the ATCA failed because the American government claimed he "might be entitled to diplomatic immunity."[33] Yet, as I discuss in Chapter 9, Mugabe was one of the worst postcolonial abusers of Africans' human rights.

Transgenerational Justice

Aside from the legal difficulties it presents, the debate about whether Africans are owed reparations for past harms raises philosophical questions about transgenerational justice. In broad terms, the central question is whether there is such a thing as collective responsibility for past actions. Are collectivities, such as all citizens of a state, responsible for the crimes committed by some individual citizens, or are only those individuals responsible? This question has been central to ethical and scholarly thinking about Nazism since the time of the Nuremberg trials. One answer to it is that only individuals should be liable for criminal penalties. Many Germans opposed Nazism, and many others simply did not participate in the genocide: therefore, they were not responsible. In this view, individuals do not bear responsibility for the activities of the groups, including states, of which they are members if they did not participate in the crimes committed.[34]

Nevertheless, it is generally acknowledged in law and practice that states are continuous entities: "just as people do not disappear and reappear, the 'national person' is thought of as continuous."[35] Current governments of African states are liable for the debts of preceding governments, even if those debts were incurred by their predecessors by illegitimate means. Similarly, current governments of Western states may be thought liable for wrongs committed by preceding governments, whatever the responsibility, or lack thereof, of their individual citizens or indeed of the individuals who comprise the governments.

Some philosophers argue that individual citizens have a duty to ensure that the states they reside in act upon their responsibilities because those citizens are who they are in part because of their membership in those states. Alasdair MacIntyre argues, "I belong to this clan, that tribe, this nation. . . . As such I inherit from the past . . . a variety of debts, inheritances, rightful expectations and obligation."[36] Kok-Chor Tan argues in favor of transgenerational responsibility for colonialism. The cost of reparations, he says, is borne by the former colonial country, even if the individual citizens whose taxes pay that cost are not descendants of the colonizers. Neither the citizens of the nation that provides reparations nor their biological ancestors need be (or have been) personally liable for the act of colonization. Rather, "it is a civic duty . . . for persons to share in the burdens of justice of their society even if they are not personally responsible for the injustice that needs correcting. . . . Citizens have the duty to help sustain the justness of the institutions of their society by virtue of their being citizens, not by virtue of their past actions."[37]

Thus, in the view of these philosophers, transgenerational justice does not require that citizens bear personal responsibility for past actions. Rather, they argue for individual and collective responsibility to ameliorate the consequences of those actions. Sometimes individuals who are members of groups express vicarious shame about the group's actions,[38] even if the actions happened when the individuals were not group members—for example, because they were not yet born. Sometimes such individuals will assume that as members of a group, they bear responsibility for its actions. This is especially so when "the innocent individual is tied to a guilty collective through family relations and/or a common history, religion and culture."[39] Such is the situation in which many Westerners find themselves today, suffering "membership guilt":[40] to them, "a wrongdoing is an inheritance."[41] On the other hand, some individuals reject membership guilt, arguing that they were not born when the events occurred or that it was not their own biological ancestors who caused harm.

Philosophical questions pertain not only to who is responsible to offer reparations but also to who is entitled to receive them. Philosophers often ask if one can call for reparations for past actions in the absence of which one would not have been born. This is called the "nonidentity" problem.[42] One cannot regret, say such philosophers, those events that gave one life. Such a logical argument might well seem specious to real individuals, who might deplore the evils inflicted on their ancestors, even if without those evils they would not have been born. Many Africans, it can be surmised, are saddened or angered by the exploitation of their ancestors, even if they would not have been born without it. They all suffer, as it were, from the "contagion of injustice."[43] This contagion, argues Janna Thompson, might be considered damage to "family lines": even if an individual exists in part because of an unjust act, her family line was damaged by that act. Family lines, says Thompson, are "transgenerational relationships with a long history."[44]

Nevertheless, in law and practice reparations are normally (although not always) confined to the actual victims of injustices and their immediate families, as the *Basic Principles* previously cited confirm. In practice, reparations have been granted to Jewish and other victims of Nazism or their survivors, to Japanese Americans and Japanese Canadians interned in camps during World War II, and to various other immediate victims of injustices. The exception to this rule concerns treaty rights and property claims, which are not the concern of African reparationists.

A final philosophical, and also empirical, question about transgenerational justice concerns the reliability of counterfactual assumptions. Reparationists assume that Africa, its states, ethnic groups, and individuals would have been better off without contact with the West. But perhaps some would have been worse off. Perhaps because their ancestors sold slaves some Africans are now better off than they would otherwise have been. Perhaps others are better off because they were able to attend schools opened by Christian missionaries. Perhaps the introduction of modern commercial agriculture, industry, transportation, and communications has rendered the continent as a whole better off than it would have been had it remained at subsistence level for the last 500 years. Even if this last suggestion appears outrageously counterintuitive, it points to the difficulties of making counterfactual assumptions. Counterfactual assumptions are, in general, subject to "imperfect knowledge. . . . The counterfactual standard therefore cannot produce determinate restitutional sums."[45] Moreover, "there can be no empirical guide to choosing the appropriate counterfactual."[46]

These philosophical difficulties suggest that Africans who seek reparations are more likely to be successful if they focus on specific wrongs against specific individuals, perpetrated by specific institutions at specific times, rather than general reparations for five hundred years of exploitation. I make the case for this proposition in Chapter 4. It would be extremely difficult, and possibly unjust, to seek blanket reparations from all Western nations, or indeed from individual nations, for the entire history of their interaction with Africa. The call for blanket reparations for historical relations is fraught with difficulties, which I discuss further as this book progresses. The claims of distant descendants of those who suffered become thinner and thinner as the causal chain of the present situation of African descendants of victims of historic harms becomes more and more complex. Debates about, and evidence concerning, the history of Africa's relations with the West proliferate. Some counterfactual scenarios are favored and others are discarded. On the other hand, all human beings, everywhere, are entitled to distributive justice. If Africans were to enjoy their rights to distributive justice, many of their claims for reparative financial compensation would be rendered irrelevant.

A Human Rights Approach

The international law of human rights provides a better framework for rectification of Western-African relations than financial reparations. Demands for financial reparations are actually calls for the West to remedy the unequal distribution of the world's wealth, which confines Africa to the bottom of the continental heap. In this discourse, reparative justice stands in for distributive justice. Yet, as I discuss in Chapter 12, it is much easier to make a case for distributive than for reparative justice. Whatever the debates about the causes and consequences of the slave trade, colonialism, and postcolonial Western-African relations, there can be no doubt that the enormous suffering and severe neglect of Africans in the early twenty-first century urgently requires the world's attention and resources.

Despite this focus on financial reparations, it is useful to consider the entire range of reparative measures from the perspective of human rights. As discussed previously, reparations can also include acknowledgment of and apology for past harms. Acknowledgment is a means to set straight in the public record facts about historical and contemporary relations. In Chapter 11 I discuss whether a truth commission for Africa could serve this function, although I am skeptical that any satisfactory "truth" could be found that would satisfy all those interested in reparations. Apology functions as a signifier that African suffering is taken seriously; apology may act as a mechanism whereby "a line can be drawn under history, thus allowing . . . parties to 'move on.'"[47] Chapter 10 looks at Africans' opinions of the meaning of apology and whether apologies to Africa can or should be offered.

The arguments I make for acknowledgment and apology stem from my reading of the international law of human rights. This law is predicated on the principle of human dignity. Its founding document is the Universal Declaration of Human Rights (UDHR), adopted by the United Nations General Assembly in 1948. The first statement in the UDHR's preamble reads, "Whereas recognition of the inherent dignity and of the equal and inalienable rights of all members of the human family is the foundation of freedom, justice and peace in the world." Article 1 of the UDHR continues, "All human beings are born free and equal in dignity and rights. They are endowed with reason and conscience and should act towards one another in a spirit of brotherhood." Reference to human dignity also appears in many other places in international law and in national constitutions.[48] The 1981 African Charter on Human and Peoples' Rights, quoting from the charter of the then Organization of African Unity (OAU), notes that "freedom, equality, justice and dignity are essential objectives for the achievement of the legitimate aspirations of the African peoples."[49]

No one can provide "factual" verification of the universal need for and entitlement to human dignity, nor is there an acknowledged definition of it. I believe that human dignity requires "personal autonomy, societal concern and respect, and treatment by others in society as a social equal."[50] An amorphous ideal of human dignity can be found in many religions and philosophies: this ideal often evolves as societies change and more and more people demand equality, personal autonomy, and social respect. The principle of dignity, however derived, moves activists all over the world to promote human rights for all.

All individuals are entitled to their human rights by virtue of being human. All individuals, moreover, are entitled to recognition as human, as beings worthy of respect and dignity. As Charles Taylor puts it, "a person or group of people can suffer real damage, real distortion, if the people or society around them mirror back to them a confining or demeaning or contemptible picture of themselves."[51] Following Taylor's logic, the West demeans Africans by not acknowledging and not apologizing for the intense suffering they and their ancestors have experienced over almost six centuries, at least in part as a consequence of their relations with the West. Nonrecognition of this suffering implies they are a lesser form of being, perhaps not quite human. As Govier notes, "Systematically to discredit or question every claim made by a person is to deny her status as a person, to treat her as a being incapable of perceiving, remembering, feeling, interpreting, and claiming from a point of view in the world."[52] Individuals' accounts of their life stories and suffering must be taken seriously.

Moreover, both philosophical and legal speculations on the nature of human beings assume that the individual's membership in larger collectivities is important to her dignity.[53] Thus, the destruction or distortion of African family lines or communities as a result of relations with the West is also a basis for reparations. Collective, family, and communal identities include memories of injustices. Respect for the dignity of these identities may require symbolic reparations to acknowledge past wrongdoing.

Apologies are crucial to an individual's sense of dignity. If she is harmed but no one recognizes that harm, she will feel that she is disregarded, not part of society, not worthy of the respect that an apology might show. As Aaron Lazare suggests, "Many offenses are experienced as assaults on the offended party's self-respect or dignity, and so a successful apology must somehow restore these vital aspects of the self."[54] Apologies are incomplete unless the individual, institution, or state who apologizes first acknowledges the harm done. Thus, acknowledgment is an intrinsic part of the process of repair of an individual's dignity and an essential part of reparations.

Human dignity also requires that individuals have access to the truth about what has happened to them. A victim of human rights violations cannot feel dignified if the society around her ignores her story or denigrates her experiences. Her story may include the story of injustices to her group or to her ancestors, and her experiences may have been partly determined by the injustices to them. Thus, the basic argument for reparations for past injustices coincides with the basic argument for human rights, namely, the need for human dignity.

The principle that everyone should enjoy economic rights also derives from the ideal that everyone should be treated with dignity. "A person in abject condition, deprived of adequate means of subsistence . . . suffers a profound affront to his sense of dignity."[55] Economic rights reflect, in large part, basic human physiological needs. They include rights to food, health care, shelter, social security, and an adequate standard of living. They also include the right to education. Hundreds of millions of Africans endure severe poverty, in which basic needs are not fulfilled. This poverty is partly rooted in Africa's pre-independence history of the slave trade and colonialism, as well as in some of the present interactions between Africa and the West. Poverty is also rooted, however, in sometimes misguided and sometimes intentional policies imposed on their citizens by Africa's post-independence leaders, as well as in deliberate corruption. Given this mix of causes, it is impossible to calculate the extent to which poverty is derived from Western-African relations, but such a calculation is, in any case, irrelevant to the human rights of Africa's citizens. Article 28 of the Universal Declaration of Human Rights mandates that "Everyone is entitled to a social and international order in which the rights and freedoms set forth in this Declaration can be fully realized."

Thus, international human rights law and principles provide a solid foundation for the contention that the Western world must concern itself with economic rights in Africa. This law avoids the problem of making claims for financial reparations based on counterfactual historical assumptions. We can ascertain who needs what in Africa in the present; we can estimate rates of poverty, illiteracy, homelessness, and disease. All Africans are entitled to lives in which they do not suffer these disabilities, regardless of counterfactual arguments about what might have happened if their continent had not suffered from the slave trade, colonialism, or postcolonial interactions with the West.

Civil and political rights are also crucial. All individuals possess rights to personal physical security; to the protections afforded by the rule of law; to political participation; and to freedom of speech, expression, and religion. Without these rights, they do not live a life of dignity. Africans taken as slaves enjoyed none of these human rights, and Africans living under colonial rule enjoyed few of them. Unfortunately, though, even since independence many Africans have been deprived of civil and political rights. This is not solely a function of continued Western interference in postcolonial Africa. African leaders must accept responsibility for the injustices they have perpetrated against many tens of millions of their citizens since independence, and they must be willing to repair them. It is the obligation of African leaders, not of the West, to provide this form of reparation.

One might argue that to suggest replacing the African call for reparations with a call for all states, institutions, and individuals to respect and promote Africans' human rights is a form of Western imperialism. Few sub-Saharan Africans participated in the formulation of the UDHR, as almost all of sub-Saharan Africa in 1948 was under colonial rule. Perhaps, then, the universal law of human rights is actually a particular law, reflecting "Western" views of human dignity. Yet the OAU and its successor organization, the AU, have drafted many human rights documents since 1981, often drawing on international law.[56] Many national constitutions in Africa include human rights, even though they were honored more in the breach than in the observance in most of Africa during the first two decades of independence.[57]

Many millions of Africans, moreover, value their human rights and make huge sacrifices to protect them. Hundreds of thousands of African human rights activists have been murdered, tortured, exiled, or otherwise oppressed by dictatorial states. There is a large social movement for human rights in Africa, and there are many African nongovernmental organizations whose mandate is to pursue human rights. While some African commentators, philosophers, and legal scholars may dispute particular aspects of international human rights law,[58] constitutional and legal developments within Africa,[59] as well as practice "on the ground," show that to evaluate the African reparations movement through the lens of international human rights law is to reflect African values. The lens of international human rights also avoids many of the philosophical difficulties I discuss.

Reparations and International Relations

I have noted that the call for reparations to Africa for the slave trade, colonialism, and postcolonial relations between the West and Africa is still weak. It is easy to ignore this call or to regard it as a fringe social movement that has no influence in international circles. On the other hand, in the twenty-first century the world appears to have entered a new political phase, characterized by severe resentment of the West. Inhabitants of the poorest areas of the world appear to be attracted more and more to a violent, symbolic politics of despair. Perhaps, therefore, African views of past Western exploitation should be taken seriously. Even if we have no personal ethical belief that such exploitation of Africa should be recognized, atoned, and compensated for, we may find it sensible to acquiesce to some of the ideas and demands of African reparationists. If Africans are convinced that Westerners are not paying attention to them, then they are more likely to support anti-Western political movements and less likely to have any trust in the West.

Yet trust is the basis for international relations, as it is for any interactions among human beings.[60] Trust is social glue, whether among individuals, groups, or large corporate entities.[61] As Trudy Govier states, "In trusting another person, we confidently expect that he or she will do what is right for us."[62] Such confidence is not always evident in relations between Westerners and Africans. Although individual Africans often trust individual Westerners, it often seems that as a group, Africans do not trust the West. For trust to emerge and to endure, it is sometimes necessary to acknowledge and apologize for past wrongs. If Africans repeatedly tell Westerners that they have been hurt, and are still hurt, by centuries of exploitation, then perhaps Westerners ought to take their stories seriously. The West's acceptance of African testimony, and acknowledgment of its partial responsibility for Africa's current tragic situation, may be a necessary component of trust-based relations between African and other nations. Reparative actions by Western actors, in particular states, might be considered a necessary part of contemporary international relations, insofar as such actions help to "[re-establish] relations of respect and trust between former victims and perpetrators."[63] It might be in a western state's interests to "renounce [its] previous image" since "a connection to the wrong might endanger the perpetrator state's relations with other states."[64] In return, however, victims "ought not to be intransigent"; they must be willing to "re-establish relations of respect" once perpetrators have engaged in acts of repair.[65] Such a cooperative attitude might lessen the chances of future conflict.

Samuel Huntington has discussed the possibilities of civilizational-based international conflicts in the twenty-first century.[66] Africa is too weak an actor on the world stage to instigate such a civilizational war. Nevertheless, inattention to Africa might increase resentment of the West. Many Kenyans, it seems, were angry that the United States paid very little attention to the African victims of the bombings of U.S. embassies in Kenya and Tanzania in 1998,[67] yet it expected African support when the United States was attacked in 2001. If, in the post–9/11 era, the West views Africa primarily as a security threat, "a place where terrorism flourishes and a potential safe-haven for radical Islam,"[68] then Africans may feel that whatever residual Western concern with the amelioration of African poverty exists is merely a sham. Acknowledgment of the responsibilities of all parties for Africa's underdevelopment might help defuse such resentment, as might actual apologies. This might also establish moral equivalence among actors. Once Westerners and other non-Africans view Africans as equal partners in discussions of world affairs in a solidaristic, not merely a political, sense, more rational decision making might occur.

For some analysts, though, trust does not imply mutual regard; it is merely an interest-based social relationship. Both sides enter a bargain in which they trust each other for pragmatic reasons because each knows it is in the other's interest to adhere to that bargain.[69] In international relations, much trust is interest-based. Between the former colonizing and the former colonized world, however, interest-based trust might not be adequate, the interests of the former colonizers not being sufficiently engaged in the rehabilitation of the former colonies. A moral dimension to trust must also exist. In the African case, acknowledgment of moral responsibility for slavery, colonialism, and underdevelopment might improve the chances of building an international moral community.

From the point of view of some embittered or angry Africans, perhaps such an international moral community is not a worthy goal. Why, after so many centuries of slave-trading and exploitation, should any African feel part of a moral community that includes the West? One might wish to dismiss those Africans who reject an international moral community as merely those who profit from promotion of an ideology of victimhood. Such politics of resentment seem to permeate much of the international discussion of relations between the West and "the rest." The African social movement for compensation might seem merely to be a means to perpetuate Africa's underprivileged status instead of making the political, legal, and economic changes necessary to develop.

Social movements do not come from nowhere: they include interpreters who name injustices and define the sought-for solutions. A cynic might reject such namers of past injustices merely as moral entrepreneurs, carving places for themselves in the international community through invention of claims that did not previously exist. A realist, however, might wish to take into account that the moral entrepreneurs of today are sometimes future political leaders.

If politics is an art, then in the twenty-first century it is in part the art of grievance. As Tariq, an ambassador, told us, Africans could use emotional blackmail, pointing to the dangers of terrorism, refugee flows, and transmission of AIDS, unless Westerners devote more attention to helping Africa. Indeed, there are rumors of a "growing terrorist network . . . in the Sahel" region of Africa.[70] The Western world takes seriously the grievances of some people within its own boundaries. It ought to take equally seriously the grievances of those outside its boundaries whom it conquered and exploited. Global political and economic relations in the twenty-first century will be more peaceful if the idea of global justice is accepted by all actors. The historical hypotheses on which claims for reparations are based are certainly questionable, but, as I explain in this volume, contemporary law, philosophy, and morality suggest universal responsibility to ameliorate suffering, regardless of who is suffering where and regardless of the historical or contemporary causes of that suffering.

Chapter 2
African Voices

This book presents my analysis of the African reparations movement and my views of what reparations the West may owe to Africa. In order to formulate those views, however, and in an attempt to be respectful of Africans' opinions, my research assistants and I also interviewed some Africans about reparations. I formulated my views in part through the process of interviewing the people introduced here and later analyzing their responses. Although I do not agree with everything they say, my discussions with them convinced me that the West ought to pay more attention to what it owes Africa, either as reparation for past wrongs or as a matter of contemporary distributive justice.

The views of the Africans we interviewed are contained in several of the following chapters. Although as I explain below they were members of the elite in their own societies, in international terms these Africans were citizens of a marginalized continent. It is imperative, I believe, that those who make or—as in my case—recommend policy have some contact with the people whom that policy might affect. Therefore, I present the respondents' views in discrete sections so that the reader might become aware of their concerns, their fears, and sometimes their anger, expressed in their own voices.

The Interviews

Between June 1, 2002, and March 31, 2004, two graduate assistants, Anthony Lombardo and Kristina Bergeron, and I interviewed seventy-one Africans in either French or English. We also elicited opinions from three other Africans, one French speaker and two English speakers, via email. Lombardo conducted fourteen English interviews and accompanied me at many of the interviews I conducted. Bergeron conducted fourteen French interviews. I conducted the remaining nine French interviews, as well as thirty-four English interviews. I translated into English all quotations in this volume from the French interviews.

We defined Africans as anyone who held citizenship in any African country, regardless of that individual's "race." Some might argue that only "indigenous" Africans, not individuals of European or Indian descent, should be considered African. In our view, however, citizenship overrides ethnicity. We would no more confine the term *African* to people with indigenous (black) ancestry than we would confine *British* to people with indigenous (white) ancestry.

We refer to the people we interviewed as respondents, meaning that they responded to the questions we asked them. Although many respondents agreed to be interviewed on the record, I do not identify any except the three remaining active members of the Group of Eminent Persons for Reparations (GEP)—Jacob Ade Ajayi, Ali Mazrui, and Dudley Thompson—whose views are a matter of public record. As I explain in Chapter 3, the GEP was established by the Organization of African Unity in 1992 to seek reparations from the West to Africa. I identify all other respondents by pseudonyms, which correspond to the sex, language, and religion (when known) of each respondent.

Because the reparations debate is a debate among activists and academics, we wanted to interview Africans who were somewhat knowledgeable about it. Aside from the three GEP members, we interviewed forty-one human rights activists; twenty-two academics, some of whom were also activists; and eight African ambassadors to the United States. We interviewed human rights activists to understand how members of civil society (that is, citizens active in their communities or countries) thought about reparations. We interviewed academics, whom we defined as anyone affiliated with a university, (as professor, researcher, or graduate student) because they constitute one of the few influential professional groups in Africa and could provide us with scholarly analysis in addition to their personal views. We chose ambassadors in order to ascertain official state positions on reparations as well as to ascertain their personal views.

To locate respondents, we used a sociological method known as purposeful sampling, in which the researcher looks for a group that can offer answers to her theoretical questions.[1] A purposeful sample is not statistically representative, nor does the researcher attempt to reach all sectors of society. Our sample focuses on members of the African elite and civil society. We sought respondents through whom we could "learn a great deal about issues of central importance to the . . . research."[2] Our recruitment of respondents also relied partially upon snowball sampling, the process of selecting respondents by availability and referral. Such an approach is often used to compile a sample of hard-to-reach respondents.

We recruited respondents by their interest in participating in the project and their availability to us. Although the majority had heard of the idea of reparations to Africa, few, other than the three GEP members, had given it much thought before we invited them to participate. Nevertheless, of those approached, a high percentage agreed to be interviewed; however, some were not able to obtain visas to visit the venues in North America and Europe where we had intended to meet them.

We conducted semistructured interviews that followed a predesigned questionnaire. Semistructured interview questionnaires guide the questions to ask but allow the respondent plenty of leeway to reply as he sees fit. I devised the original questionnaire, and Lombardo and I tested it on the first sixteen respondents in June 2002. We then revised and expanded some questions before settling on the final questionnaire, used for all interviews after June 2002. Interviews typically ran about one to one and a half hours, but occasionally time constraints cut them short and we were unable to ask all our questions; in particular, we were not always able to obtain the demographic information we sought. Often, we varied the order of questions to keep the interview moving smoothly when respondents independently raised topics we were interested in investigating. Also, we reconfigured some questions during the interview, depending on how knowledgeable a respondent was about reparations.

We took extensive written notes on each interview and made oral comments on tape after the majority of them. Each interview was professionally transcribed, with the exception of two respondents who did not consent to be taped and one interview where the tape was damaged. In these cases, I rely on our notes. Lombardo analyzed forty-one of the English interviews using a qualitative data analysis software package, NVivo 2.0. With his permission, I draw from his master's thesis for quotations from these interviews.[3] I analyzed the remaining ten English interviews and the twenty-three French interviews "by hand" and also drew on the interviews Lombardo had already analyzed for additional material. There was very little disagreement among our respondents; rather, the interviews appeared to reflect a consensus of opinion on reparations to Africa.

Thus, we used sociological sampling and interview methods to gain insight into the larger legal, philosophical, and political questions about reparations discussed in this book. As noted, I did not want to offer my opinions about Western reparations to Africa without first discussing the matter with knowledgeable Africans. In parts of this book, I present their views. Elsewhere, my views are influenced by my reflections on encounters with them.

The Respondents

The best way to describe our respondents is as members of the African elite. All of the sixty people who gave us details about their education possessed university degrees. Twenty-one possessed bachelor's degrees; fifteen, master's degrees; eighteen, doctorates; six, professional degrees. In the context of African society, possession of a university degree puts one in a small, fairly elite group. However, our respondents were not remote from the lives of ordinary people. Many had parents who possessed no education or were educated only at the primary level. Many still had regular contact with the villages from which their families came. Some had sad stories of how they themselves, family members, or people they knew had been affected by recent economic policies such as privatization of resources and cutbacks in official employment.

During oral presentations of our research, Lombardo and I were sometimes asked why we did not include "ordinary" (not elite) Africans in our sample. Unfortunately, it was not feasible to interview ordinary Africans. Physical, financial, and organizational constraints prevented our travel to various countries in Africa to conduct interviews: the research travel would be too expensive, time-consuming, and occasionally unsafe to be practical. Conversely, it is highly unlikely that ordinary Africans would visit North America and be available for interviews. In any case, interest in reparations, as it currently stands, exists almost solely among the elite. If reparations become a salient issue in international relations, it will be because African elites have raised it.

When I began this project, I had hoped to conduct interviews in Africa. I wanted to speak to people from many countries and thought I might be able to do so by attending African conferences or meetings, for example, the annual meetings of the African Commission on Human Rights, which many representatives of African nongovernmental organizations attended. This proved impractical because people attending such conferences are too busy to speak to researchers. We therefore decided to contact Africans who were visiting North America or Europe to attend academic conferences or short courses on human rights. We also drew on prior contacts to approach these individuals, respecting their privacy in accordance with Canadian research ethics standards.

We began our research at the Canadian Human Rights Foundation summer human rights training program in Ste.-Anne-de-Bellevue, Québec, in June 2002, where Lombardo and I interviewed sixteen individuals and perfected our questionnaire. Lombardo and Bergeron interviewed another fourteen people at the foundation's 2003 summer school. Lombardo and I interviewed six academics and the three members of the GEP at the annual meeting of the (U.S.) African Studies Association in Washington, D.C., in December 2002. In June 2003, Lombardo and Bergeron interviewed two people at the annual meeting of the

Canadian Association of African Studies in Halifax, Nova Scotia. Bergeron interviewed six French speakers at an academic colloquium at Laval University in Québec in 2003.[4] I interviewed eight ambassadors and one activist in Washington, D.C., between January and April 2003. Lombardo and I interviewed nine more people at a short course on human rights at the Raoul Wallenberg Institute, University of Lund, Sweden, in March 2004. We conducted six additional interviews of individuals whom we had contacted or who, in two cases, had contacted us. Finally, three people answered an email version of our questionnaire, but these interviews were much less detailed than those we conducted in person.

All but seven respondents were permanent residents of Africa, including the eight ambassadors. Two of the seven nonresidents had arrived in North America within the preceding three years, one as a refugee. There were twenty women and fifty-four men in the group. This gender imbalance reflected African social reality, in which men are still more likely than women to be ambassadors, scholars, and leaders of civil society. Among the fifty-eight who gave us their ages, the range was from twenty to sixty years, with the exception of Dudley Thompson, who was eighty-five years old. There was no discernible difference in views according to age, gender, educational level, religion, or language.

Before the interviews, I was very slightly acquainted with four of the scholars we interviewed, all now permanent residents of Canada or the United States. In addition, the nine people we interviewed in Sweden came to know me rather well during the course of the interviewing week. In negotiating with the Raoul Wallenberg Institute for permission to approach the Africans whom they expected at their March 2004 human rights training session, I had offered to trade three hours' teaching for the institute's assistance. In the event, I taught the nine respondents we met in Lund for nine hours, although none of the teaching addressed reparations to Africa. Lombardo and I also stayed in the same hotel as the African visitors to Lund. We do not believe that this acquaintance affected the content of the interviews, other than to increase the level of trust between us and our respondents.

Our respondents came from twenty-six African countries and one outside Africa. Dudley Thompson, though a member of the GEP, is Jamaican; however, as a result of decades of Pan-African work, he had contributed heavily to the movement for reparations to Africa, and his views are therefore included in this analysis, notwithstanding his citizenship. In alphabetical order, with the number interviewed from each country after its name, the African countries were Angola, 1; Burundi, 3; Cameroon, 6; Democratic Republic of Congo (formerly Zaire), 5; Republic of Congo, 1; Egypt, 1; Eritrea, 1; Ethiopia, 2; Ghana, 5; Guinea, 1;

Kenya, 8; Liberia, 1; Malawi, 2; Mauritius, 1; Morocco, 2; Niger, 1; Nigeria, 8; Rwanda, 2; Sierra Leone, 1; South Africa, 6; Sudan, 1; Tanzania, 6; Togo, 4; Uganda, 1; Zambia, 1; and Zimbabwe, 2.

This distribution reflects linguistic and political realities. English speakers were more likely than others to attend conferences and short courses in human rights in Canada, the United States, and Sweden: French speakers also attended conferences and short courses in Canada. The post–9/11 atmosphere created more difficulties than previously for Africans to obtain visas to the West. Nationals of some countries also were less likely than others to obtain visas because of the likelihood that once in Canada, the United States, or Sweden, they might seek refugee status. In any case, there is no discernible difference in views among our respondents by place of origin other than that those who had recently experienced genocide or civil war, such as those from Rwanda, Burundi, Congo, and Sierra Leone, were more likely to focus on current political events than on historical or economic matters.

We posed four sets of questions in our interviews. The first queried respondents about their knowledge of and participation in the movement for reparations. Questions included whether respondents had heard about the idea of reparations, and if so, how, and whether it was something they talked or thought about in day-to-day life. We also asked whether respondents were involved in any reparations-related work and if they were aware of any other instances of reparations claims. With regard to this last question, we waited for them to name precedents; although if they could not think of any, we sometimes asked if they were aware of reparations to Jewish victims of the Holocaust.

The second section formed the bulk of the interview. Here we asked respondents what the term *reparations* meant to them. We asked how they thought Africa had been affected by its relations with the West, probing for their perspectives on the slave trade, colonialism, postcolonial relations, and any other topics they deemed relevant. We posed our questions in neutral terms, not suggesting that Africa had necessarily been harmed by the West, and also asked if the respondents believed there were beneficial aspects of Western relations with Africa. We also inquired what acknowledgment and apology meant to the respondents, how they might be carried out, and how they might be made sincere. We then asked respondents about forms of material compensation, including the necessity and direction of financial compensation. We also inquired about responsibility for reparations from organizations other than national governments and about responsibility of non-Western nations, especially, with regard to the slave trade, the Arab world. Unfortunately, we neglected to ask whether the respondents thought a truth commission for Africa might be a good idea: thus, Chapter 11 does not draw from the interviews, as do most other chapters.

The penultimate section of our questionnaire asked about respondents' personal opinions and feelings about their relations with the West, as well as those of their parents and friends. The final section collected basic demographic data and asked about respondents' families, their volunteer affiliations, and other aspects of their backgrounds, to give some context to their answers.

I was very moved by my conversations with so many Africans, as I was by the transcripts of the interviews I did not conduct. Our respondents were, for the most part, very open and trusted us with their thoughts and opinions. Some had suffered terrible losses in genocide or civil war; others dealt daily with a level of poverty, illness, and insecurity entirely remote from the lives of Western academics. Some thanked us for the opportunity to talk to us. My arguments in this volume are influenced by all the interviews my assistants and I conducted; they are also influenced by memories of conversations with many other Africans over the last thirty-five years. I try to recognize the humanity of every African respondent with whom we spoke, whether or not I agree with that individual's opinions. As John, a South African scholar, told us, "People ought to be given space . . . to tell their stories . . . [to be] able to bear witness."

Chapter 3

Genesis of the Reparations Movement

The Social Movement for Reparations

In 1991 Chief M. K. O. Abiola, a Nigerian capitalist and publisher, convened a meeting on reparations to Africa in Lagos, Nigeria. Abiola had apparently been influenced to take up this cause both by a chance discussion about Holocaust reparations with a Jewish businessman and by his contacts with the Congressional Black Caucus in the United States: the caucus was interested in reparations to African Americans.[1] At the Lagos meeting, participants focused on eradication of African debt and on a proposal for an African Marshall Plan as reparations to Africa. In a speech delivered in London in 1992, Abiola said, "Our demand for reparations is based on the tripod of moral, historic, and legal arguments. . . . Who knows what path Africa's social development would have taken if our great centers of civilization had not been razed in search for human cargo? Who knows how our economies would have developed?" Abiola went on to argue that international law applied retroactively to slavery, the slave trade, and colonialism. "It is international law which compels Nigeria to pay her debts to western banks and financial institutions: it is international law which must now demand that the western nations pay us what they have owed us for nearly six centuries."[2]

The successful purpose of Abiola's private meeting was to pressure the Organization of African Unity (OAU, succeeded in 2001 by the African Union [AU]) to discuss reparations at its official conference in Abuja, the Nigerian capital, the following year.[3] On June 28, 1992, the OAU swore in a twelve-member Group of Eminent Persons (GEP), whose mandate was to pursue reparations for Africa. At the time, the president of Nigeria and outgoing chairman of the OAU was General Ibrahim Babangida, a brutal dictator. The original chair of the GEP was Chief Abiola. Its other members were the Nigerian historian Jacob Ade Ajayi; Professor Samir Amin of Egypt; U.S. Congressman R. Dellums; Professor Josef Ki-Zerbo of Burkina Faso; Mme. Gracha Machel, former first lady of Mozambique and a political activist in her own right;

Miriam Makeba, the South African singer; the Kenyan-American scholar Ali A. Mazrui; Professor M. M'Bow, former director-general of UNESCO; former President A. Pereira of Cape Verde; Ambassador Alex Quaison-Sackey, former foreign minister in the government of Kwame Nkrumah of Ghana; and longtime Jamaican Pan-Africanist Dudley Thompson.[4]

It is not known whether all twelve GEP members were present at Abuja or indeed if all were aware of their new role. As of December 2002, when I interviewed each of them, only Ajayi, Mazrui, and Thompson were still actively pursuing reparations through their writings and academic lectures. They still filed annual reports to the OAU/AU,[5] although I was unable to locate them. According to Mazrui, there was very little contact among GEP members, who acted in their individual capacities.[6]

In 1993 Chief Abiola was elected president of Nigeria but was unable to take office from General Sani Abacha, the then military dictator who refused to relinquish power. A year later Abiola declared himself president: Abacha then imprisoned him, and Abiola died in jail in 1998. Thus, the movement for reparations started inauspiciously, its chief instigator rendered incapable of any activities only two years after its first official manifestation.

While he was still president of Nigeria, Ibrahim Babangida promoted reparations and officially dedicated $U.S. 500,000 to the GEP. However, the group apparently received these funds from Abiola's private purse, not from the Nigerian government.[7] Babangida had discussed reparations as early as 1991 with the presidents of Senegal and Togo, the three agreeing that African debt "should be written off as part of the reparations due for 500 years of slavery of Africans in Western Europe and America."[8] Given Babangida's record as dictator of Nigeria, one can speculate that he was using reparations as a political device to deflect attention from the atrocities and corruption Nigeria was experiencing under his rule.[9]

From April 27 to 29, 1993, a "Pan-African Conference on Reparations" was held in Abuja, sponsored by the GEP and the Commission for Reparations of the OAU.[10] An official proclamation issued at this conference referred to the "moral debt" and "debt of compensation" owed to Africa.[11] The compensation envisaged was "capital transfer and debt cancellation," as well as a reordering of international relations to give Africa more representation in the "highest decision-making bodies," in particular, a permanent seat on the United Nations Security Council.[12] In late 2006 there was much discussion of reform of the U.N. Security Council, but allocation of a seat to any African country seemed very unlikely.[13]

In 1999 a "Truth Commission Conference" was held in Accra, Ghana. This commission apparently comprised private individuals from nine

African countries, as well as participants from the United States, the United Kingdom, and three Caribbean countries.[14] It concluded that "the root causes of Africa's problems today are the enslavement and colonization of African people over a 400-year period"; that Africans were owed $U.S. 777 trillion in compensation plus annual interest; and that, presumably in consequence of nonpayment, there was no African debt to outsiders.[15] The final Declaration of the Truth Commission Conference gives no indication of how it derived the figure of $U.S. 777 trillion. By way of comparison, the United States' gross domestic product in 2005 was estimated at $12.455 trillion, so that the claimed reparations would be approximately sixty-two times the U.S. 2005 GDP.[16]

The huge figure claimed by the Accra conference undermines any chance that reparations to Africa might include financial compensation. No matter what their justification, when victims claim material compensation, the amount they demand must be seen as reasonable and as payable without significant disadvantage to those making the payment (discussed in Chapter 12). This may not be a morally or philosophically defensible stance, but it is pragmatically sensible. In any case, the members of the GEP themselves did not assign a value to the reparations they sought. As Thompson argued, "Once you begin to do that you . . . trivialize reparations and what it stands [for]. . . . It is impossible to put a figure to killing millions of people, our ancestors."[17]

When Thompson discussed ancestors, he used the GEP's broad definition of "Africa" to include people living in both Africa and the African diaspora. As Mazrui put it, "We define *Global Africa* as the continent of Africa *plus* the Diaspora of enslavement (descendants of survivors of the Middle Passage [transatlantic slave trade]) and the Diaspora of colonialism (the dispersal of Africans which continues to occur as a result of colonization and its aftermath)."[18] This was also the view of the British jurist, Lord Anthony Gifford, who spoke at the 1993 Abuja conference on reparations: "All Africans, on the continent of Africa and in the Diaspora, who suffer the consequences of the crime of mass kidnap [*sic*] and enslavement, have an interest in this claim. . . . All Africans around the world have been affected in some way by the crime of slavery."[19]

The idea of a global Africa draws upon the earlier Pan-Africanist tradition started by the Caribbean American Marcus Garvey in the 1920s. For Garvey, slavery was a collective trauma, which influenced all succeeding generations of Africans and people of African descent. "Slavery . . . was more than theft and the loss of freedom in forced labor, it deprived a people of their dreams and stripped them of their civilization."[20] The Pan-Africanist movement was revitalized in the early postcolonial period by Kwame Nkrumah, first president of independent Ghana. Dudley

Thompson's involvement in the Pan-Africanist movement began during his days as president of the West Indian Students' Association in Britain in the 1940s, and he used Nkrumah's phrase, "We can no longer afford the luxury of delay" to support the urgency of reparations.[21] In Thompson's view, there was a "primordial debt" owed to Africa.[22]

As of 2003, the GEP had had little success in starting a widespread movement for reparations to Africa. In 2003 there were a few small groups actively dedicated to reparations. A British group, the African Reparations Movement (ARM), campaigned in the late 1990s and early twenty-first century for the British Museum to return the Benin bronze sculptures to Nigeria.[23] The movement's objectives also included reparations for slavery and colonialism. Although ARM had been very active on the Internet, it was less active in 2003 as a consequence of the death of a financial benefactor who apparently had supported its website, which became inactive.[24] There was also a small movement in Accra, Ghana, whose Declaration on Reparations is discussed above, and a Kenyan chapter of ARM primarily concerned with apology for slavery and colonialism.[25] A "Jamaican Reparations Movement," naming Dudley Thompson as its patron and connected to the Rastafarian religious movement, issued statements at the time of the Durban Conference on Racism and beyond, but this group's goals were specific to the enslavement of Africans in Jamaica and their descendants.[26] Up to 2002, and presumably beyond, the three active members of the GEP gave lectures, especially at universities, and tried to encourage students to form their own branches, for example, in Brazil.[27] In 2003 a "Proposal for a Permanent Organizational Structure for the African and African Descendant Caucus" was circulated via the Internet.[28]

In 2005 the AU revived the call for reparations. Its 2004–2007 strategic plan includes for 2005 "debate in all African parliaments on slavery," with the objective to "declare slavery a crime against humanity and discuss the nature of reparations."[29] The reference here is to slavery in the past and should read "to declare *past* slavery *to have been* a crime against humanity" because contemporary slavery is a crime under international law. The AU also issued a report on the "First Conference of Intellectuals of Africa and the Diaspora," held in Dakar, Senegal, in October 2004. The report includes a section acknowledging the harm to "both continental Africa and her children" caused by the transatlantic slave trade, and it advocates "reparations including but not limited to debt relief, return of artifacts and archives, and monetary relief."[30]

As the bicentenaries of the British and American abolition of the slave trade in 1807 and 1808 approached, so did a renewed interest in reparations among Africans and people of African descent. In 2006 N'Cobra, an American group advocating reparations to African Americans, announced an "International Conference on Pan-African Reparations for Global Justice" in Accra, Ghana, set for July 21 through August 2, 2006.[31] Another organization, the Global Afrikan [*sic*] Congress (GAC) announced the "2006 International Family Gathering and Conference" in Harare, Zimbabwe, to take place October 1–6, 2006, where the focus was to be exclusively on reparations.[32] The GAC was launched at a conference on reparations in Barbados in 2002,[33] following a meeting of about 135 activists in Vienna in April 2001, which had produced a "Vienna Declaration and Program of Action," using the same title as the 1993 United Nations Conference on Human Rights in Vienna.[34] The 2006 conference in Ghana apparently took place.[35] I have not been able to ascertain whether the announced conference in Zimbabwe took place, although plans for it were severely criticized by Free Zim-Youth, a group of Zimbabwean youths living in the United Kingdom. Free Zim-Youth noted that the GAC appeared to have been persuaded by Zimbabwe's President Robert Mugabe that problems in his country were the result of a British and American imperialist plot. In fact, argued Free Zim-Youth, Mugabe was "a leader who has literally destroyed the country," and "the real story in Zimbabwe [was] the police and army brutalities."[36] Indeed, it seemed that the GAC was engaged in willful blindness in its determination to interpret events in Zimbabwe (discussed in Chapter 9) as the result of imperialism.

The revived interest in reparations to Africa, as the bicentenaries approached, did not mean that the movement had yet reached a point at which it could actually influence the policies of Western governments. One reason that there is not a larger movement for reparations to Africa may be that the GEP and other leaders of the movement have not decided on a clear set of aims.

Intellectual Basis of the Reparationist Position

The GEP used the term "reparations" to mean financial compensation. As discussed in Chapter 1, in international law reparations include a variety of activities meant to repair relations between two individuals or groups, one of whom has victimized the other. These reparative activities include symbolic reparations such as apologies. This more encompassing meaning appeared to be of little interest to the GEP, yet it had not decided by 2002 on the form of financial compensation it did want.

A popular call by nongovernmental organizations (NGOs) and others concerned with poverty in Africa was for reparations to take the form of cancellation of Africa's foreign debt (discussed in Chapter 8). Eradication of the debt was also a preoccupation of the 1991 Lagos meeting. But both Mazrui and Thompson felt that debt cancellation was unnecessary. As Mazrui explained, he was "less persuaded" by debt relief owing to a "sneaking suspicion the debts will never be paid anyhow."[37] The GEP preferred capital transfer in the form of a Marshall Plan for Africa, harkening back to the Marshall Plan that assisted Europe after World War II. Mazrui called this the Middle Passage Plan after the notorious Middle Passage voyage across the Atlantic endured by enslaved Africans brought to the Americas.[38]

Nor was the GEP interested in the finer points of legality of compensation. In his case for reparations, Abiola claimed that there was a principle that "a state is liable for any injury suffered by another [state] or by the other's [state's] nationals, such injury arising from the breach of any international obligations or from the breach of any principle of international customary law [by the state that caused the injury]."[39] But this is a retroactive attribution of contemporary international law and the contemporary world structure of states to a period when neither existed. The slave trade was not legally abolished until the early nineteenth century; slavery itself was abolished later. Arguing that the law requires reparation for colonialism, which was legal under international law until 1945 at the earliest (discussed in Chapter 7) is even more difficult.

There did seem to be general agreement among members of the GEP and others interested in reparations that African underdevelopment was caused by European exploitation and that the Western world had been enriched by exploitation of Africa. The three active members of the GEP referred frequently to the influential work by Walter Rodney, *How Europe Underdeveloped Africa*. As Rodney put it, "What was a slight difference [in levels of development] when the Portuguese sailed to West Africa in 1444 was a huge gap by the time that European robber statesmen sat down in Berlin 440 years later to decide who should steal which parts of Africa."[40] We cannot know what Rodney himself might have thought about the reparations movement. A highly respected historian, he was assassinated in Guyana, his native country, in 1980.[41]

The idea that African underdevelopment was and is caused by its relations with the West has powerful rhetorical appeal. The "Proposal for a Permanent Organizational Structure" for people calling for reparations attributed almost all the ills of Africa today to the slave trade and colonialism.

> These odious and premeditated crimes, which have been unequaled in history, have led to the exploitation of African nations for centuries, leaving them economically crippled and the vast majority of our people both on the African continent and in the African Diaspora in poverty, undereducated, economically, physically, psychically, politically, and culturally subordinated, subjected to institutionalized racism, vulnerable to the intersections of race and gender.[42]

In Thompson's view,

> The highly industrialized nations of the West . . . interrupted normal historical development, indigenous development by the Africans, and particularly West Africa. They interrupted it by the heinous crime of slavery. With[in] over four centuries they abducted the strongest and the best and some of the youngest life blood for coming generations. . . . They debilitated Africa."[43]

These ideas provide a relatively simple explanation for the tragic economic and political state of much of Africa today. So does the idea that Western development, conversely, was a result of exploitation and underdevelopment of Africa. Mazrui argued that "Africa developed the West": "The labor of Africa's sons and daughters was what the West needed for its industrial take-off," he asserted, referring also to the "extractive imperative" as Africa's agricultural and mineral wealth was removed for Western use.[44]

Although the three active members of the GEP in 2002 agreed that Europe had been responsible for underdeveloping Africa, they nevertheless could not agree on those aspects of European-African relations for which reparations should be sought. The three proposed, at minimum, reparations to Africa for the slave trade. However, they disagreed as to whether reparations were also owed for colonialism or postcolonial relations. Mazrui felt that to extend the claim beyond slavery to colonialism would weaken the case for reparations. "It makes it difficult to win on both by mixing the two."[45] He believed that the claim for reparations would be most viable if it focused on the slave trade. "Being enslaved is almost uniquely black in modern history. Once you broaden the agenda [for reparations] and it's no longer uniquely black then you're being rhetorical because people will say we can't deal with two-thirds of the human race."[46]

Ajayi, by contrast, believed that reparations were also due for colonialism. Only Africans, Ajayi argued, had endured the double burden of being both enslaved and colonized, in contrast to other parts of the world such as India. "It's only . . . when you link the slave trade with colonialism that you begin to get the more correct focus," he said. "Colonialism in Africa is not the same as colonialism in India. . . . The British went to India to trade. . . . But because of the racism that is involved in colonialism in Africa, there was no interest in developing trade that was there before."[47]

Extending the reparations claim even further than Ajayi, Thompson argued for reparations for the postcolonial period. "Colonialism," he said, "is just a half step from slavery." As for the postcolonial period, "they gave us a crown [independence] but they kept the jewels." Moreover, in Thompson's view, even the present era of globalization mandates reparations. "Globalization is a crime. . . . Slaves and ex-slaves, we're far behind . . . and the technological age is moving us further and further away."[48]

Whatever claims they wanted to make, the GEP and other actors in the reparations movement were convinced that there was transgenerational responsibility for Africa's underdevelopment. They were not interested in philosophical arguments about historic responsibility, although they were willing to differentiate between guilt and responsibility. The framers of the Abuja proclamation, for example, were "emphatically convinced that what matters is not the guilt but the responsibility of those states and nations whose economic evolution once depended on slave labor and colonialism."[49] Likewise, article 29 of the African Regional Preparatory Draft Declaration to the Durban Conference maintained that states that had pursued racist and/or discriminatory policies such as slavery and colonialism "should assume their full responsibilities and provide adequate reparation to those States, communities or individuals who were victims of such racist policies or acts, regardless of when or by whom they [the policies] were committed."[50]

Both Thompson and Mazrui contended that responsibilities for harm are handed down, or "inherited," through social citizenship. "You, who have the profits in the white world," wrote Thompson, "have inherited the responsibility of what your forefathers did to us. For it is the responsibility you have and not the guilt, by which we approach you."[51] Mazrui agreed that "the struggle for Black reparations is not based on Western guilt but on Western *responsibility*. While guilt need not be inherited from generation to generation, rights and responsibilities *are*."[52] Mazrui expanded upon this point during his interview.

> Do you [Americans] deny that you are entitled to the rights provided by a constitution which was written two hundred years ago? . . . Do you . . . deny the assets side of being an American, even if the assets side is much older than your presence here? If you don't deny your asset side, why should you deny your liability side, because you're not entitled to deny that. For as long as you are accepting the asset side, you should accept the other side, the liabilities [i.e., responsibility for the harm caused to Africa].[53]

This rhetoric of reparations, however, may not outlive the three active GEP members. In 2002 all were elderly. One must ask, therefore, what the future of a movement for reparations to Africa is likely to be once they can no longer continue their work. As discussed above, the AU still mentions reparations, but they do not appear to be a priority. Moreover, as Thompson noted, reparations are not a concern for most Africans, who are preoccupied with mundane, day-to-day survival. "There's a vast majority, a large part . . . who feel that this is a matter of such a long time ago . . . that we should forget about it."[54] The genesis and activities of the GEP may be remembered as a mere comment on Western-African relations, absent the organizational resources to enlarge upon their activities.

In 2001 it seemed that the United Nations' Conference at Durban might become the locus of the demand for reparations to Africa and that advocates for reparations might organize in its wake. Despite considerable interest in reparations at Durban, that did not occur.

The Durban Conference Against Racism

Officially known as the World Conference Against Racism, Racial Discrimination, Xenophobia, and Related Intolerance, the Durban Conference took place from August 31 to September 7, 2001. At Durban, there was much discussion of the proposition that the Western world owed reparations to Africa. These reparations would be for the slave trade and colonialism and even for the postcolonial era. In general, according to the Brazilian diplomat who first proposed the world conference to the United Nations, "reparations meant for the States of the African Group compensation to be effected by inter-State donations, pardon of the foreign debt, or increased economic assistance";[55] this resembled the GEP's focus on economic compensation.

The claim for such financial compensation seemed self-evidently just, given the enormity of the historic crimes committed against Africa. The final declaration of the conference states:

> We acknowledge that slavery and the slave trade . . . are a crime against humanity, and should always have been so, especially the transatlantic slave trade, and are among the major sources and manifestations of racism, racial discrimination, xenophobia and related intolerance. . . . We recognize that colonialism has led to racism, racial discrimination, xenophobia and related intolerance.[56]

Moreover, the declaration states that persons whose human rights had been violated as a result of racism and related wrongs should have "the right to seek just and adequate reparation or satisfaction."[57] In addition to these official concluding statements, "a long line of government ministers from developing countries [said] . . . that the problems facing their nations . . . stemmed in part from slavery and colonialism. . . . The wrongs . . . could only be righted by clear acknowledgments of the past by oppressing countries, and by creating schemes for compensation."[58] For example, Enoch Kavindele, vice president of Zambia, demanded reparations, arguing that all other victim groups had been adequately redressed for past wrongs, while Africans had not.

We have come to Durban to liberate ourselves from the historical injustices of slavery and servitude and now want to emphasize that slavery should be remembered not only as an appalling tragedy, but also as a factor which for centuries deprived Africa of her human and natural resources. Africa requests an audience, so the world can take responsibility for the crimes of slavery and colonialism. . . . The slave trade was the greatest practical evil which has ever afflicted the human race. And though we agree that many other peoples and races have been victims of discrimination and intolerance, the cry on the continent is that while every one of those groups have [*sic*] been adequately redressed for wrongs committed in the past, Africans continue to suffer.[59]

President Olusegun Obasanjo of Nigeria, the democratically elected successor to the dictator Abacha, also spoke at Durban. Although Nigeria did not seek financial reparations, asking only for apology from the slave-trading and colonial powers, he also attributed much of Africa's suffering to the past.

It is imperative to recognize that the legacies of several centuries of racial exploitation, brutalisation and dehumanisation of Africans and people of African descent, through slavery, slave trade and colonialism, have had deep and fundamental consequences of poverty, underdevelopment, marginalisation, and de-linkage from the global march of human civilization. . . . Today, Africans and people of African descent, still live with the consequences that the criminal nexus of slavery, slave trade and colonialism has wrought on our continent. Let me name a few: social instability; depopulation; destruction of African traditional institutions; underdevelopment; mental slavery; looting of African resources; dehumanisation of the African persons; loss of self-confidence and lack of self-esteem; and dependency syndrome.[60]

Both of these statements reflect the official viewpoint put forward prior to the Durban Conference by the African Regional Preparatory Conference for the World Conference. This preparatory conference affirmed "that [the] slave trade, particularly of Africans, is a unique tragedy in the history of humanity, a crime against humanity which is unparalleled."[61] It made an explicit connection between the slave trade and Africa's current problems.

The consequences of this tragedy [the slave trade], accentuated by those of colonialism and apartheid, have resulted in substantial and lasting economic, political and cultural damage to African peoples and are still present in the form of damage caused to the descendants of the victims by the perpetuation of prejudice against Africans in the continent and people of African descent in the Diaspora.[62]

In an interview prior to Durban, Secretary-General of the OAU Amara Essy said that the Conference should declare slavery a crime against humanity, noting that such a statement "would serve as a psychological and moral reparation for African countries." He also argued that as reparation the Western countries should cancel African debts because "three-quarters of African debt is iniquitous and unjust."[63]

Thus it appeared that most Africans who participated at Durban accepted the development of underdevelopment thesis, as propounded by Rodney. The representative for Sierra Leone said that

> African human and natural resources were exploited by the slave traders and colonialists to develop their countries. . . . Europe contributed immensely to the present underdevelopment in Africa. The world must therefore accept[,] especially the beneficiaries of the slave trade and colonialism[,] that grave injustice was done to the African.[64]

A representative of the national human rights commission of Niger went further, including in the list of wrongs the structural adjustment programs that African countries adopted, under pressure from international financial institutions, in the late twentieth century.

> The dramatic situation confronted by the peoples of Africa . . . cannot be disassociated from the three successive scourges that have devastated Africa over the centuries: . . . three centuries of raids and of the trans-Atlantic trade, seventy years of colonial occupation, and structural adjustment, which with their consequences of poverty and pauperization ruined the masses, . . . among whom are the most vulnerable.[65]

There appeared to be little disagreement about the detrimental effects of the slave trade, colonialism, and postcolonial relations with the West among most of the African representatives gathered at Durban, although the democratically elected Liberal president of Senegal, Abdoulaye Wade, chose to also discuss contemporary forms of racism in Africa, forms that could not be attributed to Western interference. Wade said, "There ought to have been an interest [at Durban] in identifying all forms of racism, of xenophobia, the old and the new, in our countries as well as elsewhere, and in searching for solutions. Unfortunately, our conference has not permitted serious work on these particular points."[66] But Wade's was a minority viewpoint.

Many African and African American NGOs participated in discussions of reparations before and at the Durban Conference.[67] The international NGO Forum at the Conference concluded that

> Slave-holder nations, colonizers and occupying countries have unjustly enriched themselves at the expense of those people that they enslaved and colonized and whose land they have occupied. As these nations largely owe their political, economic and social domination to the exploitation of Africa, Africans and Africans in the Diaspora they should recognize their obligation to provide these victims just and equitable reparations.[68]

Western states at Durban did not accept the NGO viewpoint. Many Western delegates viewed the strong rhetoric about the evils of the slave trade and colonialism as an attempt to obtain redistribution of the world's wealth by illegitimate means. They objected to the emphasis on the historic slave trade while slavery and slavelike practices still occurred in fifteen African states, according to the U.S. State Department's human rights reports for 2000.[69] They also noted that there had been African collaborators in the slave trade,[70] a matter I discuss in Chapter 5. Moreover, the Western powers found it "misleading to attribute all of Africa's tragedies solely to the legacy of slavery and colonialism," and they noted that the descendants of those taken as slaves lived in the Americas not in Africa.[71] Against this, the representative of the government of Ghana at Durban said:

> It is necessary to discuss ways of combating contemporary forms of racism, but it is also essential to focus on the equally important past manifestations of racism, especially the slave trade. . . . To attempt to combat contemporary forms of racism without giving due attention to the tragedies of the slave trade which devastated the continent of Africa, destroying its population and economies . . . will be an exercise in futility.[72]

Despite some Western states' objections to the demand for reparations, some acknowledged the damage caused by the slave trade. The Minister for Urban Policy and Integration of Ethnic Minorities for the Netherlands expressed at Durban the Netherlands' "deep remorse about enslavement and the slave trade." The British Minister for Africa said, "The British Government and the European Union profoundly deplore the human suffering, both individual and collective, caused by slavery and the slave trade," presumably speaking for both entities.[73] Neither of these statements was an apology. Rather, they deplored past wrongs without taking responsibility that might be used by African states or activists as a basis for future claims for material compensation. In a discussion in the United Nations General Assembly in November 2006 on a draft declaration to commemorate the two hundredth anniversary of the abolition of the slave trade in March 2007, the Western states reiterated their position that they had no liability for the slave trade. Speaking for the entire European Union, the representative for Finland said:

> Nothing in the Durban Declaration or Programme of Action can affect the general legal principle which precludes the retrospective application of international law in matters of State responsibility. Likewise, those documents cannot impose obligations, liability or a right to compensation on anyone. The same is true of this draft resolution.[74]

The representatives at this debate from the United Kingdom, France, and the Netherlands all carefully aligned themselves with Finland's position, and the representatives from the United States and Canada made similar statements.[75]

None of the declarations emanating from the Durban Conference had any force in international law; they had only political intent. The NGO declaration was just that: a declaration by private civil society groups. Nor did the official declaration carry force of law.[76] Moreover, there was no call at Durban for reparations to current victims of slavery,[77] although slavery was clearly illegal in 2001 and victims would have had a very strong case for reparations. Since much of the world's slavery in 2001 took place in Africa and other "developing" countries, it was not difficult to accuse African spokespersons of hypocrisy in showing so little interest in the human rights abuses and racism in their own countries at the time of the Durban Conference. There was no official mention at Durban of internal slavery in African countries such as Mauritania.[78] Nor did there appear to be any mention of the historic Muslim slave trade from Africa[79] (discussed in Chapter 6).

The Durban Conference ended just before the September 11, 2001, attacks on the United States by the terrorist group Al-Qaeda, which preempted follow-up media attention to reparations.[80] Moreover, the conference itself was marred by the absence of the United States, which withdrew in protest both because of the proposed discussion of reparations to African Americans and because of its disagreement with the focus on the Israeli-Palestinian dispute.[81] Indeed, one commentator on the conference referred to it as a "calamity."[82] There is little evidence of official attention in the West to the movement for reparations to Africa since 2001. Because of this, Robert, an activist from Togo, told us that Durban was merely a "provocation by the West; the West continues to taunt the rest of the world." Some private reparationist groups, however, continued or intensified their activities after 2001. For some, the focal point was the bicentennials of the British and American abolition of the slave trade, as discussed previously. Despite the lack of official follow-up, discussion at Durban also both reflected and promoted discussions among private citizens. Most of our respondents were familiar with the proposal for reparations to Africa, which many favored.

African Voices

Aside from the three GEP members, most of our respondents had not been active in the movement for reparations to Africa. Many had heard of the debate about reparations, but only a few had thought seriously about it prior to their interviews. Some had seen reference in their national presses to reparations or had read about the reparations movement on the Internet. Angela, a young lawyer, had read in the Nigerian press about the 1992 OAU conference and had asked her father to explain it to her. Dorothy, a Kenyan civil servant, was one of the few respondents, if not the only one, from outside Nigeria who knew about the 1992 conference. Some respondents from French-speaking countries knew of a debate in the French parliament to declare the slave trade a crime against humanity. Some knew of the African American movement for reparations but connected it only loosely, if at all, to continental Africa.

A few respondents had had some connection with preparations for the Durban Conference. Matthew, an ambassador, had helped to prepare his president's speech at Durban. Some respondents who were members of African NGOs or African human rights commissions had been involved in preparations for the NGO conference, although they had not attended the conference itself. Some of these individuals were not interested in reparations; instead, they focused on more current human rights problems: Ahmad was concerned with the persistence of slavery in Niger; Patrick's focus was the need for human rights education; Theresa wanted to educate youth about racism and xenophobia; and Dorothy was preoccupied with the atrocious prison conditions in Kenya. David, from Cameroon, was interested in racial discrimination against diaspora Africans. Among all our respondents, only Alain from Togo had attended Durban, although several had hoped to attend but lacked funds to do so. Several activists who were also civil servants said they were prevented by their positions from attending the conference or otherwise being involved in the movement for reparations.

A few respondents had thought quite a lot about Durban before their interviews. Étienne, a scholar from Congo, considered the conference a waste of time. "Personally, for me, the problem of reparations . . . is a false problem. . . . I don't expect anything from Durban. . . . It's as if someone oppresses you and you ask him not to oppress you any more. It's illogical. . . . One shouldn't dream." On the other hand, Hamza from Niger told us that he had discussed reparations with his colleagues, particularly journalists. He reported that "the question of reparations was quite fashionable, and many African organizations were created to pursue reparations because people think that's the best way to repair the injustices against the African continent."

Insofar as they were aware of the reparations movement, our respondents agreed with the GEP and the Durban activists. They viewed reparations as a way the West could repair the damage it had caused Africa over several centuries. As Ahmad said, "I know that many people now are more concerned with the debt of the West to Africa than the debt of Africa to the West. . . . Many African intellectuals have seriously asked that the Western countries repair the [damage of] five centuries of enslavement that Africa has suffered." Angela said, "Among the people I speak to, I haven't met anyone that does not think that the West owes Africa. Every one of them believes that there should be some reparation coming to Africa."

Two ambassadors also spoke favorably of the movement for reparations. Maria noted, "In Durban, . . . the West really denied to recognize . . . slavery . . . as a crime against humanity. So since then, . . . the position of the African governments was 'OK, so let's ask Bush or ask for more aid or support for development for Africa.' . . . I think that actually it is important to keep pushing this debate, so the Western [world] will be able to fulfill their responsibilities to the development of Africa." Geoffrey suggested that reparations were owed for the postcolonial period, as well as for the slave trade and colonialism, and also suggested that there was a case for individual compensation. Such individual compensation might be possible for people killed or tortured during the colonial period or for their immediate descendants, as I discuss in Chapters 4 and 7. Said Geoffrey,

> The demand is . . . the need for the West . . . to . . . put back some of the wealth which they took from Africa by . . . aid and investment and so on. . . . And in general the Western powers, the former colonizers, have recognized their responsibility to their former colonies, and that is clearly one form of reparation which has been accepted all along. But, as discussed at Durban, the concept has got much wider connotations . . . that people suffered and suffered greatly, in some cases were killed, and that those people if identified . . . are eligible for compensation.

Almost all respondents interpreted reparations as rectification of past wrongs. Edward, a Tanzanian activist, said, "Reparations . . . means to be compensated for the atrocities which have been done to your forefathers or to your brothers, your sisters." Dawn, a Kenyan activist, said that reparations were "going back through history and trying to rectify the mistakes that were made against the people of Africa, to their economic, social, and cultural lives." Linda, a Ghanaian academic, argued that reparations were "making good in the form of money to people against whom crimes have been perpetrated."

Some respondents interpreted reparations as a measure to eradicate the gap between the West and Africa rather than as a means to rectify past wrongs. As Charles, a Zimbabwean activist, remarked,

> First of all, [reparations] brings to my mind the gap that exists between the West and Africa. . . . You can talk about . . . education, standards of living, . . .

shelter, accommodations, health. . . . There are big differences. You talk about skills. . . . We talk about even the advances in technology. We don't have those things in Africa. . . . It's preventing people from making progress in their own lives.

In general, our respondents' opinions were that justice and morality required the West to act on its responsibility to Africa, as Philip, another Kenyan activist, put it.

For me reparation is, I should not walk away, I should look at the inconvenience I cost you, the harm I cost you and . . . pay [you] back, not even [only] in monetary counts [terms], but even [just] acknowledge to you that, "Brother I subjected you to this situation, I'm sorry. . . . I think I have an obligation to do all that there is in my situation . . . to make sure that the injustices that I committed against you are redressed."

Very few respondents explicitly discussed the difficulties attendant on transgenerational responsibility. However, we did not routinely ask about this philosophical question; those who discussed it raised it independently. A typical opinion was that even if present generations of Westerners were not directly responsible for past wrongs, they nevertheless had a moral obligation to address them. As Bartholomew, the acting director of an Ethiopian NGO, said,

The wrong was done centuries back, and those who did [it] are not now alive and we can not really . . . make responsible . . . the new generation for the things done in the past. Now this is a question of moral ethics . . . it's a question of justice, [a] sense of justice morally and those who did wrong are no longer alive and those who are, of course, [were] created by their ancestors and I think they have an obligation . . . to help one another if we're going to create a peaceful world, a stable world. . . . The West seems to me not responsible, but I think has got a moral . . . obligation to do that.

For our respondents, then, as for the GEP, there was a morally compelling case for reparations to Africa from the West. Like some participants at Durban, some respondents knew that other people, especially Jewish victims of the Holocaust, had received compensation for past ill-treatment. They asked why they were not as deserving of reparations as these other persecuted people. In Chapter 4 I offer an explanation of why the social movement for reparations to Africans has so far not been as successful as the social movement for reparations to Jews.

Chapter 4
The Social Movement for Reparations to Africa
Comparison to Holocaust Reparations

The call for reparations to Africa is an emotional one.[1] This is particularly so because it seems to many African reparationists that other victims of injustice received reparations merely on the basis of the moral legitimacy of their claims, whereas Africans did not. But in fact, each case required considerable social mobilization, organization, and tactical maneuvering before reparations were granted. In this chapter, I use the literature on social movements to show the difficulties the African movement for reparations encounters. I focus on a comparison with the Jewish social movement for reparations for the Holocaust of World War II because that is the comparison with which our respondents were most familiar, to which African diplomats at Durban most often referred, and which writers on reparations to Africa most frequently cite. The purpose is to show why the Jewish movement succeeded, while the African movement has, so far, enjoyed little success. This analysis might also serve to give African reparationists some clues as to how they might be more successful in the future.

African Perceptions of the Jewish Precedent: Activists and Diplomats

Holocaust reparations are the gold standard of reparations claims. Reparations to Jews influenced later claims for reparations by "alter[ing] the structure of political opportunity new challengers face"[2] and setting a precedent. Indeed, many activists, and many of our African respondents, sought to align their frame of reference to the Jewish case. They wanted to show that their claim paralleled the Jewish claim or even exceeded it in moral force.

Reparations to Jewish victims of the Holocaust resurfaced in international discussion in the 1990s, when Jewish groups began to demand that unpaid life insurance policies on victims of the Holocaust be paid to their heirs and that monies deposited in European banks by Jews before and during World War II be paid to survivors or their descendants. Jewish and other groups also demanded compensation to living individuals, whether Jewish or non-Jewish, who had been abused as slave laborers by the Nazis. Thus, Africans became aware that "some" people, especially Jews, seemed to be entitled to reparations while others were not. To some Africans, it appeared that "white" victims of mass atrocities were entitled to compensation while nonwhite victims were not.

Thus, Ali Mazrui compared the African claim for reparations to the Jewish claim. He also compared the African claim to other, seemingly lesser cases of persecution that had resulted in reparations. I do not discuss Mazrui's other examples in detail in this chapter, as African reparationists usually compare their claim for reparations to Jewish reparations. Mazrui's other examples are the American internment of persons of Japanese ancestry during World War II, Japanese colonization of Korea from 1910 to 1945, Japanese use of Korean and other women as sex slaves during World War II, and the reparations that Iraq was ordered to pay to Kuwait for invading that country in 1990. Mazrui asked,

> How do twelve years of Jewish hell, seven years of injustice toward Japanese-Americans, decades of Korean colonization, four years of female exploitation and seven months of Kuwaiti indignity compare to several centuries of Black enslavement?
>
> Compensation and reparations seem rational to observers in one case after another, until the principle is applied to Black suffering. Suddenly what is rational becomes absurd; what is compelling for Jews or Koreans becomes comic or "uneconomic" for Blacks.
>
> Is this the latest hereditary indignity to befall Black people? Is this the latest form of racism? Restitution to Jews, comfort women, Japanese internees, Kuwaitis—even though the suffering was for a shorter time—is considered right, moral and plausible, while restitution for the centuries of damage to the African Diaspora is considered a ridiculous pipe-dream.[3]

In his interview with us, Mazrui clarified that his comments on Jews were not meant as a criticism of the Jewish movement for reparations. "I have nothing against the Jews trying to do their bit," he said. "I complain about our not doing our bit." He continued, "So in general we use the Jewish example more in terms of adroitness in getting compensation, in holding future generations responsible for past wrongs. . . . So it's the performance of Jews that sells, rather than what was done to them." Mazrui did note that in his view, the Jewish community had more influence in world affairs than Africans. "We don't have Jewish power or Jewish influence; we may outnumber Jews numerically but we're a fraction of their relevance to the world system, and we don't have the United States behind us, which the Jews have. . . . Half the Jewish demands would not be met if the United States was not behind them."[4]

Other activists in the African movement also referred to Holocaust reparations as a precedent. Chief Abiola, the instigator of the OAU call for reparations, shortened the period of Jewish suffering to the "six-year holocaust perpetrated against Jews by Hitler."[5] Joseph Ndiaye, curator in 1998 of the *Maison des esclaves* (House of Slaves) on the Island of Gorée off Senegal, from which he claimed slaves were shipped to the Americas (discussed in Chapter 10), offered a similar opinion. He said, "We never stop hearing about the Holocaust, but how often do we dwell on the tragedy that took place here over 350 years; a tragedy that consumed tens of millions of lives?"[6]

This sense of discrimination pervaded the Durban discussions. The African Regional Preparatory Conference for Durban noted that "other groups which were subjected to other scourges and injustices have received repeated apologies from different countries as well as ample reparations."[7] At Durban itself, Jakaya Kikwete, then Tanzanian minister of foreign affairs and later president of Tanzania, compared attention to the Holocaust with neglect of Africa. "The Jews are being compensated for crimes committed against them during the Holocaust. . . . We do not understand why there is total hostility to the idea of reparation and compensation to Africa. What is it that is so blasphemous about it? . . . Africans deserve this—it is a matter of principle."[8]

The Zimbabwean Minister of Justice, Legal and Parliamentary Affairs P. A. Chinamasa asked the same question at Durban, although, like Mazrui, he also referred to other cases of reparations.

> We draw the attention of this Conference to the fact that the issue of reparations is now internationally recognized as part of our legal jurisprudence: German reparations to the State of Israel, for the Holocaust; United States reparations to Japanese Americans for illegal internment and reparations by the people of New Zealand through their government to the Maori people. And I ask a poignant question, why reparations to Jews, American Japanese, and not to African Americans and Africans? Why the double standards. Is this the message that we are to take back home that weak nations and weak people have no place in the sun?[9]

All of these statements that compare Jewish and African suffering reveal an understandable lack of knowledge of the historic situation of Jews in Europe. If one were to bring together their entire history of expulsions, mass murders, and discrimination, one could argue that the Jews, like Africans, suffered for centuries, not for only six or twelve years. Moreover, 80 percent of those who received funds from the 1990s settlement for slave laborers were non-Jews from Eastern Europe.[10] But the historical "truth" of the situation of Jews and others persecuted by the Nazis is unlikely to affect such opinions as are noted above. More important is the sense that Jews take up an inordinate amount of the Western world's attention and sympathy, while Africans are ignored. The Africans whom we interviewed also sensed this difference.

African Voices

Our respondents' knowledge of reparations precedents was similar to that of the activists and diplomats cited previously. We asked respondents whether they knew of any reparations precedents, without mentioning specific cases. Quite a few volunteered that Jews had received reparations for the Holocaust. Most seemed more familiar with the recent claims against private entities, especially Swiss banks, than with reparations paid to individual survivors and to the state of Israel in the 1950s. As Ahmad put it, "The Jews' gold was confiscated; it lies in the coffers of the Swiss banks. . . . I think that's a precedent." Hamza referred to apologies to the Jews. "When you look at history, the idea of official acknowledgment comes down to the Northern countries [acknowledging] the harm that was done to the Jewish people. I don't see why they won't, or can't, acknowledge the harm that was done to Africa, make a public apology, acknowledge and take measures for honorable amends, to correct and remedy the damage they did." Some respondents also knew of other precedents. Several mentioned the African American movement for reparations, with which they had become familiar through press and Internet discussion of the Durban Conference. One or two who lived in North America were aware of specific reparations to African Americans, such as President Bill Clinton's official apology to African Americans who, without their knowledge, had been denied treatment for syphilis in the Tuskegee medical experiments from the 1930s to the 1970s.[11] Several respondents also mentioned Japanese Americans and Japanese Canadians who had been interned in their respective countries during World War II, and several mentioned reparations to native Canadians or Americans in the form of treaty and land rights.

Some respondents mentioned Japanese relations with Korea and China, although they were not always sure which country was asking for reparations for what. One or two had heard of the Korean sex slaves, and a few had also heard of the Japanese massacre of the citizens of Nanking in 1937–1938, thinking that the Japanese had paid reparations for these events. Several thought that the American government had rebuilt Japan after World War II as a form of reparation for the bombing of Hiroshima and Nagasaki, and a few thought that the United States was investing in Afghanistan and Iraq as reparation for the destruction of those countries following the post–9/11 invasions. These respondents thought that the reconstruction could serve as a precedent for reconstruction of Africa. Some of the people we spoke with, however, knew of no reparations precedents. When they could think of no cases, we sometimes asked if they had heard of the Jewish reparations claims. Most then answered that they were aware of that case.

Some of the individuals we spoke with, particularly the ambassadors and the more highly educated people, were very diplomatic in their references to the Jews, expressing admiration for how well they had organized to obtain reparations. Paul, an ambassador, attributed the African reparations movement directly to the Jewish precedent. "I can say that the whole clamor for reparations for Africans . . . became born as a result of reparations that were made to the Jews. . . . [There was] a lot of emotive talk . . . as to whether or not the same measures should be applied to Africans and Africa." Benjamin, a West African professor living in the United States, said that "we Africans . . . are not organized, we've not used our numbers very well. . . . When the German companies had cold feet or were resisting the efforts to compensate some Jewish group, I think one of the [Jewish reactions] was . . . them [Jews'] withdrawing their pension funds from banks or businesses and immediately the Germans responded. It's a question of political mobilization and building coalitions." For these respondents, then, the Jewish movement for reparations was an example to be emulated. For others, though, the success of the Jewish movement was evidence of continued worldwide discrimination against black Africans.

There was a common misperception among our respondents that in contrast to the African movement, Jewish activists had merely had to name the injustice they had suffered to receive reparations. Angela attributed the reputed wealth of American Jews to their success in receiving reparations. "Today the Jews, they have been repaid. I mean, in America now, if you're talking about very rich people, they're the Jews." As Geoffrey put it, "The Jews, they seem to have had no great difficulty in proving and showing that wrong was done to them . . . and that reparation was due to them."

Geetu, a South African, concluded that the speed with which the West settled Jewish claims showed that it valued "white" Jews more highly than it valued blacks. "People of Jewish descent had sued the Swiss government for [with]holding all funds from people who . . . [suffered] atrocities in World War II, and how quickly this case was resolved, and . . . reparations were granted. . . . For me, it's something that I believe deeply, that white lives are more important to Western governments than black lives." Omar, a North African who had some distant Jewish ancestry, exaggerated the amount paid to the Jewish community and implied that Jewish suffering was taken more seriously than African suffering. "The Germans paid an enormous amount for five million Jews, almost more than the debt for all of Africa. Yet what happened during the period of slavery in Africa and during colonialism is worse. Worse, and as harsh, and as vile as what the Nazis did against the Jews. So, why not [compensate] Africa?"

These comments on the Jewish and other precedents show that both reparations activists and other educated Africans are acquainted with the movement for reparations that has swept the world in the last twenty-five years. In several cases, though, they thought that reparations had been paid when they had not, as in the case of the destruction of Nanjing. In almost all cases, respondents did not realize how much effort, both organizational and legal, had gone into obtaining reparations, nor how small were the individual awards. For example, in the forced labor settlement of the 1990s, Jewish victims were entitled to about $7,500 each because they had been targeted for extermination; some non-Jewish victims not targeted for extermination received about $2,500.[12]

Criteria of Success for Reparations Movements

The question, "Why the Jews, why not us?" implies that the moral case for reparations to Africa is as strong as, if not stronger than, the case for reparations to Jews. Africans, contend reparationists, were persecuted for several centuries. Moreover, the facts regarding the African slave trade and colonialism appear clear and unassailable. Yet these facts are not enough, in and of themselves, to generate a positive response to the social movement for reparations to Africa.

A social movement can be defined as "a collection of formal organizations, informal networks, and unaffiliated individuals engaged in a more or less coherent struggle for change."[13] The movement for reparations to Africa so far consists of only a few individuals and a very small network with no formal organization. Despite the absence of an organized movement, our interviews evoked a generalized sense that something is owed to Africa. Our respondents, activists at Durban, the three members of the GEP, and many others, were part of an "unmobilized sentiment pool,"[14] a group of people who shared opinions but had no formal connection to one another.

One reason that the African movement for reparations is so small is that it has not yet persuasively framed its demands. One important function of a social movement is to "frame, or assign meaning to and interpret, relevant events and conditions in ways that are intended to mobilize potential adherents and constituents, to garner bystander support, and to demobilize antagonists."[15] Framing requires decisions about who is the perpetrator of a wrong, who is the victim, what exactly is the wrong to be compensated, and what are the desired reparations.

Reparations claims are a kind of symbolic politics that involve "the maintenance or transformation of a power relationship through the communication of normative and affective representations"; thus, symbolic politics relies heavily on "the subjective influence of ideas, learning and information."[16] Those who engage in symbolic politics often have to offer a new, counter-hegemonic narrative. This narrative must produce an emotional and moral resonance in the people from whom reparations are claimed, as well as in the people making the claim. Thus, advocates of reparations to Africa must determine if their principal audience is representatives of Western (slave-trading and slave-owning and/or colonial) states; (white) Westerners as a whole; African Americans; or fellow Africans. Claimants for reparations to Africa can draw on "symbolic value congruence"[17] with African Americans, and possibly with some Jews, but not with whites as a group.

The reparations movement is also hampered by the fairly weak international law of reparations. At best, the law specifies an evolving international norm, as in the 2006 United Nations General Assembly Declaration of basic principles for reparations (discussed in Chapter 1). A norm is "a rulelike prescription which is both clearly perceptible to a community of actors and which makes behavioral claims upon those actors."[18] The Durban Conference was the only venue at which advocates for reparations to Africa had gained "agenda entrance"; that is, they achieved "inclusion in the list of issues that compels attention."[19] Ideas that gain attention often have a feedback effect,[20] but the anticipated effect of the Durban discussions was eclipsed by the events of September 11, 2001. Moreover, the principal actor promoting reparations was the United Nations High Commission on Human Rights, which organized the Durban Conference. Other agencies of the United Nations, such as the Sub-Commission on Economic, Social and Cultural Rights, also issued statements promoting this new idea.[21] But agencies of the United Nations are not as strong as state actors. At most, statements in favor of reparations at Durban represented very weak "symbolic concessions"[22] to the reparations movement. There was no taken-for-granted "consensual knowledge" that Africans deserved reparations.[23]

Nor was there yet a strong epistemic community, a "network of knowledge-based experts" supporting reparations, which could influence national or international public policy.[24] After their appointment in 1992, the three GEP members tried to function as "cognitive baggage handlers,"[25] generating an epistemic community in favor of reparations, but they garnered very little support. There are no national advocates of any strength for reparations to Africa. There are no influential policy entrepreneurs[26] or idea "brokers"[27] who can advocate for reparations, with the exception of the three members of the GEP and legal norm-changers in the United Nations.

Aside from these organizational, legal, and normative problems, reparationists encounter difficulties in persuading outsiders of the legitimacy of their demands, especially at the level of "diagnostic framing," the "identification of a problem and the attribution of blame or causality."[28] Certain aspects of a claim for reparations bear more moral resonance than others. If the action caused "bodily harm" and if it offends "legal equality of opportunity," the social movement is more likely to succeed.[29] If an action for which reparations are claimed was illegal at the time it was committed, moreover, the claim has more resonance than if the action became illegal only after the fact or indeed is still legal at the time the claim is made. Finally, loss of property seems to impel public sympathy because private property is a core value, at least of the modern Western world.

The framing of claimant and respondent is also key to a successful social movement for reparations. The claimant must represent a clearly identifiable group. Leaders must be strong, united, and recognized as legitimate by those they claim to represent. They also need influential allies. To find these allies, they must minimize any likelihood that the claimants themselves might be seen as partly responsible for the harm they say they have suffered. The respondent to the claim must also be clearly identifiable. A claim is more likely to succeed if there is a recognizable responsible authority, such as a government, to whom it can be addressed. If the claimants can gain allies within that government or its bureaucracy, they can use those allies to influence policy. These allies, in their turn, might be able to generate public support by rendering their offices as legitimate venues for making claims. One difficulty faced by African reparationists is that their claims are transnational: they are not voters in the countries from which they want reparations. Few, if any, members of Parliament in the United Kingdom or elected senators or representatives in the United States speak for them.

In order to build a community of claimants, as well as a community of those receptive and capable of responding to the claim, reparationists must also convincingly show the causal chain between initial actions and later damage. The shorter the causal chain[30]—that is, the fewer the actors involved in causing the damage—the easier it is for the link to be established and for those against whom a claim is made to accept responsibility. The length of time since a wrong was committed also helps predict the success of a reparations movement. If the victims or their immediate descendants are still alive, reparations are more likely to be considered legitimate than if the potential beneficiaries are many generations removed from the ancestors who were wronged. It is also necessary to show a direct link between those accused of perpetrating a wrong and the living activists who claim to have been victimized. If many actors were involved in the process of wronging the alleged victims, then it is difficult to find a precise respondent to the claim. When the "actors" include structural variables rather than identifiable human beings—as in the case of postcolonial poverty in Africa—the chain is even more complicated.

The type of reparation demanded affects the likelihood of success. If the claim is only for acknowledgment of a past wrong or even for an apology without material compensation, it is more likely to succeed than if there is also a demand for monetary payment. If material compensation is claimed, its reasonableness will affect the outcome. The amount must be one that is payable without a high cost to those making the payment.

The claims-making organization also needs effective tactics. One tactic is to shame a respondent into replying to a claim. The effectiveness of such a technique often depends on whether the social movement can find a "condensation symbol," a concrete event or individual that becomes publicly symbolic of the perpetrated harm.[31] "We think about politics in stories, and our consciousness is changed when new stories persuade us to adopt a new paradigm."[32] The aim of any reparations movement is to create a new and legitimate story, thus acquiring "symbolic capital," a form of authority and competence recognized by the wider society, so that the claimants' demand for reparations is considered an accurate representation of history.[33] Such symbolic capital can assist claims-making groups to engage in "frame extension"[34] practices, building coalitions with groups with similar aims, such as the movement for reparations to African Americans.

Below I assess the Jewish and African reparations claims along the criteria I have set out here. I show that unless they frame their demands more clearly, the small groups currently advocating reparations to Africa are unlikely to succeed. The social movement for African reparations consists of disparate groups that promote incongruent ideas. It has not yet been able to mobilize the rather large sentiment pool of supporters of reparations.

Jewish Victims and Post-Holocaust Claims

Those who ask, "Why the Jews, why not Africans" probably do not stop to consider that the Jews did not ask for reparations for all the injustices they suffered throughout many centuries in Europe.[35] The Jews confined their claims to a discrete, short, and easily identifiable period—that of Nazi rule in Germany and elsewhere (1933–1945).

There were two waves of claims for reparations to Jews. The first was the immediate post–World War II claim and the second was the new claims against private businesses, banks, and insurance companies in the 1990s. During the first wave, Jewish claims for reparations had a high moral resonance. The judges at the Nuremberg tribunal made a strong, though not uncontroversial, case that genocide had been illegal under international customary law at the time of the Holocaust; moreover, genocide was explicitly outlawed in international law by 1951, at the time the Jewish claims for reparations began.[36] The Jews suffered direct physical harm: they were murdered, starved, tortured, sterilized, raped, and used in "medical" experiments. Nazis' treatment of the Jews violated the equality principle that by the latter part of the twentieth century was at the heart of Western culture, although at the time of the Holocaust it was not so deeply entrenched. The Jews also lost property, a loss that became central to the second wave of reparations claims; for example, the heirs of Jewish art collectors asked for return of their artworks.[37]

During the first wave, claimants were easily identifiable: the survivors had just emerged from their prison camps and hiding places. Moreover, they were not perceived to bear personal blame for what had happened to them. After some negotiations, two groups were recognized as the legitimate representatives of these dispersed survivors, namely, the state of Israel and the Unified Claims Conference of fifty-two Jewish organizations in Western countries, which represented the "stateless, dispossessed Jews in Europe."[38]

The causal chain of harm to Jews was short and uncomplicated. There was an easily identifiable entity against which Jewish claims could be made. The Nazi state was the chief perpetrator: the government of the Federal Republic of Germany was the successor government to the Nazis. On September 27, 1951, President Konrad Adenauer of Germany, successor to Hitler, acknowledged the brutality of the Holocaust, only a little more than six years after it ended.[39] Adenauer had his own motives for this acknowledgment; without it, Germany was unlikely to receive Marshall Plan aid from the United States. Adenauer also wished to facilitate Germany's reentry into the "civilized" (Western) world.

The first-wave compensation eventually received by both individual Jewish victims and the state of Israel was generally acknowledged as legitimate. Direct victims were compensated for their suffering in the concentration camps, their loss of property, and other aspects of their persecution. It has been estimated that by 2000 West Germany alone would have paid Israel and individual Jews a little less than 103 billion

Deutschmarks, or about $U.S. 47.6 billion, in compensation.[40] This figure, however large it may seem, is far less than the hundreds of trillions of dollars demanded by some activists for reparations to Africa.

The second-wave Holocaust reparations claims appeared to be less legitimate. Both perpetrators and victims were less easily identifiable. More and more alleged collaborators with the Nazis were discovered, including private American corporations such as IBM.[41] Many, if not most, of the direct victims of the Nazis were dead: sometimes the heirs who claimed insurance payments or return of property were the grandchildren, or even the great-grandchildren, of the victims. Thus, accusations of a "Holocaust industry" emerged, along with the perception that many distant and prosperous descendants of the victims were exploiting the Holocaust for their own material ends.[42] These perceptions of the lessened legitimacy of second-wave Holocaust claims hint at the difficulties that Africans experience in making claims for wrongs perpetrated many decades and centuries ago against distant ancestors.

During the first wave, Jewish claimants for reparations were able easily to mobilize the tactics of shame. Many Christian leaders and churches in the formerly Allied and occupied countries were embarrassed by their inaction during the Nazi period.[43] Several key condensation symbols existed for the first wave of reparations. These included photographs and films of victims as they were being liberated from concentration camps such as Bergen-Belsen and the diary of the teenaged victim Anne Frank. Before and during the second wave of reparations, the mass media contributed a television series, *Holocaust* (1978), and a major motion picture, *Schindler's List* (1993). These media events once again condensed the genocide of the Jews in a manner that refocused Western attention on it.[44] As Ali Mazrui noted in his interview with us, the Jewish claimants and the state of Israel also enjoyed the support of the government of the United States. The Jewish community within the United States and internationally had also consolidated itself into an effective lobbying group.

Reparations to Africa

To assess the African reparations claim as a social movement, one must consider separately the claims for three historical stages; the slave trade, colonialism, and postcolonialism. These three periods are discussed in detail in Chapters 5 through 9; here I discuss the possibility of reparations from the point of view of social movements theory.

The strongest moral claim for reparations to Africa stems from the transatlantic slave trade. In modern times, to take people as slaves is self-evidently a moral wrong. The condition of slavery is a gross violation of an individual's right to life, a gross violation of the rights to physical integrity and freedom of movement, a gross indication of discrimination, and a gross violation of an individual's property rights in his or her physical self and capacity to labor.

Nevertheless, as I discuss in more detail in Chapter 5, the slave trade and slavery were not illegal throughout the entire period that they occurred. Moreover, those entitled to reparations for the slave trade are not readily identifiable. The victims of the trade and their immediate descendants are long dead. Their distant descendants are generally unidentifiable as individuals, although in some cases African ethnic or clan oral histories contain mediated memories of ancestors taken as slaves, and in other cases historians can refer to shipping or sales records or records of groups or locales from which slaves were taken. Those responsible to make reparations are more easily identifiable. As discussed in Chapter 1, the responsible authorities are the successor governments of slave-trading and slave-buying countries, especially the United Kingdom, France, Portugal, Spain, the Netherlands, and the United States.

The causal chain of African suffering is long and complex, contributing to the difficulty in obtaining reparations. The transatlantic slave trade spanned over four hundred years. Many individuals were involved, from Europeans and Africans who raided for slaves, to African sellers, to European and African buyers, to European traders resident in coastal African ports, to the ultimate purchasers in Europe and the Americas. Thus, the question arises whether some Africans owe reparations to others or whether continental Africans as a collectivity owe some sort of reparation, perhaps an apology, to diaspora Africans descended from individuals sold as slaves.

The few activists for reparations for slavery have not availed themselves of all the tactics that help social movements succeed. So far, the major tactic appears to have been shaming, which had some success at Durban, where some European countries expressed regret for the slave trade. There is no large base of activists who could engage in other tactics, such as political demonstrations, which in any case would be hindered by the fact that reparationists would be demonstrating against foreign powers, not in their own countries where, assuming an effective democracy, they might have some political influence. There has been very little media publicity, which might interest the public in respondent countries in the case for reparations. In the 1970s, Alex Haley's novel *Roots*, and a television series subsequently based upon it, roused some interest in the slave trade, but other films about the trade, such as the 1997 *Amistad*, did not have the same effect. Nor have reparationists been very successful in their use of the Internet. The London-based

ARM published some essays by a few activists, including Mazrui and Thompson. *Transafrica Forum*, based in Washington, also published some material on reparations to Africa but did not otherwise attract a large activist base. In 2007, however, interest in the slave trade grew as the British celebrated the two hundredth anniversary of its abolition; one result (discussed in Chapter 10) was a spate of apologies or near-apologies for the trade. Nevertheless, on the whole, activists possess few resources to organize political movements, citizen boycotts, or any other punitive tactics.

The demand for reparations for colonialism faces different obstacles than the demand for reparations for the slave trade. Although colonialism was not as self-evidently a moral wrong as the slave trade, it did violate many of the central moral principles of the modern world. Colonialism was by definition predicated on conquest, a moral evil in the post–World War II world in which acts of aggression are outlawed by the United Nations Charter (Chapter 1, article 1). While inhabitants of some colonies, such as Ghana, lived in comparative security during colonial rule, in others, such as Namibia and Congo (discussed in Chapter 7), the European rulers were extremely cruel and exploitative. In any case, even the least abusive colonialism violated the principle of equality, insofar as Europeans ruled over Africans and treated them in a discriminatory manner. Property rights were also violated under colonial rule, most especially but not solely in settler colonies such as Zimbabwe, Kenya, Algeria, Namibia, and South Africa. The practice of forced labor in some colonies also violated the principle that individuals possess property in their own labor power. Nevertheless, as with the slave trade, colonialism was not illegal during much of the time it was practiced.

The causal chain of damages resulting from colonialism is more recent than the slave trade, and it is not as complex. The relevant colonial powers can be identified easily. It is more difficult to identify the victims, however. Although many who lived at the time or their immediate descendants are still alive, not all Africans suffered under colonial rule; indeed, some benefited. Some individuals considered by the indigenous political system to be slaves became emancipated by conversion to Christianity. Some availed themselves of new opportunities to acquire education, accumulate wealth, or work in the colonial civil service. Moreover, it is difficult to sort out the costs and benefits of the colonial and the postcolonial periods. Individual victims of colonialism still alive have been living under independent, postcolonial rule for twenty-five to fifty years, depending on the country. Postcolonial rulers were violators in their own right of the principles of bodily integrity, nondiscrimination, and private property.

Yet, although the claim for reparations for colonialism seems tactically stronger than the claim for reparations for the slave trade, even the three active members of the GEP could not agree whether to ask for reparations for colonialism. There is less support for reparations for colonialism in part because there are few, if any, condensation symbols around which to rally Western public opinion. In 1998 Adam Hochschild's best-selling *King Leopold's Ghost* brought to the Western English-speaking reading public's attention the horrible terrors perpetrated upon inhabitants of the Belgian Congo during the reign of King Leopold II. In Belgium itself, the condensation point was Ludo de Witte's *De moord op Lumumba* ("The Death of Lumumba"), about Belgium's alleged participation in the murder of Patrice Lumumba, the first president of independent Congo.[45] Publication of de Witte's book was one impetus to the Belgian apology to Congo for its part in Lumumba's death.

The claim for reparations for postcolonial relations is even more difficult to justify than that for the slave trade or colonialism. While the most obvious difference between the West and Africa in the twenty-first century is the gap in wealth, there is no international law requiring material equality among citizens of different regions. Nor is economic inequality generally considered a gross human rights violation in the same manner as is a direct attack on an individual's life or physical integrity. Indeed, even failure to provide basic economic rights does not lead to easy acceptance of claims. Many victims of postcolonial relations are alive. But the victims are also innumerable, responsibility for their suffering is diffuse, and their poverty is caused as much or more by systemic reasons as by identifiable perpetrators. Most important, African as well as Western states and leaders are partly responsible for many of the poor economic decisions taken during the postcolonial period. Africans themselves are at least partly responsible for the corruption, lack of good governance, and lack of transparency that have characterized postcolonial rule and resulted in suffering for hundreds of millions of people.

Although reparations claims for general postcolonial relations have very little hope of success, certain specific actions or relations do violate basic principles of justice and might persuade many members of the Western public that reparations are owed. Direct attacks on property rights are one example. If a government, private corporation, or institution can be shown to violate property rights, for example, by illegally dispossessing peasants to explore for oil, then a case for compensation might be as clear in Africa as would be a legal case demanding compensation for similar abuses in North America. Other activities that have taken place in Africa since the end of the colonial period, such as diamond smuggling, are clearly illegal (discussed in Chapter 9). Since, however, it is not states that officially sponsor these activities, the remedy would not normally be via interstate reparations. Rather, ordinary criminal or civil trials are the preferred route, difficult as it would be for African victims to initiate such trials without assistance from lawyers or advocacy organizations in the West. By contrast, however, much of what some activists consider "neocolonialism," such as investment in Africa by transnational corporations and economic structural adjustment programs, is legal and thus subject neither to reparations nor to criminal trials.

Limited Reparations Claims

I have compared the Jewish and African social movements for reparations in order to explain why it is very difficult for Africans to imitate the Jewish movement. African reparationists face problems that Jewish activists did not face. Many of the victims of Western-African relations are long dead, there are too many of them, and they cannot easily be identified. Although institutional successors to perpetrators can be identified, the exact injuries they caused are less easy to specify. The causal chain between past injuries and present victims is very long and complex, with many actors and events implicated. By contrast, reparation for the Holocaust was easily framed.

This analysis suggests that while the West may offer symbolic acknowledgments of, and perhaps even apologies for, the damage caused to Africa by the slave trade and colonialism, large amounts of financial compensation are unlikely. On the other hand, certain discrete injuries that violated key moral precepts and that occurred within living memory may result in some financial reparations. To experience success comparable to the Jewish movement's, claimants for African reparations must present clear, limited demands for recognizable wrongs caused by recognizable agents and events. Most likely to succeed are claims for reparation for actions that were illegal at the time they were committed or at least are illegal now, for violation of the right to life or bodily integrity, for violation of the equality principle, and for violation of property rights. The victims must be a finite group of people living in the present. Some such cases exist in Africa and have garnered or could garner reparations.

In France, activists in 2002 won more than $70 million in increased benefits for colonial veterans of French wars, including World War II and the Algerian war of independence.[46] These African veterans had taken the same risks and suffered the same hardships as French soldiers, yet had originally received much less in pay, health benefits, and pensions; thus, the injustice was obvious. The French government was clearly responsible for this injustice, which continued for decades. Articles in African and French media and on the Internet about suffering elderly veterans or their widows acted as a condensation point for public support for compensation. The total amount paid did not seem an unreasonable burden on the French purse. At first, however, the French government "adjusted" the pensions to take account of Africa's lower cost of living, but further public outcry forced it to pay the full amount, budgeted at about $510.7 million a year, to provide pensions to 80,000 people in twenty-three countries, as of late 2006.[47] Part of the impetus for this decision was a film about North African soldiers in France's World War II army, *Indigènes*, which acted as a condensation point for French and African public opinion.[48]

Another claim that may have a chance of success is the Kenyan "Mau Mau Reparations and Recognition Project," which wants reparations for the maltreatment of suspected "Mau Mau" warriors and supporters. The Mau Mau battled for independence against the British during the eight-year (1952–1960) state of emergency that preceded Kenyan independence. The term "state of emergency" refers to the colonial government's declaration of an emergency, in response to the militant anticolonial movement among Kenyans. In 2005 Caroline Elkins published a Pulitzer-prize–winning account of the maltreatment, *Imperial Reckoning*.[49] Elkins's book is based on documentary evidence and interviews both with survivors of British prisons and detention camps and individuals who committed the tortures she documents. British and African guards incessantly beat, tortured, mutilated, and raped their victims. Many men were castrated. Men and women had to carry buckets of human excrement on their heads, the excrement spilling over into their faces. Prisoners had to dig huge trenches and then refill them every day or had to senselessly carry heavy piles of stones from one place to another. Hundred of thousands of Kenyans were enclosed in "protected" villages, where they were subject to the capricious, brutal, and total control of their guards, many prisoners dying of malnutrition and disease.

Imperial Reckoning garnered its share of controversy: Elkins was particularly criticized for ignoring atrocities committed by the Mau Mau itself, exaggerating the numbers of victims, and accepting oral testimony without criticism.[50] Nevertheless, she and other historians[51] have provided enough evidence that one can certainly argue that the British knowingly violated their own laws. British officials held discussions to determine how they might evade the international and European Union laws protecting prisoners from abuse, to which the United Kingdom was party.[52] The Colonial Office in London protected the governor in

Kenya, even when members of the opposition complained in the House of Commons about abuse and torture.[53]

From the point of view of social movements theory, the case for reparations to victims of the British during the Kenyan state of emergency is strong. There were clear perpetrators, namely, the British and colonial governments, British officials, and some Kenyan settlers, although the matter is somewhat complicated as the British were also assisted by "loyalist" Africans, known as the Home Guard. The number of victims was relatively small, and the time period over which the atrocities occurred discrete. The crimes, murders, and violation of bodily integrity were of the worst kind. The actions were illegal at the time they occurred, and the perpetrators knew they were illegal.

In 2000 the Reparations and Recognition Project petitioned the British Embassy in Kenya for $30 billion compensation to Mau Mau members and their families.[54] The later publication of Elkins's book provided a condensation point for the movement. *Imperial Reckoning* was widely reviewed, so that many tens of thousands of members of the Western reading public became aware of the British atrocities. This knowledge should assist the reparations movement, which by 2006 had prepared a case against the British government.[55] That government rejected the case, claiming that the Kenyan governor, not the British Colonial Office, was responsible for any alleged atrocities and that the successor independent Kenyan government is therefore the entity to which Mau Mau reparationists should present their claims.[56]

An alternative to reparations claims might be trials. In other cases, legal means have been devised to try quite elderly men for crimes of the distant past. Maurice Papon was tried in France in 1997 for his role in the deportation of Jews from France during World War II.[57] There were also attempts in the late 1990s to try the former Chilean dictator Augusto Pinochet for crimes he allegedly committed in the 1970s and 1980s.[58] Elkins interviewed elderly British men who gave her details of the tortures they had perpetrated. Even if such individuals, if convicted, would never be imprisoned, a trial might have the important consequence of publicly acknowledging crimes concealed from public consciousness for fifty years. Victims might also derive some satisfaction from seeing their torturers publicly shamed.

The demand for reparations is complicated by the fact that the Mau Mau had also committed atrocities. If trials were held, however, Kenya could try those members of both Mau Mau and the Home Guard who were accused of committing crimes during the Emergency. Both trials and reparations, however, might stir up resentments among various groups within Kenyan society. At the time of independence, Kenya's first president, Jomo Kenyatta, preferred forgetting to remembering, propagating a myth of unified Kenyan resistance to colonial rule.[59] The colonial ban on Mau Mau was not rescinded until the introduction of substantive democracy to Kenya in 2002, when Kenyans began the process of debating their own past.[60]

Whatever Kenyans decide to do within their own country to come to terms with the state of emergency, the former colonial ruler, Britain, has clearly been indicted as a perpetrator of crimes against Kenyans. Britain's crimes are similar to those committed by Nazis during World War II against non-Jewish subject populations, especially in Eastern Europe. Thus, both post–World War II trials and reparations to victims of Nazis serve as useful precedents for the Kenyan reparations movement. On the other hand, the example of reparations to Jews shows the difficulties that African reparationists might expect to encounter in asking for reparations for the slave trade, colonialism, and postcolonial relations, subjects to which I turn in Chapters 5 through 9.

Chapter 5

Reparations for the Slave Trade

Law and Rhetoric

During the first four months of 2003, I was a visiting professor in Fredericksburg, Virginia. Fredericksburg is a delightful small town blooming with red, pink, yellow, and white azaleas, a popular tourist destination for those interested in both the Revolutionary War against the British and the American Civil War between the North and the South. Walking one day from my home to the tourist shops, I passed a wooden stump embedded in the sidewalk. On it was a plaque explaining that it was the stump on which slaves stood when they were being auctioned for sale.

Some of those Fredericksburg slaves might have been brought to the United States by ship from Liverpool, one of the largest centers of the British slave trade. In 1752 eighty-seven ships sailing from Liverpool were capable of taking 25,000 slaves across the Atlantic. More than two centuries later, in the early 1970s, "nearly every old-established Liverpool family . . . [could] trace its history (and many a family its prosperity) to the slave trade."[1] Liverpool slave traders subdued their human cargo with a variety of instruments of torture, including heavy leg shackles, neck shackles, and mouth pieces: the latter prevented slaves from talking or eating and could choke them to death.[2] Upon their sale in the Americas, slaves were often branded with hot iron, as cattle were branded. Production of these instruments of torture would have provided employment to some of Britain's new class of industrial proletariat.

The casual capture, torture, rape, sale, and murder of enslaved Africans shocks thoughtful individuals who encounter this sad history today. Yet the question remains, in the twenty-first century is anyone owed reparation by anyone for this dreadful crime of the past?

During World War II, non-Jewish Eastern Europeans were enslaved to work in German factories, on German farms, and as domestics in German households. Non-Jewish men, women, and children from Poland were loaded on railway cars and shipped west. En route, many froze to death. Bodies were tossed out of railway cars to lie on the side of the tracks; children died of starvation.[3] As one German official said, "The Slavs [Eastern Europeans] are to work for us. In so far as we don't need them, they may die. . . . As for food, they won't get any more than is necessary. We are the masters, we come first."[4] Fifty years later, the approximately one million non-Jewish survivors were eligible to receive $2,500 each as compensation (discussed in Chapter 4). If individuals enslaved by the Germans during World War II were found in the 1990s to be entitled to compensation, why, ask many reparationists, are not the descendants of enslaved Africans also entitled to compensation? In Chapter 4 I use social movement theory to explain the difficulties of obtaining reparations. In this chapter I consider rhetoric about, and the law concerning, the slave trade and reparations. But first, a word from the past.

Forty years ago, Frantz Fanon, the Martinican psychiatrist whose *The Wretched of the Earth*[5] became the literary symbol of the anticolonial movement, argued against seeking reparations for slavery. Said Fanon,

> In no way should I derive my basic purpose from the past of the peoples of color. . . . I will not make myself the man of any past. . . . I have neither the right nor the duty to claim reparations for the domestication of my ancestors. . . . Am I going to ask the contemporary white man to answer for the slave-ships of the seventeenth century? Am I going to try by every possible means to cause Guilt to be born in minds? . . . I do not have the right to allow myself to be mired in what the past has determined. I am not the slave of the Slavery that dehumanized my ancestors.[6]

By the beginning of the twenty-first century, Fanon's attitude was rendered obsolete by the rhetoric of reparations to Africa.

Rhetoric and the Slave Trade

Much of the discussion of the slave trade among reparationists and those who attended the Durban Conference is ridden with inflated figures of how many people were transported across the Atlantic as slaves. Summarizing several decades' worth of quantitative research by historians, the respected scholar of the slave trade, Paul Lovejoy, estimates that 11.3 million people were transported across the Atlantic from Western Africa from 1450 to 1900. He suggests that during the period 1600 to 1800 another 15 to 20 percent might have died during the crossing. If we add the higher of these two estimates, 20 percent, to the entire number in the 1450–1900 period, the number of Africans who either died during the Middle Passage or reached the shores of the Americas is 13.6 million. This number is far lower than the figures often cited in the debate on reparations.[7]

Lord Anthony Gifford acted as an advocate for reparations in an unusual debate in the British House of Lords in 1996. He overestimated the numbers who were taken to the Americas and who died in transit, claiming that "around 20 million young people were kidnapped, taken in chains across the Atlantic and sold. . . . Millions more died in transit in the dungeons of the castles [in West Africa] . . . or in the hell holes under the decks of the slave ships."[8] Although Gifford's figures bear some resemblance to those upon which scholars of the slave trade agree, other spokespersons for reparations cite much larger figures. Tseliso Thipanyane, a South African, relies on an unnamed source cited in an article in the *New African*[9] to claim that "about fifty million Africans were shipped out of the continent during the Atlantic slave trade alone." He disregards the conservative estimate of 12 million cited in the same article.[10]

These rhetorical differences between scholarly and other figures were reflected at Durban. The representative from Niger referred to "hundreds of millions of Black victims, dead as a consequence of deportation, slavery and colonialism."[11] The representative from Angola asserted that "it is estimated that from 1500 to 1900 more than a 100 millions [*sic*] Africans were transported across the Atlantic to the Americas."[12] The NGO Forum at Durban also claimed that "the Trans-Atlantic Slave Trade and slavery . . . forced the brutal removal and the largest forced migration in history (over one hundred million)."[13]

Some of the speakers at Durban might have been motivated by interests other than reparations. To blame most of Africa's problems on past relations with the West is to absolve current leaders of their responsibilities. An egregious example is that of Sudan. At Durban, Sudan's Minister of Justice Ali Mohamed Osman Yassin explicitly linked the slave trade to Africa's current problems.

> The slave trade, particularly against Africans, was an appalling tragedy in its abhorrent barbarism, enormous magnitude, institutionalized nature, transnational dimension and particularly in its negation of the essence of the victims. Africa's economic marginalization started with the deprivation of its manpower by the slave trade, followed by uneven exploitation and the siphoning of its natural resources during the colonial era. It is culminating today in economic globalization, where Africa lacks the capacity to compete commercially in the world economy.[14]

Yet Sudan itself was historically implicated in the slave trade; "dozens of Sudanese kingdoms . . . prospered over the centuries from their role as middlemen in the slave trade between Egypt and sub-Saharan Africa."[15] The Sudanese elite was embroiled in the slave trade in the nineteenth century;[16] even in the twentieth century some Sudanese slave owners making the *Hajj*, thc pilgrimage to Mecca, would sell slaves who had accompanied them.[17] There was still widespread slavery in

Sudan in the 1920s, enforced by Muslim *shari'a* courts controlled by slave owners.[18] As late as the 1980s, some members of Sudan's ruling elite were descendants of slave traders.[19] But the Muslim slave trade was barely mentioned at Durban, which focused almost entirely on the transatlantic trade.[20] Nor was the continued slavery in Mauritania mentioned in the official discussions at Durban, although it was mentioned in the final document of the parallel NGO conference.[21]

It seemed particularly opportunistic for the Sudanese minister of justice to have discussed the horrors of the transatlantic slave trade in 2001 when Sudan was still in the midst of a long-standing civil war between north and south. During the war, the central government encouraged abduction of southern Dinka and Nuer women and children as slaves. Yet the government was still denying that enslavement had occurred, although it was cooperating with an international and local effort to locate and free abducted southerners.[22]

Although it might be considered egregious, the example of Sudan nevertheless highlights the political interest in blaming the West for the transatlantic trade while disregarding African and Muslim slavery (discussed further in Chapter 6). Discussions of law pertaining to slavery also focus disproportionately on the transatlantic trade.

International Law and the Slave Trade

The rhetoric at Durban discussed not only the numbers of persons enslaved for the transatlantic trade but also how contemporary law ought to be applied to that trade. Many African diplomats and others believed that present-day laws establishing crimes against humanity ought to be retroactively applied to the slave trade so that those "responsible" for it—that is, Western states and other social institutions—could be punished, much as if they were trading in slaves today. Some Western diplomats and legal scholars replied that although the slave trade ought to have been considered a crime against humanity, at the time it occurred it was not so considered. Therefore, the law could not be applied retroactively and, by logical corollary, Western nations were not liable to pay compensation for the trade.

Part of this debate concerned when slavery and the slave trade became illegal under international law. Legal scholars agree that the two practices were not firmly and universally illegal until 1926. This is the date of signature of the League of Nations Convention to Suppress the Slave Trade and Slavery, which defines slavery in its article 1(1) as "the status or condition of a person over whom any or all of the powers attaching to the right of ownership are exercised."[23] Even this supposedly definitive convention, however, contains very weak enforcement measures.

It sets no time limit for the eradication of slavery, and measures for enforcement of abolition and for monitoring of progress were rejected as violations of state sovereignty.[24]

The Convention to Suppress the Slave Trade and Slavery culminated a process of eradication that had spanned some 150 years, as various countries abolished first the trade, then slavery itself. By the time the 1926 convention was declared many states had already outlawed the slave trade and slavery. Thus, activists might demand reparations from states now in existence that were also in existence at the time of abolition but that tolerated violations of their own laws. These states might include the United Kingdom, the United States, the Netherlands, France, Portugal, and Spain.

The first African slaves arrived in the Americas in 1502.[25] For the next 270 years, the slave trade and slavery itself were legal everywhere in Europe and the Americas. In 1772 an English judge ruled that "any slave who touched British soil was automatically set free," but "the decision prohibited neither the slave trade nor colonial slavery,"[26] and subsequent to 1772 the status of slaves in Britain was still debated.[27] In 1777 Vermont became the first American territory to ban slavery;[28] gradually some other parts of what became the United States banned the trade, although many retained slavery. Britain abolished the slave trade in 1807, followed by the United States in 1808 (although the United States had decided to abolish the slave trade before the British did).[29] The Netherlands abolished the trade in 1814, and France abolished it in 1818.[30] In the 1820s several Latin American countries, on gaining independence from Spain, abolished the slave trade and slavery.[31] In 1815 the Congress of Vienna, an international diplomatic conference of European powers called to settle territorial and other matters at the end of the Napoleonic Wars, declared slavery "repugnant to the principles of humanity and universal morality," but did not ban it.[32] In 1820 a U.S. congressional act declared the slave trade to be piracy, punishable by death.[33] Nevertheless, it is difficult to argue that customary international law condemned slavery and the slave trade in the early nineteenth century.[34] For example, in 1825 the chief justice of the U.S. Supreme Court ruled that the slave trade was legal, despite the fact that there was already widespread public "international condemnation of its immorality."[35]

In 1833 Britain emancipated slaves in its West Indies colonies, South Africa, and Mauritius.[36] However, Britain did not abolish slavery in its protectorates, including the protectorate of Sierra Leone in Africa, where slavery continued until 1928.[37] Portugal abolished slavery within its territories in 1854, but its former colony, Brazil, did not abolish slavery until 1888.[38] France emancipated the slaves in its colonies in 1848,[39] followed by the Netherlands in 1863.[40] In 1862 during the American Civil War, the United States and the United Kingdom made a "Treaty for the Suppression of the African Slave Trade,"[41] and in 1863 the United States abolished slavery; this abolition was confirmed by the Thirteenth Amendment to the U.S. Constitution in 1865.[42]

Subsequent to these many national decisions to abolish the slave trade and slavery, international activity continued. The General Act of Berlin in 1885 and the General Act of Brussels on the Slave Trade and on the Importation into Africa of Firearms, Ammunition, and Spirituous Liquors in 1890 both provided for cooperation to end the slave trade,[43] although the Berlin Act pertained only to the international slave trade, not to trade within states.[44] Finally, as noted, by 1926 the slave trade and slavery were firmly illegal under international law.

The call for reparations for the slave trade and slavery is, then, in legal terms at least partially a call for the retroactive application of laws not in effect at the time of the alleged crime. Retroactive application of law is generally prohibited. Yet, as Spitzer states, "international law is not a fixed body of rules. Rather, it is an evolving, dynamic indicator of the collective moral progress among and within nations."[45] Spitzer also notes that during the eighteenth and nineteenth centuries, international law "developed according to treaties made among five or six of the great powers of Europe," treaties that often justified conquest, slavery, and colonialism.[46] Consequently, reparationists might hesitate to accept international law as authoritative. The laws the European powers made often furthered their own interests. The British used the Berlin Conference to further their prestige as an anti–slave trade power,[47] at the same time as the conference confirmed their colonial interests in Africa. King Leopold of Belgium agreed to hold the 1890 conference in Brussels in part to further his own claim to the Congo,[48] where his agents treated the Congolese as brutally as any American slave master treated his slaves. This fact was not lost on Pierre, one of the Congolese we interviewed, who noted, "Leopold II . . . said that the [Belgian] occupation of the Congo was a vital necessity for the Congolese, who were dominated by the Arabs, because the Arabs also traded [in slaves]. So, to justify colonialism, he said, 'we must go there to deliver them, to liberate them from Arab slavery.'"

Referring to the 2001 Draft Articles on Responsibility of States for Internationally Wrongful Acts, Shelton argues that there might be some way to apply laws against slavery if one could show its continuous effects. "Any rule which relates to the licit or illicit nature of a legal act shall apply while the rule is in force, but any rule which relates to the continuous effects of a legal act shall apply to effects produced while the rule is in force, even if the act has been performed prior to the entry into force of the rule."[49] Thus, reparationists might argue that Africa's present poverty is an ongoing effect of the slave trade, so that current laws about effects of past actions—even if the actions were not considered crimes at the time—should be applied. Yet the problem of the long and complicated causal chain remains. It would be very difficult to prove that but for the crime (the slave trade), the harm (poverty) would not exist in Africa today. As Shelton notes, "causation in fact does not suffice to entail reparations, because the injury may be too remote . . . or indirect for legal causation to be attributed."[50]

Britain, moreover, could argue that it has already made reparation for the slave trade through its attempts to abolish it in the nineteenth century. Lord Wilberforce argued in the 1996 debate on African reparations in the British House of Lords that "ever since 1833 when slavery was abolished in the British Empire, British governments have striven by law, by force, by use of their navy, by influence and by the expenditure of money, to have slavery abolished in African countries, to stop the trade in human beings, and to mitigate the consequences."[51] Indeed, for fifty years the British navy devoted its considerable resources to wiping out the trade, in the face of much hostility from other nations and at high cost to its own men, although its actions off the coast of West Africa also helped to consolidate the British Empire.[52] Similarly, the United States could argue that the 600,000 dead in its civil war of 1861–1865, during which slavery was abolished, was sacrifice enough, without reparation in the twenty-first century.[53] The import of these arguments is that if historical wrongs are to be retroactively judged, then so should state actions taken to rectify those wrongs, however historically remote they may now be.

Several scholars suggest other legal avenues to buttress claims for reparations. Laremont suggests that the slave trade could be prosecuted as conscious genocide. He states that thirteen million Africans were loaded in Africa onto ships for the Americas, but among these it is estimated that 13 percent, or 1.72 million, died while crossing the Atlantic. From this he deduces that West African states could bring a charge of genocide against "the colonial powers . . . responsible for African deaths that occurred during trans-shipment."[54] Yet, 87 percent of those trans-shipped survived, according to Laremont's own figures, as did those Africans not taken by slave traders who remained on the continent. In any case, a charge of genocide requires intent to destroy a racial, ethnic, religious, or national group.[55] A better case for genocide might be made against those who raided particular African ethnic groups for slaves if, in doing so, they also intended to destroy the group. However, some of those raiders were Africans, not Europeans; thus, successor African states might be just as liable to a charge of genocide as successor Western states.

Some reparationists refer to the transatlantic slave trade as an instance of "unjust enrichment."[56] This term possesses a certain moral cachet: it implies that slave-trading and slave-buying nations immorally enriched themselves at the expense of Africa and Africans. However, Bossuyt and Vandeginste state that "while this notion is . . . legally recognized under various domestic legal systems . . . there is no public international legal foundation for such claim" and, in any case, there are statutes of limitations on claims of unjust enrichment in domestic law.[57]

In actual domestic practice, moreover, "unjust enrichment" means that an individual has unjustly violated a contractual agreement in such a way as to unfairly enrich himself.[58] If this is the case, historical documentation of the slave trade might be used to show that contracts between willing African sellers and willing European buyers were made and respected, each party obtaining what it had expected from the other party, neither unjustly enriching itself. Indeed, arguments could even be made that individual Africans unjustly enriched themselves at the expense of individual Westerners. In 1804 an African seller failed to supply all the rice and slaves he had contracted to deliver to an American slave buyer, Jonathan Sabens, of Bristol, Rhode Island. The shortfall was about 20 percent of what he had promised.[59] This might constitute unjust enrichment on the part of the African party to the contract.

The concept of unjust enrichment might be confined at present to domestic law; however, sometimes domestic legal principles are transferred to the international realm as jurists revise their views. *Black's Law Dictionary* defines unjust enrichment as a "general principle that one person should not be permitted unjustly to enrich himself at [the] expense of another," further explaining that "unjust enrichment of a person occurs when he has and retains money or benefits which in justice and equity belong to another."[60] This definition refers to persons, not corporate entities such as states. But reparationists might argue that the general principle of unjust enrichment having both been acknowledged and applied within domestic jurisdictions, it should also be applied to international legal relations.[61]

The major legal claim made at Durban by those seeking reparations was that "slavery and the slave trade are a crime against humanity and should always have been so, especially the transatlantic slave trade."[62] For example, the Kenyan spokesperson of the African group said "it [the slave trade] is not a crime against humanity just for today, not just for tomorrow, but for always and for all times. . . . Crimes against humanity are not time-bound."[63] Crimes against humanity have been illegal under international law since 1945, and since 2002 individuals accused of crimes against humanity can be tried by the International Criminal Court (ICC). The statement at Durban that slavery and the slave trade "should always" have been crimes against humanity was a compromise between African and other states that wanted them recognized as crimes against humanity and Western states that were afraid such recognition would result in their legal liability. But the term "crimes against humanity" was also a rhetorical device to bring these historical events into the contemporary discourse of gross human rights violations. The official declaration that ended the Durban Conference acknowledged the "massive human suffering and the tragic plight of millions of men, women, and children caused by slavery, the slave trade, the transatlantic slave trade,"[64] but no apology was offered by the slave-trading states. The declaration called on states only to "honor the memory of victims of past tragedies."[65]

Adopting language similar to that used at Durban, the government of France had passed a law a few months before the World Conference acknowledging slavery as a crime against humanity but using the present tense. The French law used the word *reconnaît* (from *reconnaître*, "to recognize"), thus acknowledging the crime but not apologizing for it. The French also referred to the slave trade in the Indian Ocean as well as the transatlantic trade.[66] The French law created no material or other obligations;[67] nevertheless, in 2006 France introduced a national day of remembrance for the victims of slavery, and commemorative events were held in several cities.[68]

By agreeing at Durban that the slave trade "should" always have been a crime against humanity, Western states implied that it was not a crime against humanity at the time it occurred; thus, they carried no liability. Without this phraseology, for example, European states might be liable in the United States under the Alien Torts Claims Act, which allows a plaintiff to sue a defendant for committing a crime against humanity. Such liability is far from certain, however, and would also have to overcome the Foreign Sovereign Immunities Act, which generally grants foreign states immunity from prosecution in the United States.[69]

Camponovo argues that even if retroactivity were not a problem, it is factually inaccurate to characterize the slave trade as a crime against humanity. Citing the Rome Statute of the ICC, he notes that the term has a specific legal definition: "any of a series of identified acts, including enslavement, 'committed as part of a widespread or systematic attack directed against any civilian population, with knowledge of the attack.'"[70] If this is the case, then as with genocide, not only Europeans but also Africans might be retroactively liable for crimes against humanity. At times Europeans raided directly for slaves, but at other times they bought slaves from Africans who often raided each other for human captives.

While persuasive to many Western diplomats and lawyers, these legal discussions are greeted with impatience by some reparationists. Thipanyane rejects the principle of nonretroactivity as it pertains to slavery and the slave trade. He believes that the reason there were no international treaties or customary laws outlawing slavery at the time it occurred was that "the Western states that were the driving forces behind the development of international law did not recognize the fact that the enslavement . . . of Africans . . . [was] unjust and morally wrong." He concludes that "legal technicalities cannot and should not be used to deny justice to victims of harmful wrongdoing."[71] For similar reasons, Roger Wareham, an African American activist, objected to the report that the Dutch legal scholar, Theo Van Boven, submitted to the United Nations in 1993. Van Boven argued that "it would be difficult and complex to construe and uphold a legal duty to pay compensation to the descendants of the victims of the slave trade and other early forms of slavery."[72] In Wareham's view, "Once again a different standard was being applied to African people [by van Boven]."[73] The arguments of both Thipanyane and Wareham reflect Walter Rodney's view of international law. Rodney commented that "the so-called international law which governed the conduct of nations on the high seas was nothing else but European law. Africans did not participate in its making, and in many instances African people were simply the victims, for the law recognized them only as transportable merchandise."[74]

Nevertheless, international law, like all other law, evolves and changes; thus, even if it was originally formulated by a small group of Western powers, African and other states can now influence it. Spitzer suggests that there are ways African states could sue for reparations for slavery in U.S. courts. He argues that slavery was illegal under *jus cogens* long before it was declared illegal in treaty law. *Jus cogens* refers to laws "accepted and recognized by the international community of States as a whole from which no derogation is permitted."[75] Further, argues Spitzer, African states might argue that they could not sue the United States until international law caught up with the moral reprehensibility of slavery.[76] Only now that international law has changed (for example, with the creation of the ICC) has the clock started ticking. African states might now, according to Spitzer, have the chance to sue other states in international courts for the past crime of the slave trade.

Restorative Justice

The debate about the relevance of international law to the slave trade restricts reparations to criminal acts. Reparations, however, can also be seen as an aspect of restorative justice. Restorative justice does not necessarily arise from obligations under the law; it can just as easily arise from an ethical commitment to right wrongs. A state, corporate entity, or individual decides on moral or ethical grounds that it is responsible for past wrongs and would like to make amends. The principle of nonretroactivity of law imposes no restrictions on restorative justice, as Shelton notes. "Reparations other than prosecution are considered restorative rather than punitive and should not be affected by bans on ex post facto offenses."[77] There is plenty of room, then, for Western states and other corporate entities to try to repair their relations with Africa on the basis of the need for restorative justice.

As mentioned, by 1825, when the chief justice of the U.S. Supreme Court ruled slavery legal, there was already international condemnation of the slave trade. In the eighteenth century, Enlightenment philosophy had introduced the principle of the equality of man, although it took many decades before that principle extended beyond property-owning white men to the poor, to women, and to people who were not of European descent. It requires no rhetorical flourish, then, to argue that for well over a century, the West violated its own core philosophical principles in its continued practice of slavery and the slave trade. This is a strong moral argument for retrospective justice to Africa, whatever international law may require.

But if we are to look to questions of morality as well as to questions of law, then it is legitimate to ask why only Western states are considered responsible for past crimes and not other states that engaged in slave trading and slavery. This is one of several debates about this history of the slave trade and slavery that are discussed in Chapter 6.

Chapter 6

Reparations for the Slave Trade

Historical Debates

Western, Muslim, and African Slavery

Reparationists focus their demands on the transatlantic slave trade. The West is asked for reparations because Europeans and Americans bought African slaves. This focus on Africa's relations with the West, but not on its relations with other regions, raises some uncomfortable questions. Not only the Western world, but also the Muslim world, enslaved Africans. Moreover, there was slavery within Africa. In both the Muslim world and Africa, slavery preceded, coincided with, and postdated the transatlantic trade.

Some reparationists may be under the impression that Europeans enslaved many times more Africans than did Muslim traders. This is erroneous. As noted in Chapter 5, estimates of the numbers who crossed the Atlantic Ocean, including those who died in transit, are often grossly exaggerated; a high estimate for landings plus losses at sea is 13.6 million. Relying, again, on several decades of quantitative analysis by himself and his colleagues, Lovejoy estimates that 4.8 million people were victimized by the trans-Saharan slave trade from 650 to 1600 and 2.4 million were victims of the Red Sea and East African trade between 800 and 1600. Another 2.2 million slaves, Lovejoy estimates, were exported across the Sahara, the Red Sea, and the Indian Ocean from 1600 to 1800, with 347,000 slaves exported from East Africa to Arabia, Persia, and India from 1801 to 1896.[1] Thus, Lovejoy's total for the Muslim trade, from 650 to 1896, is 9,747,000, about 72 percent of the estimate (including losses at sea) of the transatlantic trade, although over a much longer period. With regard to slavery within Africa, a much more difficult matter to quantify, Manning, also a professional historian, suggests that from 1500 to 1900, 8 million people were "enslaved and retained within the African continent," while "an estimated total of 4 million people lost their lives as a direct result of enslavement within Africa."[2]

Despite these figures, both Mazrui and Ajayi justified focusing only on the Western slave trade. Mazrui believed that the Muslim trade was qualitatively different from the transatlantic. Western slavers were the more race-conscious, asserted Mazrui, whereas "Islam went further than others to encourage *emancipation* of slaves" and had several other customs that made it possible to integrate slaves into free society, for example, by recognized alliances between free males and slave women.[3] As Mazrui elaborated in his interview with us, "the scale and divisiveness of the transatlantic trade was very different from the other two."[4]

Mazrui's opinion is confirmed in part by scholarly accounts. In the American system of slavery, children of free men and slave women were considered slaves. Under Islam, children of free fathers and slave mothers were considered free, if the father acknowledged them.[5] If a Muslim man married a slave woman, she was automatically freed. Slaves occupied a variety of positions and could rise to quite high status, sometimes having authority over free people. Within Muslim African societies, "slavery was conceived within a framework which encouraged conversion to Islam, allowed for the emancipation of acculturated and loyal slaves, and perpetuated a paternalistic attitude among slave masters in the treatment of slaves."[6] Islam prohibited the enslavement of Muslims by force and regarded manumission (freeing of slaves) with favor.[7] Sometimes in Africa, though, the prohibition against enslaving Muslims was manipulated to suggest that enslavement of non-Muslims was endorsed.[8]

Reparationists also justify their focus on the transatlantic slave trade by referring to the depth of racism in Europe and the Americas. Ajayi claimed that the relationship between white traders and masters and black slaves "bred racism that was never a part of the Muslim Arab world as Arabs enslaved both whites and blacks."[9] In the Arab world, white or Asian slaves were as common as African slaves were: for many centuries, there was a trade in slaves from Europe to the Arabian Peninsula. In Africa owners and slaves shared color, although Africans did not view themselves as homogeneously "black" as did their European owners in the Americas.

The argument that racism characterized the transatlantic but not the Muslim slave trade is not accepted by all scholars. Davis argues that "the Arabs and their Muslim allies were . . . the first people to view blacks as suited by nature for the lowest and most degrading forms of bondage."[10] Arab writers, Davis says, stereotyped Africans as possessing distinctive traits, including "blackness of skin and kinky hair . . . wide nostrils; thick lips . . . an offensive odor . . . inferior intelligence; and an oversized penis."[11] These stereotypes will be familiar to Western readers.

In some cases, too, enslavement by Muslims was as arduous as enslavement by Europeans. As early as the ninth century C.E., Arabs used intensive African slave labor to prepare the marshlands of Southern Iraq for cultivation.[12] In the eighteenth century, African slaves labored on date plantations in Oman.[13] On the island of Zanzibar in the nineteenth century, slaves worked for Muslim owners on clove plantations, where "physical punishment was at the heart of discipline."[14] Moreover, the Muslim slave trade from Africa continued via smuggling at least until the 1960s, although numbers traded by then were small.[15] In the 1950s slaves were still being trafficked to Saudi Arabia from Mauritania and Mali.[16] Oman was the last state to outlaw slavery, in 1970.[17] Had Europeans or Americans still been buying African slaves in the twentieth century, reparationists would undoubtedly have considered this scandalous. Yet the trade to the Arab world well into the twentieth century is unnoticed in the rhetoric of reparation.

Advocates argue that reparations for the transatlantic but not the Muslim slave trade are fair because the former was unique in its brutality. Ajayi argues that "the factor of competitive capitalism in Europe . . . turned slaves into pure cargo denuded of all humanity. Economic factors of insurance and transportation across the Middle Passage bred this practice of regarding slaves as pure cargo and no longer human beings. This was to an extent that would have been offensive in Islam and unbelievable in indigenous African slavery."[18]

It is not altogether accurate to state that all slaves in the Americas suffered extreme disabilities. Some were able to buy their freedom; Equiano, for example, bought his freedom from his Quaker master in the eighteenth century.[19] Some skilled slaves were rented out by their owners as craftsmen and were permitted to keep some of the rent money. Household slaves were sometimes favored over field slaves, and masters who fathered children with slave mothers often favored them, even if they did not formally acknowledge the children. The condition of slavery in the Americas, therefore, varied over time, space, and status.

Nevertheless, accounts by some other scholars confirm Ajayi's comparison of transatlantic and indigenous African slavery. Many people in Africa were taken as slaves in war, many were born slaves, and some became slaves when they disobeyed the law. Indeed, Lovejoy argues that Africa was characterized by a slave mode of production for 900 years, from 1000 to 1900.[20] Slaves were used not only in agricultural production but also in almost all other economic activities, such as mining, handicrafts, livestock breeding, and porterage.[21]

Nevertheless, it was common for slaves in Africa to rise from slave to semifree or free status. In both Muslim and non-Muslim African societies, women and children were highly valued. Women slaves could cultivate land and produce children, who would also be used as cultivators.[22] In some African societies, free fathers of children of slave mothers recognized their children, who occupied a status somewhere on the "continuum of status disabilities" that distinguished slavery from full social incorporation into the family and kin group.[23] Slave women who were taken as wives or concubines of their owners also enjoyed some privileges. Over the generations, people of slave descent could work their way up into almost equal incorporation into the kin unit of their owners, even if they were not biologically descended from them. Indeed, the condition of "slavery" was so malleable, and chances of incorporation into an "owner's" lineage so common, that Joseph Inikori suggests this indigenous African institution might have resembled more closely Europe's preindustrial system of serfdom than America's system of slavery.[24]

On the other hand, some locations on this continuum of status disabilities could result in full enslavement. Many African societies practiced pawning, a form of debt bondage in which a child or junior kinsman might be turned over by a debtor to a creditor to work off a debt: if the debt was not worked off, the pawn could be enslaved, even though legally enslavement was not permitted.[25] Slaves in Africa were also subject to some extreme disabilities that did not apply to free people. When food was scarce, they might be sold.[26] They could be used for human sacrifice, they could be killed in order to accompany a deceased owner into the next world and in societies that practiced cannibalism, they could be eaten.[27] Slaves were sometimes worked very hard, for example, in the Asante gold mines[28] and on the plantations that developed on the West African coast in the nineteenth century, in part to provision ships coming from across the Atlantic.[29] In Africa, Lovejoy argues, "slaves were property. . . . Slaves were outsiders by origin. . . . The relationship between slave and master was ultimately based on coercion."[30]

Even in the late twentieth century, descendants of slaves in Africa suffered some social disabilities, although in many societies, such as in Asante, to mention an individual's slave background was considered extremely impolite.[31] Moreover, slavery was still practiced in the early twenty-first century in a few African countries. The 2005 United States Department of State reports on human rights noted that traditional slavery—based on the status of being born a slave—was still practiced in Cameroon, Gabon, Malawi, Mauritania, and Niger,[32] yet all these states except Gabon were signatories to the 1956 Supplementary Convention on the Abolition of Slavery, Cameroon having signed in 1984, Malawi in 1965, Mauritania in 1986, and Niger in 1963.[33] As noted in Chapter 5, this continued internal slavery was barely mentioned at Durban, except for the delegates from Niger who mentioned a new penal code to outlaw slavery so that "never in Niger will human beings, merely by fact of their birth in certain families, see themselves held in contempt by their fellow men who claim, on the basis of custom, to have rights of property over them."[34] In Mauritania, formal abolition of slavery in 1980 did not result in actual freedom for the slaves. Strong social distinctions were maintained among freemen, slaves, and former slaves.[35]

These forms of slavery are distinct from the modern forms found in many African countries and many other countries worldwide, such as trafficking in women and children for purposes of sexual, military, or labor exploitation. Nevertheless, the continued existence of traditional slavery does raise the question whether African states that countenance it ought to be liable under the kinds of laws proposed at Durban. Would African activists and diplomats be willing to accuse each other of crimes against humanity and urge the International Criminal Court to capture and try those leaders who countenance slavery? As Camponovo notes, "The Dakar documents [African Regional Conference Documents] are notable for their almost total lack of introspection."[36]

Some opponents of reparations argue that none are owed because Africans willingly sold slaves to Europeans. Against this, Ajayi argues that those who sold slaves were "as much victims of the trading system as the captives."[37] In Ajayi's view, the European demand for slaves was what caused African societies to raid one another and upset the political balance in their continent. Ajayi further argues that Africans did not have the same moral responsibility for the trade as Europeans because the latter controlled it, while "the Africans . . . had no initiative in the matter."[38] Here he goes too far. Some individual Africans did indeed profit handsomely from the slave trade; to assume that they were mere victims is to deny them the agency of intelligent, thinking beings who, like Europeans, were eager to profit in whatever manner possible. Even if, in the end, the continent as a whole was far worse off because of the slave trade, some Africans profited from it and bore moral responsibility for it, just as did some Europeans.

African Voices on the Slave Trade

Europeans who bought Africans treated them as subhuman: they raped, tortured, mutilated, and murdered their slaves with impunity. To know that one's ancestors were, or might have been, enslaved in such a dreadful way is painful. Thus, underneath the anti-Western rhetoric of reparations is the deep hurt that some Africans experience, knowing that for centuries of their continent's history, they were considered mere chattel. In the eyes of many Europeans, all Africans were things, to be bought, sold, used, and abused. That some Africans were sellers while others were slaves was a mere matter of contingency, not one that humanized some Africans while dehumanizing others.

Some of our respondents were genuinely shocked by the slave trade. It was not merely an historical event for them; it was something that was so humiliating that they were outraged. Michel, a professor from Congo, said that "slavery degraded people. . . . The slave lost his human personality. . . . Not only was he completely deracinated, but he was treated as an animal, a beast, sold as a slave, sold. And when you sell someone, my God, it's not a human being, treated as a slave, flogged. . . . He was even robbed of the fullness of thought. People said . . . it's absolutely forbidden to think."

Some respondents thought that the slave trade had stolen individuals from families that still existed and still mourned their loss. Wendy, who worked for a Nigerian NGO, remarked that the slave trade had prevented many African Americans from being able to trace their heritage. "Most people love their families. They [descendants of slaves] don't know their tradition. . . . They cannot trace their generation. . . . There's nothing like knowing that you are from somewhere and knowing your roots." Fadwa, an activist from Cameroon, talked poignantly about how families in Africa would be affected for generations by the slave trade. "For those who perhaps had relatives who were taken away by force . . . away from the African continent, to work at forced labor, those are families which are affected from generation to generation." But, noted Fadwa, "on the other hand, there are families to whom nothing happened. . . . They are not affected." Fadwa saw slavery not as a national or continental tragedy, but as a particular one that affected only some Africans.

The slave trade had directly affected the family of Gilles, one of Fadwa's Cameroonian compatriots. As he explained, "I often remember a story from my grandmother, who spoke of some of her distant ancestors who were taken and sold into slavery. . . . She always said, 'Perhaps there where the whites live, you will go one day and see one of my brothers.'" While it might seem far-fetched to believe that one would grieve for distant ancestors, readers might think of North American Jews who still grieve great-grandparents murdered in the Holocaust and consider how the grandchildren of these living Jews will remember ancestors who lived five generations before they did. Family lines can be damaged by historic injustices.

Turning from cultural to economic effects, many respondents linked the slave trade to the present underdevelopment of Africa. A recurrent theme was the loss of valuable labor power. Lawrence, from Ghana, commented that "able-bodied men were . . . transported from Africa to America to work. . . . If these people had stayed back, possibly they could have come out with their own industrial revolution, who knows?" Dawn related that "during the slave-trade time, a lot of African men were killed and women died in the process, were taken away from their countries. . . . And that meant that the people who were left behind had to find a new way of living."

Linda remarked on the loss of the "work force of whole generations" and Benedict, an activist from Kenya, lamented that "those people . . . who were taken [as slaves] were the strong people in the community." Aaron, an ambassador, said, "We [will] never know who was taken from our shores, who could have been the real geniuses . . . from our country." Aaron added that in a landscape "dominated by slavery," Africa could not focus on economic development. Gérard, a Togolese activist, noted the way that the slave trade had skewed and taken over preexistent African international trade. "Africans have been doing long-distance trade before slavery and before colonization. . . . [The] slave trade . . . cut Africa [off] from the rest of the world and then . . . [took] over African business . . . for long-distance slave trade." Angela said,

> Before [the] slave trade . . . Nigeria had empires, we had our own civilization. . . . We had our own kingdom[s], we had our own trade, things were going on well; but once the slave trade came, they carted away very well-abled people. For instance, in Benue [a state in Nigeria], the people were taken away. . . . It was like a genocide. . . . They killed a lot of people because there was a lot of resistance internally. . . . [They] left [us] with very few people, women . . . and old men. . . . So it was a loss of a whole humanity.

Several respondents agreed with Mazrui and Ajayi that Muslim slavery was of a different order than American. "[It was] a slave institution that was very assimilated and . . . didn't have the . . . strong racial undertones," said Patrick. Lawrence agreed and noted that "what the Western [world] did . . . has overshadowed whatever the Arab world did." Rashid, an ambassador, also argued that the Arab world owed no reparations because the type of slavery was completely different, especially since Islam considers all Muslims, whether slave owner or slave, to be equal.

Michel opposed this view of Muslim slavery as relatively benign, in part because of his family's experience. "My grandfather was not enslaved by the whites; he was enslaved by the Arabs." Michel also pointed out one aspect of Muslim slavery that he considered worse than anything Europeans had done. "The Arabs made us slaves . . . and even worse, worse, they took us to their homes and castrated us. Yes, they castrated the slaves so that they would not have children." Indeed, castration of male African slaves was common in the Arab world,[39] but European, as well as other, slaves were also castrated; it was thought that without children, castrated slaves were more likely to be loyal to their owners. As a result, eunuchs, castrated slaves, could rise to high positions within their new societies. Despite these alleged advantages enjoyed by castrated male slaves, Michel, unlike most respondents, believed that the Arabs owed Africa reparations. Geoffrey also argued that the Muslim slave trade had been quite cruel and that "there was slavery also by the

Arabs in a country like Tanzania. . . . It is known that they are very cruel slave-wise. They used to chop [off] people's hands."

A few other respondents also thought the Arab world owed reparations to Africa. Dorothy, a civil servant from Kenya, said, "I think they [the Arabs] are the worst. Actually the Arabs really benefited because they are the ones . . . who would come, pick these people, especially the slaves. . . . So if the West is to [make reparations], I think even the Arabs [should]." Masoud, a refugee from Sierra Leone, agreed. "You have Arab families, Arab countries that have benefited immensely from the slave trade, so they should also pay for reparations." Timothy, from Tanzania, said, "I think the Arabs also may be included in this process [of reparations] . . . because there is a lot of historical evidence that Arabs were involved in slave trade. . . . There remains in East Africa people who were taken into Arabian countries."

Even if the Muslim trade was immoral, though, some respondents saw practical reasons not to ask Arab countries for reparations. Christopher, a professor originally from Central Africa, said that the Arab trade had occurred so long ago that it had not had the same detrimental impact on Africa's chances to develop as the transatlantic trade. "One has to think about some material impact . . . which can be demonstrated, and I think it is hard to see with . . . [the] East African slave trade." Basil, an Eritrean scholar, said, "These Arab traders . . . were . . . a bridge just between the African ships and the European slave traders. Yes, partly they are also responsible. But in their present situation [it is] very difficult to say because not many slaves were retained in the Arab world." Étienne believed that the Belgian colonizers had deliberately taught schoolchildren about the Muslim slave trade to deflect attention from the transatlantic trade, although, he said, "The [Arab slave trade] . . . was amateurism, compared to the whole transatlantic trade." Dominic, from Burundi, believed that the Arabs had come to Africa only to engage in legitimate trade in goods, not to take slaves. Gérard argued that it was difficult to think about reparations to Africans taken as slaves by Arabs because "the problem is that the population has melted away in the Middle East. . . . Were they killed? Were they not allowed to reproduce? . . . We don't see a significant population of Africans descended in [the] Middle East."

There was even less concern among our respondents about slavery within Africa than about the Muslim slave trade, although a few people mentioned it. Benjamin referred to slavery among the Asante in Ghana, noting that "if a free person and a slave had a kid, the kid could be absorbed into the society. In fact we had a word . . . *donko*. . . . This word . . . was a taboo; you could not mention it. . . . *Donko* is like a former slave." Joanna, a Rwandan, thought that the forced labor that peasants had had to perform for Rwandan kings was a type of slavery, and she stressed particularly the problems that arose when the father of a family had to labor for the king because he had no sons to send. Joanna referred to the legend of a young girl, Ndabaga, who cut off her breasts so that she could disguise herself as a boy and perform the forced labor for the king that her father would otherwise have had to perform.

Anne-Marie, an activist from Cameroon, was unusual in blaming African slavery for the transatlantic trade. "Before the whites arrived in Africa, the blacks already practiced slavery, and I think that's why slavery was so easy. . . . When they made war they took prisoners, and these prisoners were traded as slaves." Masoud agreed. He noted there was "complicity of the slave trade because . . . some rulers were given a lot of presents by the slave . . . buyers." One way that sellers obtained slaves, Masoud said, was by accusing others of bewitching them.

> You can pretend to be sick and you actually charge people of bewitching you, so . . . they bring some mixture. . . . If you drink it and it stays in your belly it means you are a witch; if you throw up, you are innocent. So if thirty people are immediately needed to make a cargo you can pretend to be bewitched and you accuse thirty people. Off they go. . . . So those African families who enriched themselves years back through slavery and the slave trade, they also owe an explanation of [to] the people.

David, a young Cameroonian activist, named a particular king who had been involved in the slave trade. "King Mangabel of Doualla . . . actually helped the West in transporting the slaves from Cameroon to the West because . . . they were giving spirits, alcohol, cigarettes, all those things and since he had the kingdom he could actually . . . get people transported to the West." Christopher concluded, "So in effect you can think of it [the slave trade] in terms of collaboration between agents in Africa and elsewhere taking advantage of the weak, of the weakness of the majority."

Despite a diversity of views on the relative levels of cruelty and responsibility of the transatlantic, Muslim, and African slave trades and slavery, our respondents were almost unanimous in their beliefs about the role of the transatlantic trade in underdeveloping Africa. Likewise, they were almost unanimous in their belief that the transatlantic trade had significantly contributed to Western development.

The Slave Trade and African Underdevelopment

Although individual Africans and some African societies did profit from the slave trade, a reasonable case can be made that the overall effect of the trade on Africa was detrimental. Joseph Inikori puts the case most succinctly: the diversion of much of the continent from the socioeconomic path it might otherwise have taken, to become a supplier for the international slave trade, prevented its internal development. Inikori states, "The ultimate goal of socioeconomic development in organized societies is to raise societal capital to regularly produce goods and services, which the members wish to consume, in a steadily expanding quantity and steadily improving quality."[40] In part because of the slave trade, argues Inikori, Africa lacked the conditions that could create a capitalist market, producing an economic surplus to either be used by the producers themselves or traded with outsiders.

Inikori's argument has merit: internal markets and the creation of regional economies in Africa were severely disrupted by the externally oriented slave trade. The transatlantic trade also changed Africa's political configuration, in some instances replacing a ruling administrative class with a warrior class whose sole purpose was slave raiding. Martin Klein explains that the trade was a factor in nineteenth-century state building in the area later known as French West Africa, as putative rulers accumulated slaves to be used as soldiers in their military campaigns, as producers, and as goods to be traded with Europeans for arms.[41] Large slave populations might have enabled production of a surplus in some parts of Africa and the development of an elite that could live on the surplus produced by slaves.[42]

Some scholars also argue that Africa was depopulated by the slave trade. Manning contends that from 1700 to 1850, the population of sub-Saharan Africa as a whole either stagnated or declined.[43] In other regions and at other times, emigration—whether voluntary or involuntary—of surplus population might have stimulated economic growth, as did the emigration of British and European peasants to the Americas and Australasia in the nineteenth and early twentieth centuries. But much of Africa engaged in land-extensive, labor-intensive cultivation. Male workers were needed to clear the land, and female and child workers to cultivate it.

Depopulation also hindered the possibility of urbanization, a necessary aspect of development. Populations densely centralized in cities are markets for food and other goods produced in the countryside, thus providing an incentive for peasants to produce a surplus over their own subsistence needs. Centralized populations also permit economic, organizational, and intellectual specialization.[44] Such specialization permits individuals to exercise their creative capacities in ways that can stimulate economic growth. Thus, depopulation, either of the African continent as a whole or of certain areas in it may well have retarded African economic growth.

Some of our academic respondents were familiar with arguments about the effects of the slave trade on African demography. André, a professor from Congo, argued that there was a skewed demographic distribution in Africa: the coastal areas were heavily populated, farther inland there were markedly fewer people, and even farther inland, the population was again heavy. He explained, "The Europeans arrive with their shoddy goods, distribute them to the blacks on the coast; these blacks hunt down the blacks in the interior and trap them to take them to the coast, but some flee further into the interior, creating a band . . . less populated than the coastal area." Joseph, a Congolese lawyer, noted "the destabilization of the structure of production because the slave traders preferred strongest people."

Africa's production, markets, and polities were severely affected by the slave trade. But one cannot assume, therefore, that without it, Africa would necessarily have developed into an industrialized, capitalist economy. No one can say what path Africa might have taken. It might have remained a continent of slave-based empires, nomadic pastoralists, and subsistence agriculturalists. This is all the more likely because one of Africa's disadvantages was its low level of technological development, which predated the slave trade.[45] On the other hand, we cannot deny the possibility that without the transatlantic slave trade, Africa might have developed in a more market-oriented manner, encouraging production of a surplus, investment of that surplus in profit-making activities, and eventually, a functioning capitalist economy.

The Slave Trade and Western Development

Many of our respondents asserted that the West owed reparations to Africa because without African labor and resources, it would never have been able to develop. "The resources and labor from the African continent permitted the North [the Western world] to develop and take the lead on Africa," said Hamza. Alain, a young activist from Togo agreed: "The West should make an effort to recognize that . . . Africa invested so that the West could become what it is today." Frederick, an activist from Malawi, referred to slave labor as an investment in Western development. "The Africans need to be given a little something [in reparations] because they invested elsewhere, their labor was used somewhere." The claim for reparations, Frederick continued, was "a claim not to something that we did not contribute to, but we are making a claim to something that Africa contributed."

Not only the West as a whole, but also private corporations in the West, benefited from the slave trade, as Patrick argued. "Corporations

. . . specifically benefited from it. . . . The insurance companies involved . . . the shipping companies that were built on the slave trade." If successors to the slave-trading shipping companies from Liverpool still exist, then perhaps, as Patrick suggested, they owe reparations to Africa. Dudley Thompson pointed out that it was possible to obtain evidence of precisely which banks and corporations had profited from the slave trade. "We have traced certain banks . . . who loaned money to slave masters in Britain. And we have traced certain people who bought slave ships. We have names and we have dates. . . . Everybody who has been found to benefit from the slavery and the slave trade will be defendants [in a reparations suit]."[46] Indeed in 2007 Barclays Bank faced pressure from American reparationists who claimed Barclays had purchased a bank that had originally made its profits from the slave trade.[47]

Several of our respondents referred directly to Walter Rodney's historical research on Africa's contribution to Western development, as Mazrui frequently did in his written and oral work advocating reparations. Irwin, a South African historian noted, "As Walter Rodney said, you often feel, although it isn't exactly accurate, that the [African] farmer still just has the hoe. And there's a sense of being left out . . . a sense of wealth having been created and used in order to build development elsewhere. That's part of the real history." Rodney discussed what he called "the transfer of wealth from Africa to Europe," arguing that "Africa helped to develop Western Europe in the same proportion as Western Europe helped to underdevelop Africa."[48]

Rodney quoted Karl Marx's famous description of the slave trade. "The turning of Africa into a commercial warren for the hunting of black skins," observed Marx, "signalized the rosy dawn of the era of capitalist production."[49] While the West used African labor and resources in its own interests, it deliberately withheld knowledge and technology from Africans themselves, in Rodney's view. African chiefs and kings who attempted to buy technology from Europe to develop their own shipping and manufacturing industries were rebuffed, eventually converted by persuasion or force into being slave sellers. In the sixteenth century, for example, the king of Kongo, roughly in the area now known as Angola, asked for "masons, priests, clerks [and] physicians" from Portugal, to no avail.[50] At the same time, British and French port cities such as Bristol, Liverpool, Nantes, and Bordeaux prospered because of the slave trade,[51] as did several American port cities. The insurance firm Lloyd's of London was also set up with profits from the slave trade, according to Rodney.[52]

Other scholars have confirmed much of Rodney's history since his death in 1980. But there is still much debate about how important the slave trade and slavery were to Western development. Rodney based his work in part on an earlier analysis by the Caribbean historian Eric Williams, who argued that the development of British industry, shipping, banking, and insurance depended on profits from the slave trade. The industries that developed as a result of slavery, argued Williams, included wool and cotton manufacture, sugar refining, rum, and ironmongery.[53]

In partial confirmation of Williams's thesis, Inikori suggests that the slave trade provided the impetus for technological innovation in the cotton industry in England, which employed many thousands of newly proletarianized workers. Industrialists sold their cotton cloths to both African sellers of slaves on the coast of Africa and European buyers of slaves in the West Indies and the Americas.[54] Similarly, in the United States, the Northern cotton textile industry relied heavily on raw cotton from and textile sales to the Southern market; the Northern, Southern, and later Western states of America were one integrated market, even though slavery itself was practiced only in the South.[55]

A debate about how much the transatlantic slave trade contributed to the West's development has been raging for several decades. In the 1970s, Stanley Engerman argued that even making some very implausible assumptions about its importance, the slave trade did not contribute significantly to the financing of British capital formation in the eighteenth century, the first century of the industrial revolution.[56] More recently, David Landes has argued that "historians have tried to calculate the gains from slaving and find it far from a bonanza. . . . [The] gains were simply not big enough in total, let alone that part that went back into trade and industry, to alter the path of British development."[57] In Landes's view, the industrial revolution in Britain would have taken place even without the transatlantic slave trade. "The crucial changes in energy . . . and metallurgy . . . were largely independent of the Atlantic system; so was the attempt initially to mechanize wool spinning."[58] Rosenberg and Birdzell suggest that slavery was not necessary to the British cotton textile industry: its development might merely have been slowed a little, had the British had to buy cotton from India, not grown with slave labor, rather than cotton produced by slave labor in the American South.[59]

To summarize, let alone assess, the enormous debate on the contribution of the African slave trade to Western development is impossible in this chapter. But to make the case for reparations, one does not need to argue that without the slave trade, the West would not have developed at all. The slave trade and slavery certainly were not sufficient to start the process of Western industrialization. For example, despite having been active in the slave trade, Portugal and Spain did not become major industrial powers.[60] Perhaps the slave trade and slavery were not even necessary for Western development; the West might have developed later or in different ways or on different trajectories if the transatlantic slave trade had never existed.

But the historical fact is that the slave trade did contribute to Western development. In its early period, many people made money from the trade in slaves, from slave-produced products such as sugar, and from consumer goods, such as rum and cotton textiles, sent to the coast of Africa in exchange for slaves. Nor was this profit confined to those directly implicated in the slave trade. In the northern United States, for example, shipbuilders such as the Brown family, who later endowed Brown University, profited, even if they did not themselves own slave ships.[61] The question is not whether the slave trade and slavery were indispensable for Western development. Rather, whether indispensable or not, they did so contribute. As Bailey argues, "Had there been no slavery, the West Indies trade would not have been as substantial. And had there been no substantial West Indies trade, there would have been much less trade for New England and the mainland colonies. The result would have been a much narrower field and a markedly slower pace for the economic movement of the colonies toward political independence and industrial capitalism in a developing United States."[62]

Thus, the slave trade and slavery helped the West to develop and enriched many families, some of whose descendants still live on the wealth the slave trade helped to generate. In the early twenty-first century, the Earl of Harewood, a cousin to Queen Elizabeth II, was one of the richest people in the United Kingdom. The Earl's eighteenth-century ancestors, the Lascelles family, were intimately involved in the slave trade. They made a fortune selling West Indian sugar and lending money to slave owners. When the owners defaulted on their loans, the Lascelles took over their plantations, eventually owning thousands of slaves, especially in Barbados. The family also invested in slave ships. When the Lascelles' 1,277 slaves were emancipated in 1838, the British government paid the family £26,000 in compensation.[63]

The wealth of the Lascelles family revisits the philosophical question of transgenerational justice (discussed in Chapter 1). Do individuals whose inherited wealth derives originally from the slave trade or slavery owe reparations to Africa or to some individuals of African descent? The Harewood Trust has cooperated with historians to ascertain the Lascelles's involvement in the slave trade and has invested funds in educational projects and a local West Indian festival; it has also cooperated in the making of a very critical 2005 film, *How to Make a Million from Slavery*, about the Lascelles fortune.[64] Aside from these activities by the trust, should the Earl of Harewood pay reparations from his own personal fortune, and if so, to whom? Perhaps he should pay reparations to the government of Barbados, representing the descendants of the slaves his ancestors owned. Alternatively, he might commission a search of historical records to determine which individuals in Barbados are the actual descendants. Perhaps, as James Walvin has suggested, he should make a lump-sum charitable donation to the black community near his estate in England, that community acting as a proxy for the entire community of blacks earlier exploited by his ancestors.[65] Or perhaps he should merely keep his vast wealth on the grounds that its origins, so long ago, are now irrelevant.

If we can show that the slave trade and slavery contributed in any way to the development of the West, does this constitute a moral case for transfer of wealth from the West to Africa as a form of reparation? Counterfactual histories both of Western development and of African underdevelopment cannot be verified, but perhaps the historical record of exploitation of Africa is sufficient to persuade reasonable people of the ethical imperative to repair the material damages caused by the slave trade. Against this, Landes suggests that the entire discussion of the contribution of the trade to Western development is rhetorical. "Third World countries and their sympathizers want to enhance the bill of charges against the rich, imperialist countries, the better to justify not only recriminations but claims for indemnity," he argues.[66] Indeed, much of this debate appears to be rhetorical, disregarding both international law and historical evidence. Some prominent Africans object very strongly to the focus on reparations from the West when Africans themselves are responsible for many of their continent's present-day problems.

African Criticisms of Reparations for the Slave Trade

Under the rhetorical appeal of the call for reparations to Africa may lie an unwillingness to deal with far more complex causes of that continent's severe underdevelopment. Promotion of a bitter call for reparations is an easy way to deflect attention from internal African politics and the many ways African dictators have abused human rights. Wole Soyinka, the Nigerian winner of the Nobel Prize for literature in 1986 and a political activist in his own right, referred metaphorically to the detention of Chief Abiola, the instigator of the reparations movement, as a case of modern-day slavery. Soyinka asserted, "Abiola . . . is today himself enslaved by one of the new breed of slave dealers, who actually boasts of power over the most heavily populated, most talented slave market that the African world has ever known."[67] Thus, Soyinka argued, "Reparations, like charity, should begin at home, and the wealth of the Mobutus, the Babangidas, the Abachas . . . should be utilized as down payment."[68] Here Soyinka was referring to Abacha's predecessor as dictator of Nigeria, Ibrahim Babangida, and the long-time dictator

(1972–1997) of Zaire (now Congo), Mobutu Sese Seko. The fortunes they accumulated through corruption have been estimated to be $5 billion by Abacha, more than $5 billion by Babangida, and $8 billion by Mobutu.[69]

Soyinka also disagreed with Mazrui's comparison of the transatlantic and Muslim slave trades, arguing, "Islam . . . inaugurated the era of slave raids on the black continent for Arab slave markets. . . . Even today, you will encounter ghettoes in many Arab countries peopled entirely by descendants of those slaves. . . . It simply seems to me rather presumptuous to offer absolution to the practitioner of a dehumanizing trade through an exercise in comparative degrees of abuse."[70] If Westerners are to be responsible to pay reparations for the slave trade, then so, according to some African critics, must other actors in it.

Referring to the actual era of the slave trade, the Nigerian activist Tai Solarin in 1991 suggested that "the demand for reparation is illegitimate because it was mainly our own traditional chiefs . . . who sold us as slaves in the first place."[71] Kwame Anthony Appiah agreed that "it is not clear that the wrongs done to the enslaved were done to black people as a collectivity. The real victims of the slave trade were the enslaved. My Asante ancestor, Akroma-Ampim, captured and enslaved many non-Asante West Africans. He profited from slavery and the slave trade."[72]

Abdoulaye Wade, president of Senegal at the time of the Durban Conference, was also descended from slave owners. He noted that if reparations were to be paid for slavery, then he himself might be liable to pay them, as his ancestors had had an army of 10,000 men, of whom two-thirds were slaves.[73] Moreover, he found the proposal for monetary compensation for slavery insulting because "no relationship can be established between reparation for slavery and the new plan for development in Africa. Four centuries of slavery and colonialism that destroyed all our structures were the basis of the impoverishment of Africa. . . . This incalculable loss will pursue us always."[74] "It is absurd," he was reported to say, "that you could pay up a certain number of dollars and then slavery ceases to exist, is cancelled out and there is the receipt to prove it."[75]

President Wade's skepticism about reparations to Africa and Soyinka's scorn for it are salutary warnings about African leaders' abdication of responsibility for their own crimes. Nevertheless, in his speech at Durban, Wade agreed with Mazrui and Ajayi that the transatlantic slave trade was of a different order than the Muslim or inter-African trade. Said Wade:

> Of course, the slave trade should be considered a crime against humanity. . . . This is not a question of the slavery that all peoples of the world practiced, in-

cluding black people, at some time in their history, nor of the trade . . . from the south to the north of the Sahara, or from the center [of Africa] to the Middle East or even India, but of the Atlantic slave trade which turned the Negro into a piece of merchandise, and free labor, [and] which justified this treatment by recourse to philosophical and religious doctrines that claimed that the Negro had no soul and, consequently, could be a beast of burden.[76]

Wade's eloquent description of the transatlantic slave trade suggests that even if material reparations are not appropriate, acknowledgment of its evil and apologies from the present representatives of the states, corporations, and families that engaged in it are essential. The fact that Africans were badly treated by their own rulers or captors, or by Muslim buyers and owners elsewhere, does not absolve the West of its own responsibility. For many centuries, Westerners treated Africans as less than human, as expendable animals, whom it was permissible to rape, torture, mutilate, and murder. Regardless of whether in retrospect, it was legally a crime against humanity, this was a moral crime of enormous magnitude.

Nevertheless, Africans, as well as Europeans, were perpetrators of this enormous moral crime. In the mid-1990s Edward Ball traveled to Bunce Island in Sierra Leone to meet descendants of an ethnic group that had sold slaves. Ball was himself the descendant of a slave-owning family in South Carolina, some of whose slaves had originally been purchased at Bunce Island. He was interested in how the descendants of African sellers of slaves coped with moral questions. One middle-aged man, Maligie Kanu, said that "slavery was encouraged by the chiefs, with their warriors. If you are powerful, then you can conquer people, then you have slaves. If you went to any town, it was to conquer the town, and take some captives. These people become slaves. You could sell them, or you could use them to farm for you."[77] Kanu did not exempt himself from ethical responsibility on the grounds that the slave trade had been originally instigated by Europeans. Rather, he asked, "When you discover this collective responsibility . . . this evil act which has been committed both by the Africans and by the Americans, by your ancestors, what are you to do now to remedy it?"[78] His more nuanced ethical view of African participation in the slave trade is more persuasive of the need for acknowledgment and apology than the exculpating arguments proposed by Mazrui and Ajayi.

Chapter 7

Reparations for Colonialism

In 2002 Nelson Mandela, first president of post-apartheid South Africa and without a doubt Africa's then most respected statesman, said that the former colonial powers had a responsibility to financially assist Africa: "Africa doesn't want charity; they [*sic*] want assistance, because the colonial powers have exploited the contine0nt, and it is the time now that they put these resources back for the development of the continent."[1] The African Regional Preparatory Committee, meeting before the Durban Conference, had similarly recommended that "a Development Reparation Fund should be set up to provide resources for the development process in countries affected by colonialism."[2] Both statements imply that the former colonial powers should repair the damages caused by colonialism.

The case for reparations for colonialism is stronger than the case for reparations for the slave trade. Colonialism occurred far more recently. The states that were colonial powers still exist, and many individuals who lived under colonialism are still alive, or their immediate descendants populate the continent. As Appiah argues, "Many [Africans] who are still alive suffered directly from the official acts of colonizers. . . . And no doubt many of those who were born since independence can also plausibly claim that much in their life would have been better if the colonial state had behaved better."[3] In some cases, the harm arises from economic exploitation, as I show using the example of Ghana. In other cases, the harm includes systematic violation of the right to life and physical integrity, as the genocide of the Herero in then South-West Africa and as the deaths of millions of people in Congo exemplify. In other cases, though, the effects of colonialism are more indirect and are bound up with complex postcolonial causes of underdevelopment.

Law and Rhetoric

Ajayi argued that "colonialism was an attempt to continue the exploitation of African labor hitherto provided through the slave trade. . . . [It was characterized by] . . . racism, excessive violence and gross abuse of human rights. It was part of the propaganda of empire that Africans were lazy and had to be flogged to make them work. . . . Racist colonialism, as such, exploited, rather than developed, Africa."[4] Thus, argued Ajayi, the case for reparations for colonialism was so compelling that legal questions were irrelevant.[5] The legal questions surrounding reparations for colonialism are similar to the legal questions surrounding the slave trade. They include debates about the definition and applicability of crimes against humanity, retroactivity, unjust enrichment, and an "international" law that was primarily devised by Europeans. It is unnecessary to revisit these debates in this chapter.

Nevertheless, it is necessary to note that colonialism was legal under international law until 1945, at the earliest. The 1945 Charter of the United Nations, in article 1.2, states that the purposes of the UN include "to develop friendly relations among nations based on respect for the principle of equal rights and self-determination of peoples." Although there is no exact legal definition of self-determination, it has generally been accepted that colonized peoples have the right to independence from their colonizers.[6]

The UN charter did not envisage compulsory, universal, and immediate decolonization. Rather, it laid down principles to be followed regarding the many "non-self-governing territories" then in existence. Members of the UN responsible for "the administration of territories whose people have not yet attained a full measure of self-government" were to "accept as a sacred trust the obligation to promote to the utmost . . . the well-being of the inhabitants of these territories." This obligation included the duty to promote just treatment, self-government, and development.[7] That the charter did not forbid colonialism is not surprising. In 1945 colonial powers were influential members of the UN, whereas only four African countries—Egypt, Ethiopia, Liberia and South Africa—were members, as most of Africa had not yet been freed from colonial rule.[8]

The 1948 Universal Declaration of Human Rights (UDHR) notes (Article 2) that "no distinction [in entitlement to enjoyment of rights] shall be made on the basis of the political, jurisdictional, or international status of the country or territory to which a person belongs, whether it be independent, trust, non-self-governing or under any other limitation of sovereignty." This clause ensures that human rights are universal, regardless of whether an individual is a citizen of an independent country or merely a colonial subject. The clause is, nevertheless, a compromise. During the process of drafting the UDHR, the socialist bloc, led by the Soviet Union, pressed for a much stronger clause, designating residents of the colonies for special protection. Other countries such as Cuba, Ecuador, and Egypt agreed with the socialist bloc, but they were opposed by the United States and most European colonial countries, especially the United Kingdom, France, and the Netherlands.[9] Thus, the UDHR does not prohibit colonialism.

Nevertheless, after World War II, the principle of self-determination rapidly gained currency. Within the colonizing countries themselves, colonialism was increasingly regarded as illegitimate. India and Pakistan were granted their independence from Britain in 1947; other colonies also became independent, either through negotiation or force of arms. In 1960 the General Assembly of the UN adopted the Declaration on the Granting of Independence to Colonial Countries and Peoples. This declaration mandates immediate transfer of power from colonialists to the people of the colonial territories and immediate cessation of all repressive measures against them.[10] The principle of independence was affirmed by the International Court of Justice in cases to do with Namibia (former South-West Africa) in 1971, Western Sahara in 1975, and East Timor in 1995.[11]

If one takes the 1960 UN declaration as an authoritative law forbidding colonialism, then there might be a legal case for compensation to African countries still under colonial rule after that date or where decolonization did not occur in a timely fashion. Portugal did not give up its colonies of Guinea-Bissau, Angola, and Mozambique until 1975, after a peaceful internal revolution shortly after the death of Portugal's longtime dictator, Antonio Salazar. There might also be a case for reparations for colonial practices, such as forced labor, that were illegal under international law. Before independence, noted the Angolan representative at Durban, "In Angola the slave trade was replaced by the system of forced labour and a contractual system which obliged people to work for no pay. . . . Colonial repression became one of the bloodiest [in] Africa . . . [Portugal's policy] was to terrorize Angolans for more than three decades resulting in the killing and deportation of many people."[12]

However, this conservative view that some African countries deserve reparations for having been colonized after 1960 does not mean that the colonial powers owe compensation for the entire period of colonial rule. Rather, it implies that no compensation is due for acts not illegal at the time they were committed, however reprehensible those acts might seem in retrospect.

Despite the fact that colonialism was not declared illegal until 1960, official documents at Durban included it with the slave trade, asking for reparations for both and declaring both to always have been crimes against humanity. The African Regional Preparatory Conference declared that "the historical injustices of the slave trade and . . . colonialism and apartheid are among the most serious and massive institutionalized forms of human rights violations" and demanded that "states which pursued . . . acts of racial discrimination such as slavery and colonialism should assume their moral, economic, political, and legal responsibilities . . . and provide adequate reparation."[13] The final declaration of the world conference states:

> We recognize that colonialism has led to racism, racial discrimination, xenophobia, and related intolerance, and that Africans and people of African descent . . . were victims of colonialism and continue to be victims of its consequences. We acknowledge the suffering caused by colonialism and affirm that . . . it must be condemned and its reoccurrence prevented. We further regret that the effects and persistence of these structures and practices have been among the factors contributing to lasting social and economic inequalities in many parts of the world today.[14]

The NGO forum at Durban also referred to colonialism as a crime against humanity and claimed that failure to acknowledge and make reparations for colonialism contributed to present-day racism.[15] Some African NGOs joined in an oral intervention by the African American Policy Forum at a preparatory consultation in January 2001, stating that "the African victims of slavery and colonialism were victims then and now of grievous social and economic harms. . . . No earnings. No freedom. No political autonomy. No economic independence. No land. These and other oppressive violations created a debt that has never been paid in any form."[16]

Colonialism did not receive as much attention at Durban as the slave trade did. Many of the statements by national spokespersons referred only to the slave trade or passed directly from the slave trade to the present period, which they saw as one of exploitative globalization, without specific mention of colonialism. Nevertheless, colonialism was generally perceived to be a manifestation and cause of racism, deserving of compensatory reparation. Deputy President of South Africa Jacob Zuma stated that "the social and economic inequalities and the poverty which ravages the developing world today are deeply rooted in the history of slavery and colonialism."[17] Colonialism was an unmitigated evil in the eyes of almost all Africans who spoke at Durban.

African Voices

Our respondents had a very concrete sense of how colonialism had injured Africa, some referring to stories they had heard from their parents or grandparents. Some noted that they, personally, had been privileged to attend missionary schools or otherwise benefit from contact with Europeans, but that the vast majority of their countrymen had been decidedly worse off. Others, especially the scholars, had studied their countries' histories in detail. As noted in Chapter 2, most respondents still had contact with the villages their families came from and were well aware of the living conditions in those villages. Many had parents, especially mothers, who were illiterate, and their fathers might have attended only primary school.

For most of our respondents, the period of actual conquest was too remote to discuss, although Aisha, an activist, spoke about the devastating effects of colonial conquest in Niger. "To go from one region that resisted to another, the colonialists . . . set fire to all the villages and put poison in the wells. . . . Even if there were a survivor, the survivor had no chance after that." Several respondents noted the long-term detrimental effects of the borders that the colonialists had created. Fareed spoke about the British-imposed division between North and South Sudan. "They sowed the seeds of hatred between the two parts of the country and you wouldn't imagine how many precious lives on both sides . . . how much money, how much property . . . how that war was caused by these struggles." Several Togolese discussed the problem of family separations along the Togolese frontiers with Ghana and Benin, Alain noting that "there are people whose aunts or brothers live on the other side of the border." Aaron said that the splintering of Africa had sapped its potential. "If you trace back the history of the United States . . . [it] is much stronger now because it is an amalgamation of different states. . . . We're [Africa] weaker now because of what happened to us through colonialism, just by dividing us up."

Respondents were also aware of how colonialism had contributed to ethnic strife. Dominic, a Tutsi from Burundi, complained that the Belgian colonialists' decision to divide people in Burundi into Hutu and Tutsi by the use of identification cards was a factor causing Burundi's civil war. Stéphane, from Cameroon, blamed a conflict in Bakassi, on the border between Cameroon and Nigeria, on the colonialists' decision in 1961 to hold a referendum that resulted in some Cameroonians' being incorporated into Nigeria.[18] At the same time, Stéphane said, Cameroon suffered from the union of various groups. "The Conference of Berlin . . . [had a role in creating] a mixture . . . of tribes . . . of ethnicities, which we now know in Cameroon. . . . These differences cause havoc. . . . I am from the South of Cameroon—I accuse colonialism of having stripped my region of all its cultural substance"; here Stéphane was referring to the conflict between French-speaking and English-speaking Cameroonians. Colonialism, then, in our respondents' views, frequently created ethnic conflict by labeling people as members of different ethnic groups.

Ethnic conflict was also exacerbated when colonialists appointed chiefs, with complete disregard for the indigenous political structure of African societies. Aisha said, "When the whites arrived and conquered the territory, and when there was . . . someone in whom they thought they could have confidence, sometimes, they take a stranger. . . . In Niger . . . there are villages that have taken Senegalese chiefs. . . . That's already a social loss. There's no more confidence between the person who governs the region and its inhabitants." Conversely, as Edward said of Tanzania, if Africans opposed colonialism, "people were killed. . . . The chiefs, they were killed, and all those who opposed the colonialism were hung in public."

Africa, it seemed to our respondents, had been treated by the colonialists as a huge source of natural resources, free for the looting. Respondents noted that the colonizers had dismantled their traditional agricultural systems, replacing them with cash crops. Ruth, a young Kenyan activist, said that "billions and billions were stolen during the colonial era, in the form of raw materials, sugar, tea. . . . And the white settlers, they came and demanded the fertile land and . . . most of the Kenyans had to move to different parts of the country." Martin, a Tanzanian activist, agreed: "I think when the Western people came to Africa . . . some of them were grabbing some resources. So they exploited resources from Africa for their particular country." On the other hand, areas that did not have natural resources that the colonialists wanted were neglected. According to Frederick, "they took a lot of resources from Africa . . . for their own benefit, we as Africans never benefited. And during . . . the time of colonialism some parts of Africa were neglected. For example, Malawi . . . was neglected. . . . We did not have good minerals. . . . So . . . there was quite little that these people did put in place for infrastructure. . . . So I would feel that in a way, our country is lagging behind."

Some respondents came from countries with mild climates that had attracted European settlers. These settlers lived on land expropriated—stolen—from Africans. Respondents from Kenya, Malawi, Tanzania, and Zimbabwe were all angry about the colonial appropriation of land. As Charles said, "The British . . . took over good land . . . [and] Zimbabweans were pushed to marginal land which . . . [was] not good for agriculture, not good for subsistence. . . . They [the British] took over, I think, 90 percent of the most productive land." Charles was from Zimbabwe, where there had been many British settlers and where white ownership of land was a matter of intense controversy at the time of our interviews (discussed in Chapter 9).

The colonial expropriation of land also caused ecological devastation, like that caused by a mining company in Congo, according to Michel.

> Entire regions became deserts because the mining company exploited them. . . . The people who were the owners of the land didn't have land anymore. . . .

They had to travel over 20 kilometers to cultivate their fields. . . . They continued to live their small lives, which were completely debased. Not only had they lost their ecosystem, but they received nothing in return. . . . I know a customary chief . . . who despite all this dared to say, . . . "Listen, you have ravaged my lands. You've ruined everything. I have no more fields. . . . The game has fled because you have ruined everything; pay me." And he made trouble, the village even rebelled. What did they give him? Some corrugated iron.

The way the Europeans organized transportation routes in Africa also had long-term detrimental effects, according to our respondents. Railways were built to export primary products to the coast, not to facilitate inter-African trade, as Masoud explained. "The construction of the railway was only in areas where they can cut, they get the primary products and everything geared toward shipment. So up to this point you can see . . . commercial productivity . . . really wasn't constructed at all. It was only constructed along lines where there was production of primary products." As David noted, these colonial transport routes still affect Africans' capacity to communicate and to travel. "You can not leave Cameroon without passing through France. I can not leave . . . to go to Britain. I will leave from Cameroon to France first, if I go to another country."

Under colonialism, not only was land stolen and resources exploited, but human beings were also used in ways that would now be considered illegal and were, indeed, often illegal at the time. French colonialists used forced labor. Émile, an academic from Cameroon, told us that "one of my grandfathers died while working on the construction of the railway in Cameroon." Sayeed, from Guinea, mentioned that relatives, including his father, "spent days and nights in the bush, looking for rubber."

One form of forced labor was recruitment of Africans into colonizers' armies. Some respondents were angry that they had lost family members who fought for Europeans in the first and second world wars. Michel felt strongly that Congolese had been exploited during the 1940s for a European war that had nothing to do with them. "The entire population was mobilized. . . . Everyone was put under military rule, and the miners had to produce so much, and those who didn't produce went to prison, tortured. . . . How much . . . did the war between the Germans, the Belgians, and all the rest interest Africa? . . . It wasn't an African war!" Moreover, as Anne-Marie told us, surviving veterans of those wars from the French colonies were not paid pensions at the same rate as French veterans: "Many paid with their lives, some returned mutilated, but until this year they have not received the treatment they were owed." Anne-Marie and several other French-speaking respondents were well-informed about the inequitable treatment of African veterans of the French army as a result of publicity in African newspapers and on the Internet shortly before we conducted our interviews. As discussed in Chapter 4, the movement to obtain compensatory payments for these "anciens combattants" was successful.

Finally, some respondents discussed the lingering psychological damage of colonialism. "It hurt morally; it's a moral subordination," said Christopher, continuing, "You know you are inferior. [The British said] 'we are here to civilize you': . . .Well, that means, 'we are superior, you are inferior.'" Theresa, a Zambian activist, argued, "The fact that you are ruled by an outsider is in itself oppressive. You cannot express yourself. You are treated as a second-class citizen. You don't exist."

Thus, many of the Africans we spoke with believed profoundly that colonialism had been harmful to their countries, their families, and themselves as individuals. As Alexandre, an academic from Burundi, put it, "I think, truly, colonialism was brutal and did not recognize the value of the Other." Colonialism was, to our respondents, a continuation of the slave trade and a precursor of the present exploitative period of neocolonialism and globalization (discussed in Chapter 8). In their view, colonial powers owed reparations to Africa for the political, economic, and psychological damages of colonialism.

Colonialism and Underdevelopment of Africa

Many representatives of African governments at Durban believed that without the slave trade and colonialism, Africa would have developed in much the same way as the West. Jakaya Kikwete of Tanzania said that "the slave trade and colonization of Africa in the nineteenth century are responsible in a big way for the poverty, underdevelopment, and marginalization that enveloped that continent."[19] Most of our respondents agreed with this opinion. Dawn complained that "we can't still catch up with the rest of the world." Angela argued that indigenous technology, knowledge, and craftsmanship had been supplanted during colonialism.

> We had our own science . . . our own civilization, the families had their own irrigation system, they were already doing their farming, they had their own technology. . . . They had their own bronze, their own iron. . . . So when the West came in, they [*sic*] disrupted everything. . . . And then of course our own education. . . . When the white man came . . . he introduced . . . his own idea of education. . . . And in the process of doing that, all this evil came into Africa.

But, some of our respondents said, colonialism had also had some positive effects. Basil pointed out that colonialism had helped modernize Africa. "Colonialism helped to reform many . . . feudal sentiments, feudal administrations. . . . Colonialism created the modern working class in the cities . . . also education." In other cases, however evil colonialism seemed at the time, the situation several decades later was so unstable that some people regretted the end of European rule. Étienne, André, and Pierre were all from Congo. Étienne explained, "African society today is the result of colonization. Today there is a university . . . hospitals, all the rest, there's . . . an indirect development, because the colonizing countries . . . had to . . . develop . . . the people, because they had to be in good health and well-nourished to be able to produce. . . . Today people don't even live, they survive." André mentioned the colonialists' efforts to eradicate disease. "There were illnesses . . . sleeping-sickness . . . smallpox . . . that . . . decimated the population. So, with colonization, with the installation . . . of a sanitary infrastructure, with preventative medicine . . . mortality declined . . . and natality increased." According to Pierre, life in Congo today was so bad that some people looked back with nostalgia on colonialism, even colonialism with a whip.

> Today, when one asks people who stagnate in disorder, there are people . . . who present colonialism as having been a model society. They say, "In the time of the Belgians, it wasn't like this. . . . Our children studied for free; we didn't pay school fees." . . . They find that colonialism was an orderly system. . . . These people grew up under the discipline of work, and they liked the work. . . . Because, some say, despite the whip things were good; they were respected.

One might dismiss these three Congolese scholars' comments on the grounds that Congo is an extreme case: it suffered three and a half decades under the brutally corrupt rule of Mobutu Sese Seko, followed by a regional war and invasion in which more than four million people died. Nevertheless, in several other countries the postcolonial period has also been one of corruption, extremely mismanaged economies, famine, civil war, and genocide. The difficulty lies in sorting out what part of these terrible problems is a consequence of colonialism and what is the result of independent decisions by postcolonial rulers.

Our respondents' contradictory views about the effects of colonialism call into question the argument proposed by Rodney. Rodney views colonialism as an unmitigated disaster for Africa. British settlers, he said, stole huge tracts of land from Africans, as Lord Delamere did in buying 100,000 acres of Kenya's best land for one penny per acre.[20] Tens of millions of Africans were forced to cultivate cash crops under threat of the whip and gun.[21] Merchants from colonial countries enjoyed protected markets in the colonies, where they could sell their goods at exorbitant prices without fear of competition.[22] European firms also monopolized shipping and banking.[23]

Moreover, Rodney points out, although some Africans might have benefited from new social infrastructure such as hospitals or schools, the hospitals were segregated.[24] Gregory, a government servant from Rwanda, also pointed this out, telling us that under colonialism, the purpose of having hospitals for Africans was to keep plantation workers and miners healthy. Rodney also notes that African education was limited to that necessary to provide low-level employees for colonial governments and private corporations; there was no technical or scientific education, which might have assisted Africans in realizing their own development potential.[25]

My own research on colonial Ghana confirms Rodney's more general account. British rule there was relatively benign; after the defeat of the central Asante Empire in 1896 there were no massacres or enslavement of Africans. Yet the British colonized Ghana for their own economic interests, massively exploiting the indigenous population. Ghana's major cash crop was cocoa. A few large British firms controlled the cocoa trade, agreeing not to offer competitive prices to cocoa producers. There were similar controls on Ghana's other exports, including palm oil, palm kernels, timber, gold, manganese, and diamonds. Shipping and banking were also heavily controlled by private British firms, as was retail trade to Ghanaians. Cheap imported cloth, pots, salt, and sugar undercut Ghanaian producers of these goods, and Africans were often charged more than Europeans for the same imported products. Some banks discriminated against Ghanaian customers solely on account of race, while others would not accept Ghanaian customers because communal ownership of land meant that the Ghanaians could not provide collateral for loans.[26]

The function of the colonial state was to recruit labor and provide transportation for imports and exports; thus, all railway lines ran from the interior to the coast, not across Ghana in routes that might have facilitated intra- or intercolonial regional trade. Many African villages paid Europeans to build roads that the state would not build, while the government itself had a "road-gap" policy that forced Africans to use its railways to ship their products to the market. The colonial state relied heavily on import and export taxes to finance itself; British companies passed on the cost of import taxes directly to Ghanaian consumers, while they compensated themselves for export taxes by paying very low prices to Ghanaian producers of raw materials.[27]

Those Ghanaians who tried to compete with British investors found their paths blocked at every turn. There was a minor "gold rush" in Ghana in the 1890s: indeed, the purpose of the war with Asante was to obtain control of its ancient gold mines. The British-owned Ashanti Goldfields was given a concession of 100 square miles of land: this concession also covered timber rights and retail trade, yet African entrepreneurs could not obtain financial backing when they tried to invest in gold mines. Ghanaians were also prevented by law until 1934 from mining diamonds by modern rather than "native" methods; even if they found diamonds on their own land, they could not sell them without a "diamond winner" license. An unusually successful Ghanaian businessman, "Pa" Grant, managed to obtain about 700 square miles of concession land for timber but often could not find European companies willing to ship his logs. One W. Essuman Gwira, a government employee, invented an inexpensive method of processing palm fruit, but the government denied him leave to perfect his machine.[28]

Thus, colonial Ghana was "developed" in the interests of British capital and the British colonial state. As noted in Chapter 6, Inikori defined African underdevelopment as the incapacity to develop a regional, differentiated, market economy producing a surplus for sale and investment. There were entrepreneurs in Ghana who were interested in capitalist production and investment and in trade as equal partners with Britain and the West. But they were blocked at every turn by European buying, selling, shipping, mining, and banking monopolies supported almost always by the colonial government.

This evidence suggests that Rodney's contention that colonialism underdeveloped Africa is correct. If those Africans living under comparatively benign British rule, as in Ghana, found the path to development blocked, then we can assume a far more severe blockage in other colonies, especially those in which there were large numbers of European settlers, such as Kenya, South Africa, and Northern Rhodesia (now Zimbabwe), or in which cultivation of cash crops for export was based on forced labor, as in Portugal's colonies. This appears to be one of the major reasons why independent Africa became impoverished: its "normal" path to development had been blocked by colonialism. Mazrui, in agreement with Rodney's thesis that the West underdeveloped Africa, refers to the cultivation of cash crops for export from Africa to the West as the creation of "dessert and beverage economies."[29] He further argues that colonialism caused "damaged governance" in the continent, as "older indigenous institutions of political accountability were effectively destroyed by Western colonization."[30]

But if colonialism underdeveloped Africa, did the end of colonial rule result in development? Landes argues that there is no evidence that the former African colonies were better off after independence. Indeed, many were worse off because, for example, they were unable to maintain the infrastructure built by Europeans. In 1960, the year that Congo became independent from Belgium, it had 88,000 miles of usable road: by 1985, it had only 12,000 miles.[31] To adopt the counterfactual assumption that without colonialism, Africa would have a developed market economy, is problematic. As Landes argues, this assumption rests on the hypothesis that "these subject peoples would otherwise have been free of domestic as well as of foreign exploitation; also able to learn and change."[32] In Ghana and other parts of Africa, without colonialism the result well into the twentieth century might have been agriculturally and technologically stagnant economies. An Africa never colonized might have remained in a state of nondevelopment, rather than underdevelopment. Nevertheless, for good or for ill, colonialism did rob Africa of the opportunity of a more autonomous development, wherever that development might have led.

Colonialism and Western Development

Many of our respondents were convinced that Africa under colonialism had developed the West, continuing the contribution it made to Western development during the slave trade. As David put it, "During colonization . . . raw materials were carried from Africa and exported to the West and used in developing the Western countries . . . and the mining and the development [helped] to underdevelop Africa." Masoud said succinctly, "They come, they tell you, 'Close your eyes: we baptize you in the name of the Lord the Father'; they take our diamonds away."

David and Masoud implied that the underdevelopment of Africa was necessary for the development of the West: the wealth the West acquired externally through empire caused its own internal development. The West's wealth was facilitated by the extraction of resources, both human labor power and mineral and agricultural products, from the colonies. Rodney mentions the extraction of minerals that were very important to Western industrial development, such as manganese for steel.[33]

Yet this is a very contentious proposition. Other scholars suggest that internal changes in the West brought about capitalist growth. The evolution of internal markets, changes in land-tenure arrangements, the stratification of society into different social classes with different roles in the production process, perhaps even the evolution of new cultural norms of savings and investment all seem to have contributed to the development of rich, Western European economies.[34] Clearly, colonialism was not enough in and of itself to create a wealthy Western economy.

Landes argues that colonialism might have been profitable for some individuals, especially for those who actually traded with or invested in the colonies, such as cocoa buyers in Ghana. He acknowledges that the purposes of colonialism were trade, "managed cultivation" of crops that the colonialists wanted for their home market, mineral extraction, and just plain pillage.[35] Individual Europeans involved in these activities did indeed profit. But Landes argues that the colonial countries as a whole did not necessarily profit from colonialism.[36] Similarly, Rosenberg and

Birdzell reject the idea that colonial consumer markets were engines of development for the colonizers, arguing that "poor and underdeveloped countries do not as a rule provide markets large in relation to the output of advanced economies. . . . Markets large enough to encourage a major expansion of production in advanced countries are . . . in countries that are themselves economically advanced."[37] Nor were colonies necessary for the economic well-being of European states: witness the unprecedented growth of the former colonizing countries in the decades after decolonization.[38] The economies of the United Kingdom and the Netherlands were growing before they established colonies and continued to grow after they gave them up.[39]

Like the slave trade, then, colonialism may have been neither necessary nor sufficient for Western development. Nevertheless, colonialism occurred. Even the most benignly run colonies, such as Ghana, were essentially territories to be exploited by the colonial powers and their citizens. And in the worse cases, colonialism could mean gross human rights violations and genocide.

Colonial Genocides: The Herero and the Congo

From 1904 to 1908 the colonial German military in then South-West Africa, now Namibia, exterminated about 65,000 of approximately 80,000 members of the Herero ethnic group. German settlers wanted Herero land, and the Herero resisted giving it up. In January 1904, the Herero rebelled. The German commander, General Lothar Von Trotha, reacted with explicit orders to exterminate all Herero men, women, and children. "Within the German [colonial] borders every Herero, with or without a gun, with or without cattle, will be shot. I will no longer accept women and children," he declared.[40] The extermination of the Herero was accomplished by outright execution; dehydration after deportation to the desert; and confinement, forced labor, sexual slavery, and starvation in concentration camps.[41]

Modern Germany has recognized that its predecessor state committed this genocide. In August 2004, Heidemarie Wieczorek-Zeul, the German Minister for Economic Cooperation and Development, attended a commemoration of the genocide's hundredth anniversary, where she apologized on behalf of Germans.[42] According to Wieczorek-Zeul, "The atrocities committed at that time would today be termed genocide. . . . We Germans accept our historical and moral responsibility and the guilt incurred by Germans at that time."[43]

Not satisfied with only an apology, Herero activists also demanded financial reparations for this genocide. The amount they sought was moderate: $600 million, or about $10,000 for every individual killed.[44]

Although it is unlikely that there are any living survivors, the genocide is still within active historic memory. Although the United Nations Convention on the Prevention and Punishment of the Crime of Genocide was not proclaimed until 1948, thirty years after the genocide, the Herero refer to the 1899 Hague Convention on the Laws and Customs of War by Land, which prohibited killing or wounding prisoners of war or taking enemy property. This convention, however, applied only to the parties that signed it. Regardless of that fact, and given that neither the Herero as a people nor the territory of South-West Africa had any chance to sign the convention, the Herero claim that there is a moral case that as an indication of accepted principles of international customary law at the time, the 1899 Hague Convention should have been applied to them.[45]

With the assistance of American lawyers, who had observed the successful cases brought by Jewish organizations in U.S. courts against private corporations, in 2001 the Herero sued three German corporations in the Superior Court of the District of Columbia.[46] These corporations were Terex Corporation; Woermann Linie, later known as the Deutsche Afrika-Linie; and Deutsche Bank. Deutsche Bank was accused of being the principal financier of the colonial government, while Woermann Linie, the principal shipping line into and from South-West Africa, was accused of having benefited from slave labor and having run its own concentration camps; the case against Terex Corporation was withdrawn.[47] This lawsuit reflects a general perception that private corporations not only have deep pockets but also fear the embarrassment caused by accusations of complicity in genocide.

Chapter 4 examines the difficulties that the social movement for reparations to Africa faces. The Herero case fits several of the criteria for a successful reparations claim. The Herero ask for reparations for an acknowledged wrong of the worst kind, genocide, perpetrated by a known perpetrator, the German army, against known victims, the Herero. An extermination order exists. The genocide was against a relatively small number of people and occurred over a short period of time. The amount the Herero request is relatively small and could easily be paid without significant cost to German taxpayers. Thus, as Harring asks, implicitly referring to the Jews, "How is colonial era genocide different from modern European genocide?"[48] An answer proposed by Professor Mburumba Kerina, a reparations activist in Namibia, is "the Jews are white: we are black."[49] If the German government does not follow up its apology to the Herero with financial compensation, then it may well reinforce the perception that the Western world still regards persecution of blacks as less heinous than persecution of whites.

Thus, it might seem obvious that the German government owes the Herero financial reparations. But within Namibia itself, the Herero claim raises the question of distributive, as opposed to reparative, justice. The government of Namibia opposes financial reparations to the Herero from Germany, which is Namibia's largest aid donor.[50] It prefers aid for all Namibians rather than reparations to only a few members of a small ethnic group. There is a further problem. The South-West African People's Organization (SWAPO), the political party in power in Namibia since independence in 1990, is alleged to have committed many atrocities during its time in exile as a liberation army. Some activists in Namibia believe that there should be a truth commission to detail SWAPO's atrocities and that the government should pay reparations to its victims. If the German government pays reparations to the Herero, this will be a precedent reinforcing the demand for internal reparations.[51]

Moreover, SWAPO is dominated by the Ovambo tribe, who comprise about half the Namibian population: according to Harring, SWAPO "has . . . played a mean and petty politics of domination against other Namibian peoples."[52] The government of Namibia also argues that it has more pressing priorities than reparations, such as the need to purchase land from white Namibian farm-owners to redistribute to black Namibians. Harring, however, suggests that the Herero could use their requested $600 million to buy about 1,000 of the 4,000 white-owned farms: these land purchases would reduce the government's need for funds.[53]

A second case of severe colonial abuse was not intended to be genocide but might well be considered to have been genocidal in effect. In the late nineteenth and early twentieth centuries, Congo was the personal property of King Leopold II of Belgium. He wanted to extract from Congo as much rubber as possible to supply the growing Western industrial market. To do so, his employees turned the Congolese into slaves. As Michel said, "In this period of Leopold II . . . the blacks, the Congolese, were forced to harvest rubber . . . and this rubber harvest was subject to incredible coercion! . . . Each native had to produce a certain quantity of rubber in a certain period, and those who did not produce, they cut off their arms."

Adam Hochschild estimates that 10 million Congolese died "during the Leopold period and its immediate aftermath." He derives this figure both from a report of an official Belgian commission in 1919 and from later scholarly work.[54] The cruelty that killed so many was wanton, sadistic, and completely unchecked. Hochschild cites, for example, the eyewitness account of a Belgian prosecutor who saw a group of about thirty children of seven or eight years, waiting their turn to receive twenty-five lashes from the whip. Twenty-five lashes could render an adult unconscious. Congolese women were often taken as hostages, raped, or turned into prostitutes at the pleasure of the Belgians.

Executions were common. One Belgian officer kept a gallows in the front of his station and lined his flower bed with human heads.[55]

The Belgian government in 2002 apologized for the complicity of some Belgian officers in the murder of the first president of independent Congo, Patrice Lumumba. The Belgians also apologized for their neglect of the Rwanda genocide of 1994. But as of early 2007, they had not apologized for the criminal colonial regime in early twentieth-century Congo. Perhaps their view was that the crimes occurred when the colony was Leopold II's private property; thus, the responsibility was Leopold's. Yet even if the Belgian state at the time did not control Leopold, perhaps its successor bore some responsibility for the contributory role of a sovereign state that permitted such brutal latitude to its own king.

Should there ever be a serious call for reparations to Congo from Belgium for Leopold II's treatment of the Congolese, it will encounter a number of obstacles. No one knows the actual numbers killed, and there was no extermination order. The crime did occur within the historic memory of the grandchildren and great-grandchildren of the victims, but the consequences cannot be disentangled easily from the other consequences of colonialism, from the crimes of the postcolonial period, or indeed from the war of the late 1990s. The Belgian state could also claim that although it purchased Congo from Leopold II, it is not legally responsible for his actions. At best, a call for reparations might be based on a retrospective reading of the law outlawing crimes against humanity, as these crimes can be committed by civilians as well as by governments or military leaders.

A special exhibit at the Royal Museum of Central Africa in Tervuren, Belgium, in 2005, entitled "Memory of the Congo: The Colonial Era," was perhaps a first step to an acknowledgment by Belgium of Leopold II's cruelties. Nevertheless, at least one scholar criticized the exhibition for downplaying the violence of Belgian rule in the Congo and for sidestepping responsibility for the massive depopulation caused by direct conquest, disease, starvation, and flight.[56] Acknowledgment is often the first step to apology, but it seems that the Royal Museum's acknowledgment was weak and exculpatory. Whether new or increased funds should now flow from Belgium to Congo as reparations rather than as aid is a more difficult question. Congo, a country of mismanagement, civil wars, and political chaos is as likely to waste reparations as aid. Although one might argue that in principle reparations require no assurance of financial accountability, their purpose being to right a wrong regardless of the use to which they may be put, in practice no country and no country's taxpayers will be willing to pay reparations that will merely be wasted or illegally appropriated by those purporting to represent victims of past crimes against humanity.

Colonialism and Reparations

Like the slave trade, colonialism was not sufficient to cause Western development; nor, indeed, might it have been necessary. But as a matter of fact, colonialism did assist that development. Thus, reparationists argue, since the West stole from Africa in the past, it should return what it stole now. Once the stolen wealth is returned, it can be used to remedy Africa's present poverty. But this argument ignores the structural causes both of Western wealth and of contemporary African poverty.

Western development was a consequence of the emergence of capitalism. In capitalist societies, wealth is generated by ever more efficient methods of production. Monetary compensation for colonialism, as for the slave trade, would not necessarily result in increased efficiency in Africa. Compensatory funds, like foreign aid, could be squandered easily in temporary redistributive programs, without lasting effects on productive capacities. Improvements in productivity require changes in social and political relations, especially entrenchment of principles of accountability and transparency in administrative, legal, and governance institutions. Wealth alone is, and always has been, insufficient for development.

Any attempts to calculate just compensation to Africa for colonialism would also encounter numerous obstacles in determining an appropriate amount. As Christopher said, "I don't think that's a good idea to actually pay money [for colonialism]. . . . How do you assess that? . . . Can we go back and try to assess . . . what was the difference between what the farmers were paid for their coffee and how much the British were getting on [the] international market?" Such historical recalculation of unjust profits, unfair creation of infrastructure, inequitable tax burdens, and many other injustices would use much time and resources.

Moreover, as our respondents realized, some colonized Africans benefited from access to European education and from employment by colonial governments, missionaries, settlers, or private European corporations. Colonialists' prohibitions on indigenous slavery protected some African groups that had previously been raided by others. Individuals considered of slave origin sometimes converted to Christianity, which declared all men equal. Some women who were unhappy in polygynous marriages escaped them by converting to Christianity. Thus, colonialism was not an unmitigated evil.

As with the slave trade, any case for compensation would also have to consider which entities owed it to Africa. Should commercial firms or mines be held responsible for the exploitative practices of their institutional ancestors? Should, for example, the chocolate companies that still exist and that bought cocoa in Ghana during the colonial period be held accountable for denying cocoa growers a fair commercial price?

Should banks still in existence be expected to compensate for the preference they gave to their European over their African customers during the colonial period? Even in the present, corporations have few legal human rights obligations (discussed in Chapter 9). It would be very difficult, therefore, although not impossible, to extrapolate human rights obligations to pay reparations back to the colonial past.

Clear cases of gross exploitation, such as the genocide of the Herero and the mass murders in Congo, warrant acknowledgment, apology, and perhaps financial reparations, although, as the example of Namibia shows, African governments might prefer foreign aid to the entire country over financial compensation to particular victims of gross violations of human rights. Historic economic exploitation is much more difficult to calculate, although particular groups that suffered under colonial rule might be able to make a claim for compensation. Nor, were the economic harm of colonialism to be calculated, would Western publics necessarily accept an obligation to pay compensation to governments they know to be inefficient, abusive, and corrupt. These arguments pertain as much to the postcolonial as to the colonial period.

Chapter 8

Neocolonialism and Globalization

Reparations activists do not generally ask for reparations for the postcolonial period. The three active members of the Group of Eminent Persons (GEP) in 2002 confined their demands to reparations for the slave trade and colonialism. In part, this was because in the postcolonial period African governments were formally independent and made their own decisions. As Geoffrey, an ambassador, told us, postcolonial international economic relations were determined by contracts made by sovereign states; however inequitable or unfair the contract might seem, a state could not ask for reparations if things went wrong.

Nevertheless, many of our respondents believed that postcolonial economic relations, especially globalization, were a manifestation of continued Western exploitation of Africa. They considered the entire post-independence period to have been one of neocolonialism, an economic colonialism that granted formal political independence but nevertheless continued the exploitation begun by the slave trade and continued through formal colonialism. This perception reflects a deep sense of despair, a feeling that no matter what Africans do, they will never be able to control their own economies.

Rhetoric

The official documents of the Durban conference do not specifically mention reparations for the postcolonial period. Nevertheless, the final declaration did refer critically to several features of the world economy. Racism and its related manifestations could, according to the declaration, be aggravated by "inequitable distribution of wealth, marginalization and social exclusion."[1] The declaration also mentioned the possibly detrimental effects of globalization.

> The process of globalization constitutes a powerful and dynamic force which should be harnessed for the benefit, development and prosperity of all countries. . . . While globalization offers great opportunities, at present its benefits are very unevenly shared, while its costs are unevenly distributed. . . . The neg-

ative effects of globalization . . . could aggravate . . . economic disparities which may occur along racial lines.[2]

The declaration listed under "effective remedies" for the racist outcome of globalization a number of measures that were often mentioned by our respondents. They included debt relief, increased foreign aid, infrastructural development, and various measures to eradicate poverty, including better access to world markets. These are not, however, strictly reparative measures, although some participants at Durban so framed them. Rather, they are measures to remedy world inequalities and have more to do with distributive than reparative justice.

The NGO forum's declaration at Durban denounced globalization more forthrightly than the conference's official declaration. It declared, "Globalisation is a historically uneven process based on colonial and imperialist integration of the world economy and on maintaining and deepening unequal power relations between countries and regions of the world."[3] and continued:

> We denounce processes of globalisation that concentrate power in the hands of powerful Western nations and corporations . . . as racist and unjust. It [*sic*] widens economic inequalities within and between countries. . . . Tools of globalisation such as structural adjustment policies result in poverty, famine and the collapse of health and educational systems. . . . Globalisation is the continuation of colonial and imperial control. It is inherently racist and anti-democratic. . . . The wealth and power of globalisation is concentrated in the global capitalist class and is inherently linked to racism.[4]

Many of our respondents held views similar to those expressed by the NGO Forum.

African Voices[5]

Many of our respondents felt that they shared a common fate of misery, poverty, exploitation, and powerlessness, all connected directly to the international economy. Globalization, they thought, had put them more at risk than they would have been had their economies been more independent of interactions with the West and the international community. Jan Aart Scholte stresses the "supraterritorial" aspect of globalization, suggesting that it is characterized by "increases of interaction and interdependence between people in different countries."[6] But this definition does not elucidate the inequalities of these connections. "People" do not interact as equals but as individuals constrained by region, economy, and politics. Africans are the least able of any regional group to interact as equals in the new world of supraterritorial relations.

Richard referred to globalization as an "airborne disease." Indeed, to some respondents, globalization was almost a deliberate conspiracy concocted by Western powers and institutions to extract the maximum profit from Africa. Several specifically referred to globalization as a continuation of the slave trade and colonialism. Susanna, from Tanzania, explained, "Really, globalization is another way of colonialism. They're coming in another fashion." Stéphane said, "Globalization . . . it's simply another form of colonization . . . of the South by the North . . . a modern colonization." Even one ambassador asserted, "With the globalization we can see . . . the very same logic of colonization."

Although conceding that globalization's effects might sometimes be positive, Benedict considered them mostly detrimental.

> Globalization . . . like colonialism, it has its advantages and also disadvantages. . . . People are able to move freely, probably will get employed somewhere else . . . from African countries where the main problem is unemployment. People are also able to . . . advance in terms of technology because the West is ahead of Africa. But then there's also several disadvantages. . . . One is unfair competition . . . we do not tread on an equal footing: somehow we . . . [are] on the losing side. . . . When you look at industrialization, the products from the West, when they are brought to Africa, they kill the local industries.

Benedict was unusual in conceding any positive effects to globalization. Most of our respondents agreed with the strong, antiglobalization attitude of the NGO Forum at Durban. To them, globalization was a way to open Africa to control by international financial institutions (IFIs) and private multinational corporations (MNCs) while simultaneously driving it into deeper and deeper debt. Lawrence said,

> [My] understanding of globalization is to have what's called equal partnership, equal relationship, but I realize that the relationship has been two thirds in favor of the developed world. . . . The price[s] of commodities are determined by the developed world. . . . They [African countries] don't even get . . . enough money . . . to develop their countries because they sell based on what the buyer determines.

Ronald, a lecturer in development studies from Tanzania, said,

> When the seller is from the developed country, it's the developed country that fixes the prices. . . . In Tanzania, in my home . . . last year, 2001, the price of coffee, before June, it was around 300 Tanzanian shillings. August, the price fell . . . to 80. By November it was at 8. And the prices would not go up. Why? The WTO [World Trade Organization] can address why.

Both these quotations imply that globalization is a plot: world prices are set by self-interested Westerners or Western-dominated international organizations, not by neutral market forces.

It seemed to our respondents that there is no room for Africans to participate independently in the global market. Sayeed expressed it clearly.

> We are subjected to it [globalization] but we do not participate. Globalization should mean the participation of each state with its economic, political and cultural values. But we are subjected to it, because we have very little. . . . We have cultural goods to sell, but economic goods . . . we have very little. . . . We don't play an equal part with our partners who have their multinationals, which exploit [our] resources. So . . . we submit, but we don't participate.

Moreover, it seemed to our respondents that the West regarded Africa as an area that could be looted freely by outsiders. All of Africa's resources, they thought, were being expropriated by powerful outsiders, leaving Africans to starve. At the same time, there was little, if any, outside investment in Africa. Gérard pointed out that "Only 1 percent of external investment [is] in Africa, and output of Africa in world trade is less than 1 percent. But at the same time African resources are crucial for . . . the global economy. So, as somebody put it . . . we are sitting on gold and digging for food."[7] Yet there was no way that Africa could escape globalization because, as Étienne explained, "Globalization is a totalitarian phenomenon. . . . Africa should fight for a new international order, because the one we're in now . . . its rules were made without us."

Our respondents were particularly distressed by the structural adjustment programs (SAPs) that many African countries had adopted since the 1980s. Fiscal austerity, trade liberalization, privatization of state-owned enterprises (SOEs), abolition of state marketing boards, export-led agricultural reform, firing of civil servants, and currency devaluation were typical characteristics of SAPs. Michel said:

> We hear, "Don't hire people, don't raise their salaries." . . . They stop our services. . . . But the IMF [International Monetary Fund] doesn't help our governments solve inflation . . . with the consequence that our currency loses its value, no employment is created . . . and there is unemployment. So, these measures are imposed, perhaps to help states function better, but in reality, it's the people who have suffered. This entire history, it's suffering, from the colonial period . . . to independence.

Luke asked what made the World Bank (WB) a "world" organization. "Which World Bank? Does Kenya have a say? Is the world constituted only by the West? Who influences policies that are made by the World Bank? It can only be a World Bank if Africans have representatives."

Some of our respondents mentioned that SAPs often resulted in reduced spending on health and education or required citizens to pay user fees for them. Speaking of his native Ghana, George said, "Africans, we are poor, so if education is not free, it's difficult for people. So . . . that's created a line between the rich and the poor. . . . Rich people have access to education and the poor ones [do] not." Philip said that in Kenya, "To go to a public hospital you have to pay almost half. . . . [If you need] a bandage, you have to buy that bandage. If you had to be injected you have to buy the needle, you have to buy the serum. . . . All these things just came in a flurry after the implementation of the [SAP]."

A few respondents decried the privatization of SOEs. Their sentiments are expressed by Marc, an activist from Togo.

> In my country today, there is what we call the "new" [English in original] industrial force, where industries come from the West and establish themselves. They don't pay any taxes at all. . . . But you should see the conditions my compatriots work in. . . . The conditions are atrocious. They don't respect workers' rights at all. . . . And you should see the privatizations of our state industries. Water, for example . . . it's privatized. Electricity, privatized. . . . These corporations invade us and privatize our resources.

The economic strictures imposed by international institutions had no legitimacy at all, in the eyes of most of our respondents. Charles contended that

> These policies . . . have been creating business for the West. . . . We [Africans] don't have the capacities . . . to run a market-oriented economy because we don't own anything. The peoples who own something are the multinational corporations, which are owned by the West. They come in, they take control of the market and what happens? All the benefits go back to the West.

According to our respondents, if there were any economic justifications for the policies of IFIs, they were completely outweighed by their highly detrimental human impact. Joanna, a Rwandan, thought the international community was deepening her country's postgenocide suffering.

> Now, what's in fashion is globalization. . . . Maybe it's a good idea, but it damages life in general for Africans. Because they privatize . . . despite the people's low purchasing power. It's [globalization] caused . . . a lot of unemployment . . . and lots of poverty. . . . Globalization . . . at the level of Africa, they [globalizers] haven't considered social life, or even life itself. . . . Women prostitute themselves. . . . It's a consequence of poverty, of unemployment.

In the view of many of our respondents, MNCs worked hand-in-glove with IFIs to impoverish Africa. Dawn defined globalization as "a lot of multinationals coming in and just exploiting a lot of resources and going away." Theresa noted the tendency of MNCs to desert African communities they were once based in. "They make their profit and . . . they just leave with no qualms about the damage that they have on the people. . . . You wake up in the morning, all the companies closed. Workers . . . may not even have been paid their monthly salary."

Almost all our respondents considered globalization to have had more negative than positive effects on Africa. As Margaret angrily said,

> We are being forced, we are being plunge[d] into this globalization situation . . . And there is no way we can say, "We should not join the force." Because it stays. . . . So the Western countries are moving at . . . 5 kilometers to catch up with the globalization issue. . . . But for us, that is perhaps 2,000 kilometers for us to catch up.

Haleema, an Egyptian civil servant, agreed with Margaret, using very similar vocabulary. "OK, globalization for them means that we should go far to them, not that they are going to . . . take some steps toward us. I think we should meet in the middle of the way." Luke spoke of the inequities.

> We need to . . . construct appropriate speed governors of globalization. . . . In Kenya . . . thirty-four local industries have closed shop because the markets are flooded by cheap goods coming from the West or brought by multinational[s] who have the benefits of economies of scale, who can exploit cheap labor in Asia and bring their products in Africa. I think it is . . . fulfilling the last aspect of neocolonialism in Africa.

These comments about the speed of change echo Stiglitz's warning against the "shock therapy" style of globalization.[8]

Our respondents' comments on globalization were not merely general observations; they often arose from their lived experiences. Some had family members, colleagues, or friends who had lost their jobs because of SAPs. Edward told us his mother, a nurse, had been laid off from her job in a clinic because of the employment cutbacks necessitated by Tanzania's SAP. Angela explained that structural adjustment required that each individual literally restructure herself by tightening her belt. "We are the ones who are going to tighten our belts and structurally adjust ourself to help them pay what they have stolen."

Those who most favored globalization were several ambassadors who were fairly conversant with international trade and banking. Rashid did not object to globalization as long as everyone followed the same rules. He supported tariff and subsidy reductions to permit freer trade among countries that renounced protectionist measures. If this occurred, his own country could sell more fruit and vegetables to Europe. Paul thought that "Africa . . . want[s] to be part of the world. . . . It should be [done] in such a way that it does not profit only one side of the world." Like Rashid, he was suggesting not that the rules of the international game were wrong, but that they should be implemented fairly. This was not a perspective that most of our respondents shared, perhaps for lack of knowledge of the actual working of the world trade system.

Only a few respondents, other than ambassadors, mentioned benefits of globalization. David thought globalization meant that Africans could have more contact with the rest of the world. "Africans can have an opportunity, those who have not traveled abroad, to use the same machines. . . . It is possible . . . to import products from Europe without actually traveling to Europe." Basil thought that foreign investment would create opportunities for Africans, who would also benefit from "knowledge, interaction, experience, exchanges." Frederick believed that "because of globalization . . . our leaders have been able to interact at large with . . . their counterparts and they have learned quite a lot in terms of . . . respect for human rights"; this was an unusual comment about how globalization favors the flow of ideas. René, a scholar from Mauritius, was skeptical of the entire discourse of reparations, favoring instead the possibilities for economic development that foreign investment might bring. "One can't really repair the errors of the past," he said. "I believe, above all, in the politics of investment, so that people can enrich themselves."

By and large, our respondents believed that the West cared little, or not at all, about how globalization affected Africa. As Angela explained, "I have a problem with understanding what globalization exactly means . . . maybe trying to make a village where everybody will have access to everything." But, as Luke put it, "There is a lot of pillage that also goes on in that village." Alain told us, "I ask myself if they ever take account of the human aspect of Africa. Because with globalization, with structural adjustment programs, all that, they cry, 'No, it's for your benefit.' But at the end of the day . . . the people suffer a lot from those programs." The West, it seemed to our respondents, was incapable of treating Africans as real people.

Yet the almost complete agreement among our respondents about the negative effects of globalization does not seem to reflect general African opinion. The WB and the Royal African Society of the United Kingdom sponsored a poll of almost 8,000 Africans in eight countries from December 2003 to January 2004. Two-thirds thought that globalization had had a positive effect on their lives, this percentage rising among those with higher education and higher income. About 70 percent also favored foreign investment. At the same time, however, strong majorities felt that rich countries were not "playing fair" in trade negotiations, and this percentage was higher among more highly educated people.[9] Our respondents may have been more knowledgeable about relations between the West and Africa than less-educated Africans:

alternatively, they might also have been more exposed to criticisms of globalization, as well as to demands for reparations for past exploitation of Africa by the West.

Although reparations activists, and Africans at Durban, did not explicitly demand reparations for neocolonialism or globalization, they did, like our respondents, refer frequently to postcolonial exploitation of Africa. They conflated foreign investment, world trade, SAPs, privatization, and globalization into one economic world system whose object, it seemed to them, was to continue the centuries-old exploitation of Africa. They advocated changes to this world system as a form of reparation. One idea popular among reparationists was that the West should completely forgive Africa its international debt.

Debt Relief

Debt relief was the most popular form of reparation advocated at Durban. Gnassingbe Éyadema, then president of Togo, stated that "the high debt burden faced by some nations is no different from imposed servitude during the days of slavery."[10] Pascoal Mocumbi, prime minister of Mozambique, agreed: "The external debt burden is unbearable and renders null and void the capacity of our economies to take off towards a sound economic and social development."[11] The representative from the Commission of Human Rights and Fundamental Freedoms of Niger asserted, "Payment of the external debt has plundered Africa of the resources it needs to develop. . . . After three centuries of slavery, and seventy years of colonialism, we believe that Africa doesn't have any debt left to pay, because she's already paid too much."[12] Experts on the United Nations' Sub-Commission on the Promotion and Protection of Human Rights in 2001 also supported debt relief.[13]

Many of the respondents also spoke of the enormous African debt. The WB estimated the total external debt of sub-Saharan Africa at $203.5 billion in 2001, just before we began our interviews; by 2005, it was $215.6 billion.[14] Matthew, an ambassador, said debt hindered his country's participation in the global economy. "We cannot be a player in globalization if we carry the debt to represent 90 percent of our income." Margaret, a Malawian, said, "The . . . money which we borrowed . . . is . . . like a bondage. . . . I don't actually see my country getting out of it."

To refer to African debt as enslavement might seem simply a matter of rhetoric. Leaders of independent African states have always been formally free to accept or reject loans. No physical coercion forced them to borrow, as Ayittey notes. "Bad debts do not occur in a vacuum; it takes two to create them."[15] Nevertheless, according to debt relief activists, the accumulated loans of the postcolonial period soon imposed an almost impossible financial burden on African states, forcing them to devote large percentages of their budgets to debt servicing when funds were scarce for education, health care, and other material needs. At the end of 2002, sub-Saharan Africa's total outstanding debt was 66 percent of its gross domestic product.[16] To many activists in the 1990s, Africa's debt was the symbol of its underdevelopment and of Western cruelty to and disregard for African people. A coalition of Western and African NGOs known as Jubilee 2000[17] began a campaign to persuade Western governments and IFIs to completely cancel Africa's "odious debt."[18] According to Jubilee, "For every $1 given in aid, $1.31 is squeezed out of Africa in debt repayments to the rich countries"; thus, the African continent suffered from "debt bondage."[19]

Responding to the concern about debt, in 1996 the WB and IMF proposed the Heavily Indebted Poor Country (HIPC) Initiative. Some countries would be relieved of some of their debt if they ensured that the money saved would be invested in poverty-reduction programs.[20] By March 2007, thirty countries, of which twenty-seven were African, had reached the point at which they could receive relief, expected to amount to U.S. $25 billion for all thirty countries.[21] Moreover, in 2005 the G8 group (seven industrialized countries plus Russia) proposed to cancel $37 billion debt to the WB, the IMF, and the African Development Fund, owed by nineteen countries, of which fifteen were in Africa.[22]

The G8 decision to write off African debt seemed at least in part a response to the influence of the antidebt social movement. Both the WB and former U.S. President Clinton acknowledged its influence.[23] But even assuming, incorrectly, that all $37 billion were African debt, this is less than one-sixth of the sub-Saharan African debt of $215.6 billion in 2005. Moreover, this cancellation was to take place over forty years,[24] and aid from the International Development Association and the African Development Bank to countries granted debt relief would be reduced by the amount of relief each year.[25]

Although the campaign for African debt relief has had great international moral resonance, Serkan Arslanalp and Peter Henry Blair argue that, in fact, the African debt service burden since independence has never been particularly onerous. The outflow from Africa for debt servicing between 2000 and 2005, they say, was about 3 percent of the gross domestic product, while the inflow of capital was 15 percent.[26] The total cost of debt servicing—payment of both interest and principal—for all of sub-Saharan Africa declined from 5 percent of the gross national income in 1995 to 3 percent in 2004.[27] Arslanalp and Blair argue that the problems of Africa's HIPCs are rooted not in debt but in poor infrastructure and weak institutions. The governments of these countries "fail to provide a rule of law that protects investors, property rights and contracts . . . [and] fail to provide roads and other physical infrastructure."[28] Supporting this view, Andrew Mwaba argues that the real challenge for Africa is to create conditions that will facilitate "autonomous" (private) capital inflows into the continent; this requires governments to institute measures "allaying investor fears of macro-economic instability and government predation."[29]

I cannot assess the validity of the various arguments about the efficacy of debt relief in this chapter, other than to note that debt relief without internal reform will not result in improved African economies. Thus, conditionality on debt relief, demanding such reform, is sensible. But to some debt relief activists, conditions are a form of neocolonialism; they believe that there should be no conditionality, even if the conditions are to democratize or to spend the saved funds on development projects. Jubilee-Zambia objected in 2003 to conditionality on Zambia's debt relief, arguing that the HIPC program was "primarily a creditor's plan to assure sustainable debt servicing," not a plan to relieve their country of its "clearly unpayable" and "economically exhausting" debt.[30]

There is some rhetorical value to Jubilee's position. In the early post-colonial period, African debt was often incurred by dictators propped up by Western states. The "public" debt incurred by these leaders had nothing to do with African publics, who had no say regarding whether the debt should be incurred or how the borrowed funds should be used. As Ayittey contends, "The African people shall not be held liable to repay foreign loans contracted on their behalf without their authorization."[31] Even *The Economist*, generally considered a pro-business publication, agrees with this position. In a 2005 article on Nigeria, it wrote that "much of its debt is 'odious'; that is, it was accrued under military dictators. Since Nigerians did not choose these regimes, it seems unfair that they should have to repay the loans that foreigners were foolish enough to make to them."[32] Western governments did not attempt to stem the flow of this borrowed money into dictators' private accounts or to label the leaders who stole these funds as criminals. As a group called Africa Action noted, "The real question should be 'who owes whom?'"

> Many of the loans being repaid by African countries today were disbursed for strategic purposes, to prop up repressive and corrupt regimes during the Cold War. They were given for failed and grandiose projects pushed by creditors, most of which did not benefit Africa's people. Yet Africa's people are today expected to pick up the tab. They are required to sacrifice their own health and education to ensure that these debts are repaid to wealthy creditors.[33]

Nevertheless, such rhetorical appeal does not take into account the reality of the current political situation. Many African countries are still not democracies, corruption is still endemic in most, and even the most worthy recipients of debt relief still experience deep administrative and organizational problems. Uganda, a democracy, apparently spent $32 million on a new jet the very day it qualified for debt forgiveness.[34] According to an African Union (AU) study, every year corruption costs Africa $148 billion.[35] Nor does the rhetorical appeal against debt take into account the unwillingness of Western and IFI officials to "throw good money after bad"; unless the funds newly liberated are well spent, it seems pointless to relieve African states of debt. African development requires more than debt relief.

Prerequisites to Development: Economic and Political Reform

In Chapter 1, I suggest that focusing on economic rights is a better way to remedy Africa's economic deprivation than demanding reparations. Under international human rights law, every individual is entitled to social security, food, housing, health care, and education.[36] In international discussions, economic rights are often articulated as the right to development.

Article 1.1 of the Declaration on the Right to Development, declared by the United Nations General Assembly in 1986, defines development as "a comprehensive economic, social, cultural and political process, which aims at the constant improvement of the well-being of the entire population and of all individuals on the basis of their active, free and meaningful participation in development and in the fair distribution of benefits resulting therefrom."[37] The right to development is also a cornerstone of the African human rights regime. Article 22.1 of the African Charter on Human and Peoples' Rights states, "All peoples shall have the right to their economic, social and cultural development . . ." and continues in Article 22.2 to state that "states shall have the duty, individually or collectively, to ensure the exercise of the right to development."[38] African states also believe that the entire international community should help them develop. In 1990 Africa called upon the United Nations to "promote the application of justice in international economic relations."[39] In a 1972 resolution on the environment, the Organization of African Unity (OAU) also introduced the idea of reparations: "The responsibility of the colonial powers and other industrialized countries in the destructive exploitation and dissipation of Africa's natural resources . . . implies recognition of the right to reparation from the countries whose development has been based or is still based on this exploitation."[40] The final declaration of the Durban conference also noted a desire to "make the right to development a reality for everyone and to free the entire human race from want."[41]

Nevertheless, even if it were far more entrenched in international law than it is at present, the right to development would still be merely a statement of good intentions. The right to development cannot be ensured only by challenging the policies of IFIs, MNCs, and Western governments, as necessary as that is. African states' own policies must also change.

In the early postcolonial period of the 1960s and 1970s, blaming Africa's underdevelopment almost entirely on exploitation by the West was popular. Many scholars and activists believed that withdrawal from, or avoidance of, international (Western) capitalism would promote development.[42] Challenging this orthodoxy, in 1983 Goran Hyden argued that the path to African economic growth was a slow one and that to understand how that path might be taken, scholars had to pay attention to orthodox economic theory. He advocated a market economy, local capitalist development, and foreign investment.[43] Yet the rhetoric about underdevelopment, neocolonialism, and globalization at Durban suggests that many activists were still persuaded by the view popular in the 1970s, as were many of our respondents.

I cannot, in this volume, discuss in any depth these complex arguments about causes of poverty in Africa. Yet one cannot properly assess the causes of African underdevelopment without analyzing internal, as well as external, economic and political practices. Without a productive economy creating goods that private citizens can use or that governments can redistribute, Africans cannot overcome their underdevelopment. Democracy, good governance, and the rule of law are also necessary to promote and eventually guarantee African development. Citizens must enjoy the full range of civil and political rights, especially the rule of law; freedom of speech, press, association, and assembly; and political democracy. These rights increase the likelihood that governments will engage in accountable, transparent policy-making and will devote resources to the economic human rights of their citizens.

Many African countries underwent significant macroeconomic reform in the 1980s and 1990s, led by SAPs. Critics argue that SAPs failed Africa, especially by undermining access to economic rights such as food, health, and education.[44] Activists at the Durban NGO Forum assumed that IFIs were responsible for decisions to cut funds that supported citizens' basic needs. African governments themselves, however, not IFIs, decided to reduce spending by cutting funds to health and education instead of cutting funds to the military.[45] Nor did African governments control corruption. In any case, some aspects of SAPs did help to improve the economic performance of some African countries.

Chapter 7 discusses Ghana, a country that was colonized in a comparatively benign manner, but whose colonization nevertheless caused underdevelopment. Here I turn to postcolonial Ghana, as an example of a country whose indigenous ruling elites were at least partly responsible for its postcolonial underdevelopment. Ghana is but one example of the complex nature of responsibility, which renders implausible any call for reparations for underdevelopment that focuses only on external culprits. Ghana underwent structural adjustment in the 1980s; its experience suggests that blanket condemnation of SAPs is unwise.[46]

Before the 1980s, Ghana's economy had already been structurally adjusted twice, once during the colonial era and once during the early post-independence decades. From independence in 1957 until the early 1980s, a series of leaders, starting with Kwame Nkrumah, attempted to impose either socialist or military economic order on the country. The result was a massive decline in Ghana's economy. On December 31, 1981, Flight-Lieutenant Jerry Rawlings took power in a coup d'état: he ruled Ghana until 2001. In 1983 Rawlings adopted a SAP. This program included elimination of the state marketing board for cocoa, better protection of private property, reduction in the size of the public service, and privatization of SOEs.

One of the most devastating of Nkrumah's policies had been underpayment of cocoa producers. A state marketing board had purchased cocoa from farmers at a set price, then sold it at the world market price. The state pocketed the difference for its own purposes, which included providing jobs and goods for the more politically threatening urban populace. The price the board paid the farmers was so low that it was not worth their while to produce cocoa; but after Ghana eliminated the cocoa marketing board, it became worthwhile for farmers to resume production. Thus, the SAP partly corrected the bias against rural producers, which Hyden notes had been typical of many African states.[47]

Rawlings also attempted to better protect property rights. When small farmers or entrepreneurs are the legal owners of their land, they can safely invest in it and use it as collateral. Without private property in land, farmers in Ghana lacked incentive to invest in cocoa trees, which take several years to mature, and even lacked security in producing subsistence crops. Insecure property rights in Ghana had also caused capital flight, speculation, and "political investment," as the elites relied for financial security on political office or influence.[48]

One of the most contentious aspects of Ghana's SAP was reduction of its bloated public service. Ghana dismissed 241,000 public servants between 1985 and 1991.[49] That a quarter million individuals suddenly lost their jobs is a great tragedy, but it should also be kept in mind that by 1983 real starting salaries in the bureaucracy were below subsistence level. Nevertheless, compensatory funds could and should have been established by IFIs when SAPs were introduced, to cushion the blow to those who lost their livelihoods when the number of public servants was reduced.

Like the bloated public service, SOEs had also been a serious drain on Ghana's economy; most were very inefficiently run. Output of these enterprises increased after privatization. The privatization program was not a complete success, however, as assets were often transferred to Rawlings's ministers or supporters.[50]

Critics who decry SAPs and other policies of IFIs often forget that any population is divided into groups. Observers often concentrate on the sectors of the population who lose income: these are often urban, especially employees of the state. Observers do not notice those whose incomes rise, especially when they are in rural areas, as occurred in Ghana. Nevertheless, gains from higher agricultural prices in Ghana were offset by other SAP policies, such as withdrawal of subsidies on health, education, and agricultural inputs.[51] Even so, Ghanaians' standard of living improved after the SAP was introduced. The infant mortality rate declined from 96 per thousand in 1980 to 59 in 2003,[52] and life expectancy increased from 51.8 years in 1980 to 56.9 years in 2000.[53]

Ghana did not, however, follow a steadily upward economic path from the mid-1980s to 2000, largely because it was still a dictatorship. In the 1980s and 1990s, rule of law was precarious, and freedom of speech and democracy nonexistent. The early Rawlings regime, from 1982 to 1993, was characterized by political murders and tortures, unprecedented in Ghana's history.[54] State-approved attacks against businesspersons and market traders, for allegedly hoarding goods or charging high prices, discouraged trade and undermined the market economy.

In the 1990s, Rawlings began to understand that he had to supplement economic reform with a more accountable political system that protected the rule of law. He reintroduced electoral politics and was elected president in 1992 and 1996. An orderly transfer of power to President John Agyeman Kufuor took place in 2001. After 2000 there was much more freedom of the press and assembly, civil society organizations were much more active, the rule of law was more entrenched and respected, and Rawlings's highly abusive military and security forces were brought under control.[55] Kufuor was reelected in 2004. In 2005 Ghana was still an extremely poor country, yet 72 percent of Ghanaians who had been surveyed in 2002 were willing to "endure hardships now" in the hope of future betterment.[56]

But Ghana's success also relied on the approval of the international community, confirming, in part, our respondents' views that African prosperity was determined by international decisions. Western countries increased their aid to Ghana as a reward for its SAP; to disentangle the beneficial effects of the SAP from the beneficial effects of this increased aid is difficult, if not impossible. Presumably, changes to economic policy in Ghana not approved by IFIs and Western donors would have reduced Ghana's eligibility for aid.

Nevertheless, Ghana's economic improvement suggests that the rhetoric of the NGO Forum at Durban might do more harm than good. To completely blame outsiders for African poverty is to ignore the need for both appropriate economic policy and a concomitant democratic political system in all African countries. Many of our respondents recognized the importance of internal democracy to their countries' development. When we asked to whom financial reparations ought to be paid, should they be forthcoming, some responded that they should be directed to independent civil society organizations because governments were still too corrupt to be given these resources. As Indira, from South Africa, suggested, "The best means of distribution [is] to the greatest number of people and that used to be the state but it isn't necessarily . . . in all cases. So a combination of the state and perhaps bodies like the UN. . . [and] the organs of civil society." Stuart, an academic from Liberia, agreed. "I have a little bit more faith in leadership that comes out of civil society than . . . the regime. . . . So when I think about leadership [in distributing financial reparations], I'm thinking more about leadership from civil society."

The macroeconomic reform that Durban activists so decried can release blocked productive capacities, as it did to some extent in Ghana. As Amartya Sen argues, for development to occur, citizens must be permitted to exercise their own capabilities.[57] In Africa, these include citizens' capability to cultivate subsistence crops; to engage in local, national, or international market transactions; to engage in industrial production; and to exercise their entrepreneurial agency. When citizens can exercise their productive capacities, they can create goods and wealth for their own use rather than rely completely on national or international redistributive mechanisms.

Macroeconomic reform can also stimulate economic growth by efficient creation of and participation in a market economy that protects property rights, as the Kenyan economist Mwangi Kimenyi argues.[58] Economic growth may also contribute to economic rights, if it increases the amount of public resources that can be dedicated to education, health care, or clean water. Governments must ensure that those who cannot provide them for themselves enjoy their economic rights. This can occur, however, only if an efficient, welfare-oriented redistributive state exists. Such welfare-oriented states are few and far between in Africa, and their emergence is only likely in the event of an upward, interactive, and mutually reinforcing spiral of economic growth and political freedom.

African economic growth also requires increased foreign investment, an aspect of globalization to which many activists at Durban, and many of our respondents, objected. Foreign investment provides capital, technology, and expertise to developing economies; it also provides employment. Increased foreign investment follows domestic institutional improvements, especially establishment of more transparent, accountable governments; the rule of law; and reliable infrastructure. Improved security of tenure in land and property is also necessary to attract foreign investment, as is a better-qualified, more educated labor force.[59]

Thus, Africans need more globalization, not less, but they need it within a context of democracy, human rights, the rule of law, and citizens' active involvement in the decisions their governments make. Africans also need leaders who are responsive to their citizens and who are not corrupt. These political reforms not only protect individuals from arbitrary rule but also create the stable, reliable conditions that attract long-term investment. They also permit Africans to speak out and demand change when, as often happens, foreign investors exploit their labor and resources. The institutional reliability that might attract foreign investors ought not to be implemented at the price of Africans' human rights, but must be concomitant with them.

Internal Versus International Reform

African heads of state have acknowledged the need for internal political reform. The OAU was preoccupied with colonialism, apartheid, and preservation of state sovereignty. By contrast, the AU promotes the universal values of democracy and human rights that earlier generations of African leaders often rejected as Western impositions. Article 4(m) of the AU's *Constitutive Act* specifies that the union should function in accordance with "respect for democratic principles, human rights, the rule of law and good governance."[60]

The AU's acknowledgment of the need for internal African political reform contrasts with reparationists' focus on international reform. Mazrui advocates a "Middle Passage Plan" for Africa. This plan calls for capital and skill transfer and reorganization of IFIs so that Africa would have more voting power in the WB and the IMF.[61] The term "Middle Passage Plan" alludes to the Marshall Plan, the generous aid package offered by the United States to war-ravaged Europe after World War II, in large part to rebuild former enemies as bulwarks against the Soviet Union. Indeed, American officials discussed the possibility of a Marshall Plan for Africa in the 1960s but rejected it, presumably because Africa lacked the strategic importance of Western Europe.[62]

The proposed Middle Passage Plan is analogous to the Development Reparation Fund, proposed by many participants at Durban.[63] But even if a Middle Passage Plan were instituted for Africa, it would encounter obstacles that did not exist in post–World War II Europe. The European countries that received Marshall Plan funds had had developed capitalist economies prior to World War II. They also had advanced, well-organized government bureaucracies, and some had been advanced democracies. Thus, Europeans after World War II had already had several decades of experience with the economic, political, and legal rules and institutions that Africa, in the 1990s, had only begun to acknowledge it needed.

Yet, whatever the responsibility of some African states and elites for their countries' own underdevelopment, they are also at the mercy of world economic forces. Even if some macroeconomic change was necessary in Africa in the 1980s and 1890s, as in Ghana, this does not mean that all macroeconomic policy changes advocated, or insisted upon, by IFIs and Western donors were necessary. Many of these changes undermined Africans' economic rights in the interests of long-term market efficiency. While such efficiency is indeed necessary, IFIs and Western states ought always to be cognizant of their prior responsibility to ensure economic human rights. One does not need to believe that the West deliberately set out to impoverish Africa to accept the West's ethical responsibility to protect Africans' economic rights. Even though Tariq, an ambassador, said that Africans had to learn the rules of the economic game, he also wanted a Marshall Plan for Africa.

Caplan suggests that "the real obligation of the rich world [is] to pay back the incalculable debt we owe Africa. We need to help Africa not out of our selflessness and compassion but as restitution, compensation."[64] Yet to frame this responsibility as a question of reparations is unwise. Responsibility for the difficulties that Africa has experienced since independence is too diffuse and spread among far too many actors to easily assign culpability. Even if culpability were to be assigned and restitution calculated, most theorists of transgenerational economic justice confine restitution only to the immediate descendants of those who were wronged, not to descendants several generations removed. The way forward is to remedy poor economic policies and give ordinary Africans a political voice. Economic and political reforms must be internally driven: if they are not, they will merely be seen as another example of Africans' having to conform to alien norms.

Yet not all Africans are convinced of the need for democracy. Joyce, an activist from Burundi, considered democratization yet another aspect of nefarious globalization. "For me, really, globalization . . . I consider it like the law of the jungle. . . . It's the law of the strongest. . . . 'You come with me into democracy, or you don't come: if you don't follow, you go to the side, and at the side, you know what that means.' That's the threat that hovers over you." Alexandre, a scholar who was also from Burundi, agreed with Joyce. "There's a certain paternalism that's there . . . in the conditionalities that are specific to Africa. . . . With regard to democratization . . . there's President Mitterand . . . [who] says to the African countries, 'If you don't do that [democratize], I'll turn off the tap.'"

One ought to take seriously our respondents' deep sense of economic hopelessness and political despair. To many, it seemed that Africans remained "sitting on gold and digging for food." Globalization did not open up possibilities for them: it was an airborne disease that caused Africa untold harm. Some aspects of this hopelessness might be remediable if African economies become more efficient. Some aspects can also be remedied by more accountable, open, and democratic governments buttressed by the rule of law. But more serious attention to African poverty by the international community is also necessary. One aspect of such attention is to deepen international responsibility for human rights and extend it to more institutional actors. In Chapter 9 I consider the developing movement to impose human rights obligations on MNCs. I also consider international criminal law. Both are alternatives to the call for reparations, and may have more practical effect.

Chapter 9

Postcolonial Relations, Postcolonial Crimes

Africans can resort to means other than the claim for reparations in order to garner protection against Western states and Western-based institutions. Reparationists would like more economic justice from transnational corporations: the means to impose human rights obligations on these private organizations are still weak, but there is growing international normative pressure upon them. There is also some room to bring them to justice via civil law, especially in the United States. Some investors in Africa engage in criminal activities, and they can be pursued using already extant police procedures and criminal laws. There is also a new mechanism to bring some criminals to justice; namely, the International Criminal Court (ICC). These mechanisms, however, are not strictly reparative, because they deal with present actions and crimes. They also apply as much to African actors as outsiders. Nevertheless, they answer some of the calls that reparationists make for justice for the postcolonial period.

Corporate Reparations

Antiglobalization activists often oppose Western investment in Africa, which they perceive as inimical to Africans' interests. This is a mistake: other regions of the world, such as South-East Asia, China, and India, that attract Western investment have shown remarkable levels of growth in the last fifty, twenty-five, and fifteen years respectively. Indeed, Africa suffers from too little, not too much, globalization. It does not attract much investment, except in resource extraction. Africans are not needed as laborers for world industrial production. They are poorly educated and suffer from high rates of HIV/AIDS, as well as other diseases, especially malaria and tuberculosis. Nor is Africa a large potential market for the world's industrial goods. Moreover, the regulatory environment for business is unstable and unpredictable; yet, except for those that expect to make substantial profits in the very short term, businesses thrive when regulation is stable and clear, and the rule of law prevails.

Africa does need more integration into the world market, but the conditions under which it has so far been integrated reveal how abusive international investors can be of their workers, of the environment, of the surrounding communities in which they invest, and of national interests. Africans are not wealthy or organized enough to protect themselves from much of this abuse, nor are their governments strong and efficient enough to bargain with outside investors, even where the governing classes are not themselves corrupt.

In the 1990s South African activists began to agitate for reparations from Western corporations. Some of these cases involved standard torts, or harms, rather than claims for reparations for historical wrongs and thus could be judged under civil law. A British solicitor, Richard Meeran, brought cases against three companies, Cape Plc., Thor Chemicals, and Rio Tinto Zinc, for torts committed in South Africa. Cape Plc. was the parent company of two mines, some of whose employees developed lung diseases as a consequence of exposure to asbestos. A study at one of these enterprises, Penge Mines, showed that asbestosis caused the deaths of 80 percent of black workers who died between 1959 and 1964.[1] In 2003 the case was settled for $U.S. 12.39 million.[2] The case against Thor holdings, launched in 1992, claimed that workers at its mercury-processing plant in KwaZulu-Natal were exposed to mercury poisoning. This case was settled for 9 million South African rand.[3] In 2000 Meeran led a case in United States courts against Mobil Oil, claiming elevated rates of leukemia near a refinery Mobil had established in 1954 in south Durban.[4]

Activists in other South African cases demanded reparations for complicity in apartheid, claiming that corporate investment assisted the apartheid regime to stay in power. In 2002 four South African victims of human rights violations sued in Geneva for $50 billion in reparations from three American and Swiss banks, alleging participation in a conspiracy—namely, the apartheid system—to commit crimes against humanity. This conspiracy allegedly contravened a UN embargo against South Africa from 1985 to 1993.[5] The claimants' intent was to force these companies to provide funds to assist individual victims of human rights violations and to set up social programs. Ed Fagan, a lawyer earlier instrumental in obtaining Holocaust reparations for Jews, represented the plaintiffs.[6] In 2003 Fagan also brought a $100 million lawsuit against Union Carbide, Dow Chemical, and other companies in New York, accusing them of negligence in the management of pensions and of health, life, unemployment, and retirement funds in their South African operations.[7]

Some of these claims were brought before U.S. courts under the Alien Torts Claims Act (ATCA). President Thabo Mbeki of South Africa objected that matters of importance to South Africa as a whole should not be adjudicated in foreign courts, "which bear no responsibility for the well-being of our country."[8] This objection is similar to the position of the Namibian government against German reparations to the Herero (discussed in Chapter 7). In 2003 the South African Trade and Industry Minister said his government would not enforce the judgments of foreign courts in cases against transnational corporations.[9] Presumably, the reason for this statement was to preserve an attractive environment for foreign investors in South Africa.

Since the end of apartheid, South Africa has had a large, well-organized civil society and an open, democratic government subject to the rule of law. Its citizens' successes in reparations cases against private corporations are unlikely to be replicated easily elsewhere in Africa, where there is less access to the rule of law and governments are often not democratic. As of early 2007, attempts to force Shell Oil to pay reparations to the people of the Niger Delta area of southeast Nigeria for environmental and other damages were not successful.

Shell and other companies first drilled for oil in the Niger Delta in 1958. Oil soon earned approximately 90 percent of Nigeria's national export revenue. Shell's business practices in Nigeria show that without a proper legal and regulatory environment, private corporations will extract the maximum profit with minimum regard not only for the environment and surrounding communities but even for their own long-term security. Shell polluted the environment of the Delta region to such an extent that "farming in Ogoniland [a region of the Delta] . . . [became] an exercise in futility."[10] So much natural gas "flared" from Shell's wells that the iron roofs of local houses corroded and respiratory diseases were endemic.[11] Canal construction caused saline water to flood fresh water.[12] Despite the vast wealth extracted from it, the region had very few roads, there were few teachers or doctors, and there was very little access to electricity.[13]

One of the ethnic groups affected by Shell's policies was the Ogoni, a group of about 500,000 people.[14] In the mid-1990s, some Ogoni citizens created a peaceful civic organization, Movement for the Survival of the Ogoni People (MOSOP), to pressure Shell to clean up the environment and contribute to the welfare and development of the surrounding population, claiming that Shell had removed about $30 billion from Ogoniland since 1958.[15] MOSOP also wanted a greater share of oil revenues to remain in the region rather than be transferred to the central government;[16] at the time, oil-producing Nigerian states were permitted to retain only 1 percent of oil income.[17] Ken Saro-Wiwa, a writer, was MOSOP's leader. The government arrested Saro-Wiwa and nine colleagues in 1995, held them in military custody, tortured them, and then executed them after a farcical trial that generated international protest.[18] Shell refused to intercede with the Nigerian government to protect Saro-Wiwa and assisted the government to suppress those who were objecting to its environmental degradation.[19]

In a statement to the court before his conviction, Saro-Wiwa said, "Whether the peaceful ways I have favored will prevail depends on what the oppressor decides, what signals it sends out to the waiting public."[20] Ten years later, armed militants began to kidnap and kill foreigners in southeast Nigeria. Seven oil workers were killed in an attack on their boat in 2004.[21] In early 2006, in two separate instances, a new organization of ethnic Ijaw "youths" called the Movement for the Emancipation of the Niger Delta kidnapped thirteen people, although all were eventually released. There were about 14 million ethnic Ijaw,[22] among whom were some elders who seemed to approve of the militants' actions as the only means to draw attention to the Ijaw plight. Kidnappings continued throughout 2006 and early 2007, with forty foreigners taken hostage in January 2007 alone.[23]

One purpose of these kidnappings was to draw attention to the terrible living conditions endured by the population in the southeast[24] and to force Shell to abide by the instructions of a Nigerian court to pay $1.5 billion to Bayelsa State in compensation, an order that Shell appealed.[25] As a result of the kidnappings and other attacks on oil companies and pipelines in the region, Nigerian oil production in 2006 fell by 20 percent: this was one reason that oil prices in early 2006 were over $60 per barrel worldwide.[26] That Shell and other oil companies were able to so disregard the environment and so mistreat the citizens of southeast Nigeria was in large part a consequence of a weak and corrupt government; Nigeria ranked at 142 of 163 countries on the 2006 Corruption Perceptions Index.[27] National and local regulation of the oil giants was either nonexistent or easily disregarded.

In its defense, Shell pointed to widespread theft of oil from its pipelines and the environmental damage caused by this theft. It claimed, for example, that 50 to 60 percent of the oil spillages in the region in 1992–1993 were caused by sabotage, not by its poor environmental policies.[28] Certainly, sabotage and theft did contribute to oil pollution in the Delta region and reduced Shell's direct responsibility accordingly. Much oil was stolen from the pipelines and "bunkered," or sold to illegal buyers: it was suspected that some of those who sold this oil illegally were local or national officials.[29] Indeed, it was unclear how much of the protest against Shell was caused by genuine anger and how much was a means by which local notables could manipulate young men to steal oil. Nevertheless, one might argue that had Shell used more of its profits to benefit local Nigerians, there would have been less theft and sabotage.

The spate of kidnapping in the Niger Delta in the early twenty-first century highlighted the poor long-term planning of Shell and other oil companies in the region, including Mobil and Chevron. In fact, scores, perhaps hundreds of cases were brought against oil companies in Nigeria from 1987 on, mostly alleging damage caused by oil spills, and Nigerian judges became more sympathetic to plaintiffs as the dangers of oil spills garnered ever more world public attention.[30] It was unlikely in 2007 that anger and militancy against the oil companies would decrease without extremely concrete, visible development projects with immediate results. By taking advantage of the extremely weak regulatory environment to make as much profit as possible, these oil companies played fast and loose with their own interests. They risked finding their oil platforms and pipelines completely disrupted, their workers and executives kidnapped and murdered, and their profits plummeting.

Nor were relations between Shell Oil and local Nigerians purely a Nigerian matter. Already heavily influenced by Islamic radicalism in the North, Nigeria witnessed the introduction of Islamist ideology in the southeast. In April 2006 a new group called the Martyrs' Brigade threatened to mete out "jungle justice" against Mobil Oil, which it accused of a disastrous oil spill in 1997: the group referred to Mobil officials as "infidels."[31] This potent combination of oil and identity politics might result in a new civil war. A secessionist war in the southeast (a replay of the 1969–1971 secessionist war) could prove the last straw for a fractured Nigeria, plunging an already weak state into chaos. This chaos would cause a refugee crisis not only in neighboring African states, but also in Europe. U.S. security would also be affected: in February 2007, 11.7 percent of U.S. oil imports were from Nigeria,[32] and the figure was expected to rise to 25 percent in the ensuing decade.[33] Environmental damage could also affect world security. Massive flaring of gas that could be recovered and recycled contributes to global warming. The United States treats oil production in Africa as an urgent security concern,[34] yet does not demand that U.S. corporations operating outside U.S. borders engage in responsible behavior that could ameliorate this threat to its security.

Shell's activities in Nigeria show that corporations often refuse to take responsibility for the consequences of their actions, unless that responsibility is forced on them. Reparations seem one of the few ways that corporations can be brought to account. The official declaration at the Durban Conference mentioned the responsibility of private corporations. It urged states to take measures to "ensure that transnational corporations and other foreign enterprises operating within their national territories conform to precepts and practices of nonracism and nondiscrimination" and encouraged the business sector to "develop voluntary codes of conduct" to eliminate racism and related intolerance.[35] But discrimination is only a small part of the problem. Corporations could adhere strictly to codes of conduct regarding nonracism and nondiscrimination; for example, they could ensure that in Africa they did not discriminate among "races" or among members of different ethnic groups, but this would not necessarily affect environmental policies, payment of taxes, or corrupt interactions with local authorities.

To obtain the reforms that activists desire, corporate responsibilities must extend to a much wider range of human rights than nondiscrimination. Yet under international law, corporations are not liable for human rights violations, except perhaps with regard to a "moral and social obligation to respect the universal rights" in the UDHR.[36] One way to control their behavior is to pressure them to adopt voluntary codes of conduct. By the early twenty-first century, several such codes existed, to which many corporations claimed to adhere, but these were mainly in the consumer goods industries or in manufacturing.[37] In 2002 fewer than 10 percent of U.S.–based MNCs had human rights codes,[38] although by June 2006, ninety-nine companies listed on the Business and Human Rights Resource Centre website had explicit human rights codes, up from thirty-eight companies listed on the same website in October 2002.[39] The resource extraction industry, which is the most pervasive in Africa, did not develop codes of conduct for its transnational enterprises. Rather, "U.S. mining and oil companies forged cozy relationships with dictatorial regimes across Africa," as did oil and mining companies based outside the United States.[40]

The weakness of international law regarding corporate responsibility for human rights violations makes it very difficult for victims of corporate abuse to seek reparations. Some international documents detail minimum standards for the way corporations treat their workers, especially documents of the International Labor Organization (ILO), but there is no mechanism for legal enforcement of these standards. Transnational corporate responsibility for human rights depends heavily on pressure from international social movements, especially in the West: in the absence of such pressure, there is little incentive to change poor behavior. Yet when, as in the case of Nigerian oil, the actions of one corporate sector could affect world security, there is a strong argument to increase the international capacity to regulate corporate behavior. In such a situation, voluntary codes of conduct, consumer boycotts, and admonitory declarations from bodies such as the ILO are not enough.

None of this, however, means that African political leaders are absolved of responsibility for the abusive actions of Western corporations. If international law is not yet developed enough to ensure that corporations adhere to human rights obligations, it is somewhat more developed regarding the obligations of political leaders, whether legitimate or illegitimate. Many African leaders collude with foreign firms in ways that are criminal and are, or should be, subject to international criminal law.

Criminal Resource Extraction

Mazrui argued that African leaders were responsible for only about 15 percent of Africans' suffering since independence. He attributed 40 percent to the imperial and colonial experience and 25 percent to "the contemporary global system and political economy," leaving 15 percent to ecological conditions and 5 percent to chance.[41] These rhetorical estimates excuse the African political class from its responsibilities and exculpate African political leaders of their own agency, their independent decisions to deprive their populations of basic freedoms and economic rights.

While some African leaders have sought greater accountability, rule of law, and personal responsibility in the continent, they have often been thwarted by much less responsible individuals in positions of power. Since independence, much of what passes for political leadership in Africa has in fact been criminal activity. Some of this criminal activity is subject to international criminal law, although much is not.

The Report of the Regional Conference for Africa, prior to the Durban Conference, noted that "external interference, mainly linked to the exploitation of minerals and the arms trade" was one of the "contributing factors in the spread of conflicts and instability in Africa."[42] A covert world existed in which "an undeclared and subterranean form of warfare has erupted between organized crime groups, sometimes with the involvement of states, over wresting control of the world's illegal markets."[43] Many states in Africa could be described as "weak," "failed," or "collapsed" in that, to various degrees, they cannot effectively administer their own territories or provide security for their citizens.[44] These states are especially vulnerable to international criminal pillage when they possess sovereignty over valuable natural resources, such as oil, timber, and minerals.

Some political leaders used their resource privilege to consolidate their power by obtaining the support of either legitimate businesses such as oil companies or illegitimate businesses such as traffickers in illegal diamonds. A resource privilege is "the privilege of any person or group exercising effective power within a country to confer internationally valid legal ownership rights in its natural resources."[45] In Congo in the late 1990s, then President Laurent Kabila established state control over gold and diamonds, as well as over minerals such as copper, cobalt, and zinc, enabling him to use these resources to pay off his allies, both internal and external.[46] During the civil war in Sierra Leone in the 1990s, criminal gangs expedited export of "blood diamonds" from Africa to the international black market. There were even some allegations that these diamonds were traded by Charles Taylor, the rebel leader in Sierra Leone, to Hezbollah and Al-Qaeda.[47] Possibly Taylor was assisted by diamond merchants resident in Sierra Leone but of Lebanese extraction, who were sympathetic to Hezbollah.[48]

In most cases where such pillage occurs, state elites are involved; for example, it appears that the political leaders of Liberia and Burkina Faso helped expedite the export of Sierra Leone's blood diamonds.[49] This "'parallel financing'—the bartering of resources for armaments"[50] underwrote many African wars. Nor were diamonds the only resource that could be bartered in this manner. "Red logs," valuable forest timber purchased *inter alia* by firms from China and France, were used to finance Liberia's civil war.[51] Arms smugglers also took advantage of the opportunity to register their ships under the Liberian flag of convenience to transport their illegal goods.[52]

Whether the business is diamonds, gold, timber, or shipping, lack of international corporate accountability contributes to Africa's wars. The flow of blood diamonds lessened after the international diamond industry heeded NGO and UN calls for transparency and initiated the Kimberley Process, a procedure to ensure that all diamonds are legitimately produced, exported, and traded.[53] However, by 2006, the Kimberley Process had not been fully implemented, and blood diamonds were still entering the international market.[54]

African leaders' collusion in illegal export of valuable resources is mirrored by their collusion in the international trade in illicit drugs, which relies increasingly on trans-African routes and African traffickers.[55] In Kenya, members of the government and law enforcement agencies and their relatives allegedly were involved in the international trans-shipment of cocaine.[56] Illegal arms flows in the Great Lakes region of Africa were in part financed by the drug trade, in which leaders of the Interahamwe, the former *génocidaires* of Rwanda, were involved.[57]

These activities are subject to criminal law, not the law of reparations. In the normal course of events, the law in question is domestic African law, not international law. In some cases, however, police and elite complicity render it difficult to impose domestic sanctions on culprits. The possibility of invoking international criminal law against individuals involved in illicit trafficking in resources and arms is emerging. The ICC's jurisdiction includes crimes against humanity, war crimes, and genocide. To the extent that warlords, their allies in the African political class, or their allies in either legitimate or illegitimate international business are complicit in these crimes, they might be vulnerable to prosecution by the ICC. For example, the corporations involved in extraction of gold, diamonds, timber, and coltan (used in consumer electronic products) from Congo hired security firms that allegedly were involved in some of the atrocities there.[58] If this is proved to be true, then the corporations themselves could be considered complicit, and their representatives could be charged by the ICC. In any case, the ICC already has jurisdiction over the political and military actors with whom these corporations collude. This criminal jurisdiction is much stronger than the weak international norms of reparations and a much more effective means of punishing those who abuse Africa now.

Political Crimes

Even though the ICC's mandate, as of 2002, was limited to crimes against humanity, war crimes, and genocide, it did allow the ICC some jurisdiction over the behavior of individuals who controlled criminal states. Criminal states systematically violate the rights of their own citizens, which is a breach of international law. Two such states in the early twenty-first century were Sudan, committing war crimes and crimes against humanity in its Darfur region, and Zimbabwe, which massively deprived its citizens of food and housing.[59] The rhetoric of Durban suggested that all major catastrophes that had occurred in Africa were rooted in the slave trade, colonialism, and abusive postcolonial international relations. Some of the worst postcolonial African catastrophes, however, were caused by the African political class. Colonialism and neocolonialism set the stage for the emergence of vicious politicians in post-1960 Africa, but those leaders acted of their own volition and with motives of their own.

Responsibility for these political crimes is much more complex in the postcolonial period than it was under colonialism. In a review of two reports on the origins of the Rwandan genocide, Douglas Anglin distinguishes core, contributory, and circumstantial causes.[60] Drawing on Anglin's distinction, I consider core causes of massive political crimes to be decisions that are not inevitable, that are caused by human agency, and that further the interests of those making them. Contributory factors are short-term prior events that inadvertently cause or promote the crime. Circumstantial factors are those that are part of the underlying economic or political scene and that often reflect historical events. Responsibility for contributory and circumstantial causes does not bear the same weight as responsibility for core causes.

In the early twenty-first century, a conflict between "Arabs" and "Africans" in the western Darfur region of Sudan masked the attempt by the central government to suppress a rebellion originally motivated by a demand for basic human rights and regional autonomy.[61] African rebels sought the same concessions as had recently been offered Sudan's south, after a civil war that had lasted several decades. In response, Arab troops on horseback, yet carrying advanced weaponry, marauded through African areas of Darfur, killing, maiming, and raping; they also burned villages, killed animals, and poisoned wells. Arabs tended to be from nomadic tribes, allied with the central government, while Africans were settled tribes. All were Muslim, and there was little "racial" distinction, though they used the terms Arab and African themselves as markers of culture and identity.[62] Formerly in some conflict over land and water, by 2004 Arabs and Africans had become mortal enemies.

Core responsibility for the political crimes in Darfur adhered to the Sudanese government. No Western power had any reason to promote them, nor did any do so. Contributory factors might partially implicate the United States, which hesitated to offend the Sudanese government because it wanted to purchase Sudanese oil and because the Sudanese government had positioned itself as an ally in the American war against terrorism.[63] Circumstantial factors implicating the West include the original decision by British colonizers to create one country from such a vast territory.

One might consider whether the West bears responsibility for not stopping the crimes in Darfur. In 2004, at the United Nations, President George W. Bush used the term "genocide" to describe the crimes taking place in Darfur.[64] Yet by early 2007 the United States had taken little concrete action to protect its inhabitants. The United Nations, however, was somewhat more assertive. It imposed a ban on arms sales to all belligerents and a travel ban and asset freeze on some Sudanese: the United Nations Security Council (UNSC) also referred the Darfur case to the ICC.[65] Seven thousand African Union (AU) monitors were sent to Darfur in late 2004,[66] to be logistically assisted by the West, but they were inadequately supplied. In September 2006 the Sudanese government objected to President Bush's request to permit 20,000 UN peacekeepers into Darfur, asserting that this proposal was a result of a Zionist desire to dismember Sudan.[67] In late July 2007, however, Sudan agreed to accept UNSC Resolution 1769, authorizing up to 26,000 African Union and UN troops to enter Darfur by October 2007.[68]

If the West and the United Nations did little to help Darfurians, African leaders were no better. In May 2004, with the support of African states, Sudan was elected to sit on the United Nations Human Rights Commission.[69] At a summit with Sudan in October 2004, the leaders of Libya, Chad, Egypt, and Nigeria rejected "all foreign intervention in this purely African question," implying that African regional autonomy was more important to them than saving the lives of the people of Darfur.[70] In early 2007, however, fellow members of the African Union did block Sudan's efforts to have its president, Omar el-Bashir, elected AU chair.[71]

Other world powers also failed Darfur. In 2004 the Chinese owned 40 percent of a large oil project in Sudan and had also built a 1,600-kilometer pipeline there.[72] In exchange for access to its oil, China provided the Sudanese government with three arms factories.[73] China's interests were one reason that the Security Council did not take stronger measures against Sudan.

By mid-2007, Western states, NGOs, and the United Nations were providing some—but not nearly enough—logistical support to AU monitors. Thus, Darfur raises the ethical question of whether Western bystander states are responsible to protect Africans against their own governments. If they are responsible, then perhaps they owe reparations in cases in which they did not protect, as the OAU argued was owed to Rwanda.[74] But in international law, there is not yet any "hard" responsibility to protect citizens against their own rulers, let alone pay reparations for failure to do so.

The question whether there is an international, or Western, responsibility to protect Africans against their own governments also pertained, in the early twenty-first century, to Zimbabwe. Many Zimbabweans were suffering from a severe shortage of food, as a result of their government's policies. Robert Mugabe, Zimbabwe's president since 1980, was encouraging "land invasions" of white-owned farms by persons alleged to be veterans of the 1965–1980 war of independence. His purpose was to buy political support, ostensibly by redistributing the land to poor Zimbabweans.[75] These large farms produced much of the food that had earlier made Zimbabwe the breadbasket of Eastern Africa. The land invasions rendered unemployed about 150,000 to 200,000 farm workers, who with their families constituted about a million and a half to two million people, many of whom were immigrants from other African countries, thus not eligible for the land that was ostensibly to be redistributed.[76]

By October 2003, almost half of Zimbabwe's population of nearly 14 million were considered "food-insecure, living in a household that is unable to obtain enough food to meet basic needs."[77] The new occupants of the redistributed farms often had no idea how to farm or were subsistence peasants, unable to produce for the market. Despite the unprecedented food shortage, Mugabe distributed state-owned grain only to his political supporters and withheld it from those who, he thought, might vote against him in the farcical periodic elections still held in Zimbabwe.[78] At one point, Mugabe even denied international agencies permission to bring food into the country to feed the starving, and he intimidated, threatened, and imprisoned all opposition. The World Food Program predicted that 1.4 million people, or 17 percent of the rural population, would need food aid in 2006–2007.[79] Mugabe also exacerbated his people's woes in 2005 by engaging in "Operation Drive Out Trash," the destruction of the homes and small businesses of hundreds of thousands of urban Zimbabweans.[80] This destruction severely compromised the housing, nutrition, and health of up to 2.4 million people.[81] By 2007, there were an estimated 3 million Zimbabwean refugees in South Africa, with another 200,000 in Botswana, and many others seeking asylum elsewhere.[82]

The individuals bearing core responsibility for Zimbabwe's food deficit were Mugabe and his henchmen. A contributory factor might be thought to be the 1980 Lancaster House Agreement, which gave Zimbabwe independence. According to the agreement, the British, Zimbabwe's former rulers, were to provide funds to buy out white farmers on a willing-seller, willing-buyer basis, but not enough funds were supplied.[83] However, according to Power, two-thirds of the large white-owned farms in Zimbabwe were purchased after, not before, independence, thus holding title issued by the Mugabe government.[84] Moreover, many of the large farms taken over after 2000 were distributed to single black owners, mostly Mugabe's allies and relatives, such as the Minister of Home Affairs, who was given five farms, and Mugabe's wife, who was given two.[85]

Circumstantial factors contributing to Mugabe's decision to deprive his citizens of food include the original British takeover of Zimbabwe (then Southern Rhodesia) and its establishment as a settler colony where whites were encouraged to farm. It is ironic that the Lancaster House Agreement offered compensation to whites for loss of lands they took from Africans but did not compensate Africans for their prior losses of land to whites. A contributory cause might well be the international community's tolerance of Mugabe's violent actions. In the early 1980s, forces loyal to Mugabe tortured, killed, and starved to death thousands of minority Ndebele in Matabeleland, with little criticism by the international community.[86] Thus, perhaps, Mugabe thought he possessed an international license to maltreat his people.

Despite his attacks against his own people in the early twenty-first century, the international community did not accuse Mugabe of crimes that might be indictable at the ICC, such as crimes against humanity. The British Commonwealth suspended Zimbabwe in 2002[87] and extended that suspension in late 2003:[88] as a result, Mugabe withdrew Zimbabwe from the Commonwealth.[89] As of March 2004, the European Union had also imposed a travel ban and asset freeze on ninety-five individuals from Zimbabwe, including Mugabe;[90] by March 2007, then British Prime Minister Tony Blair was urging stronger sanctions.[91] But President Thabo Mbeki of South Africa protected Mugabe from further punishment.[92] In 2002 Mbeki claimed that attempts in the Commonwealth to ostracize Mugabe were "inspired by notions of white supremacy."[93] Mbeki claimed before the 2005 Zimbabwean elections that "nobody in Zimbabwe is likely to act in a way that will prevent free and fair elections being held."[94] In 2005 the African Union resisted calls from the United States and Britain to criticize Operation Drive Out Trash.[95] In 2006 it refused to make public a report critical of Zimbabwe's human rights record, which had been prepared two years earlier by the AU Commission on Human and People's Rights.[96]

By 2007, however, the African Union was somewhat more critical of Mugabe. Its then president, John Kufuor of Ghana, called the situation in Zimbabwe "very embarrassing,"[97] although the African Union still condemned what it saw as the European Union's double standard in denouncing Mugabe while ignoring other abusive African leaders.[98] In April 2007 leaders at the Southern African Development Community (SADC) meeting in Tanzania refused to confront Mugabe, instead "reaffirm[ing] its [SADC's] solidarity with the Government and People of Zimbabwe."[99] In May 2007 the African bloc at the United Nations successfully nominated Zimbabwe's Environment Minister, Francis Nheme, to Chair the UN Commission on Sustainable Development,[100] despite allegations that he had personally run down a previously successful, white-owned farm that had been given to him during Zimbabwe's land redistribution.[101] These inconsistent actions by various African organizations and representatives buttressed Mugabe instead of indicting him for his criminal acts. As Baker puts it, in Africa "loyalty to members of the heads of state club is still strong."[102]

The West, then, is not the only actor that ought to be taken into account when discussing political crimes in Africa. In Darfur, the United Nations bore a special responsibility. So did great powers other than the United States: China and Russia both had interests in Sudan. China cultivated good relations with African leaders to facilitate its access to African resources, to open up new markets, and to find supporters for its positions in international organizations such as the United Nations.[103] In 2005 Beijing's foreign affairs college gave Mugabe an honorary degree, and China donated $9 million for him to build a personal palace, as well as providing him with arms.[104] Regional actors also affected African affairs, as in Mbeki's support of Mugabe.

Criminal Trials, Not Reparations

The reparations discourse confuses the responsibility of Africans with the responsibility of outsiders. In the case of postcolonial political crimes, core responsibility often lies with African leaders, who are responsible for far more than Mazrui's 15 percent of the damage done to their countries. The political class is often a criminal class. Just as it submitted the names of alleged Sudanese perpetrators to the ICC, so the UNSC should submit the names of Robert Mugabe and his henchmen. The UNSC possesses the authority to refer "situations" of grave violations of international law against genocide and crimes against humanity to the ICC,[105] even if the countries involved, as in the cases of Sudan and Zimbabwe (as of January 1, 2007) are not party to the ICC itself.[106] Under the Rome Statute of the ICC, crimes against humanity are defined to include forcible transfers of population, as in Operation Drive Out Trash, and "other inhumane acts . . . intentionally causing great suffering,"[107] as in the starvation and malnutrition caused by Zimbabwe's land redistribution.

Other events discussed in this chapter suggest that there was much room in 2007 for expansion of the list of crimes for which the ICC should be responsible. For example, as Ocheje suggests, the ICC should have jurisdiction over corruption.[108] Since the African Union has adopted a Convention on Preventing and Combating Corruption,[109] perhaps such a supplemental jurisdiction of the ICC—at least in the most egregious cases—would be attractive to it. It would also be useful, in the future, to give the ICC jurisdiction over corporate entities, or their individual officers, who cooperate with African criminal gangs, rebels, or indeed state officials to plunder the continent's resources. Perhaps, indeed, plunder should be defined as a crime under ICC jurisdiction.

As of early 2007, all of the individuals referred to the ICC for trial were African. Uganda had referred John Kony, leader of the brutal Lord's Resistance Army in its north, and some of his henchmen,[110] although none of these individuals was before the court in early 2007. Some individuals alleged to have committed crimes in the war in Congo had also been referred: in January 2007 Thomas Lubanga, an accused Congolese war criminal, became the first person to stand trial at the ICC.[111] The ICC has no power to arrest alleged criminals: it can only wait for them to be arrested or surrendered by states. Although it is an international criminal court, it will, in the foreseeable future, be able to try only a small number of people.

Moreover, the ICC possesses no jurisdiction over what many Africans perceive as the most egregious crime against them, their systemic poverty. It cannot try those responsible for this poverty. Yet in a moral sense, it was a crime for the West to lend huge sums to African dictators while turning a blind eye to corruption. In a moral sense, it is also a crime for private corporations to absolve themselves of human rights obligations. There are very few structures available in international law to declare these moral crimes legal crimes, yet both contribute to African poverty. But law progresses in part because thinking individuals persuade governments and international institutions that acts previously permissible must be declared illegal. Such was the thinking that resulted in the creation of the ICC: such thinking might, in the future, result in the creation of mechanisms to try corporate and economic crimes.

Both extant and possible future criminal laws, then, can be used to obtain the kind of justice that those who want reparations seek. Since much present African suffering is caused by criminals, corrupt elites, and irresponsible corporations, the extension of international criminal law to cover more types of crime would provide stronger redress for victims than the much softer law of reparations. Western and non-Western actors would be liable for prosecution under a stronger criminal law regime. If human rights law were also extended so that corporations had stronger obligations analogous to those of states, Africans would have another avenue of redress that did not require resorting to a claim for reparations. Both African adherence to laws that currently exist and African pressure for extension of international laws are more likely to control contemporary, postcolonial abuses of human rights than calls for general reparations from the West.

Chapter 10
Remedies
Acknowledgment and Apologies

Many of those who call for Western reparations to Africa ask for acknowledgment of the ways that the West has harmed the continent and for apologies for this harm.[1] Acknowledgment and apology help repair relations between victimized individuals or groups and those who victimized them. To Africans, though, these symbolic gestures might seem insincere, or even hypocritical, without subsequent material compensation.

Social Functions of Apology

In the social world, apology is a means by which fractured social relationships can be repaired; hence, Goffman's characterization of apologies as examples of "remedial work."[2] In an apology, says Thompson, the apologizer conveys "(1) that she acknowledges that she has committed a wrongful act against the victim and takes responsibility for it; (2) that she feels remorse for her deed; (3) that she undertakes to avoid similar transgressions against the victim in the future."[3] For acknowledgment to become apology, then, requires a sense of remorse, regret, or sorrow. Remorse, regret, and sorrow are embodied not only in the act of apology itself but also in recipients' reactions. Thomas and Thomas's classic sociological dictum, "If men [*sic*] define situations as real, they are real in their consequences," is instructive here: remorse, regret, and sorrow exist as much in the recipients' subjective reception of the apology as in the apology itself.[4]

Acknowledgment and apology are assumed to have a positive effect on the psychological well-being of persons harmed by historic injustices. Govier and Verwoerd assert that "the power and importance of apology lie in its potential to offer to victims a *moral recognition* or *acknowledgement* of their human worth and dignity."[5] In this sense, acknowledgments and apologies signify the beginning of atonement for, or amending of, past injustices. As Barkan argues, "An apology does not mean the dispute is resolved, but is . . . a first step: part of the process of negotiation, but not the satisfactory end result."[6]

Sometimes, but not always, apology is followed by material compensation. Compensation occupies an ambivalent place in the reparations literature. For some, material commitments are optional. Cunningham argues that "apology . . . has the potential to improve relations between groups if the apology . . . is sincere and is acceptable to the recipients. . . . Reparation, in money or goods, may follow from this; but in practice reparation has occurred independently from apology."[7] Tavuchis likewise argues, "What is critical . . . is the very act of apology itself rather than the offering of material or symbolic restitution."[8] On the other hand, Minow notes that "unless accompanied by direct and immediate actions . . . that manifest responsibility for the violation, the official apology may seem superficial, insincere, or meaningless,"[9] and Barkan asks, "unless accompanied by material compensation or restitution, does not the apology merely whitewash the injustice?"[10]

Tavuchis notes that while apologies are inherently social acts, they need not be restricted to the personal, one-on-one, private realm. On the contrary, collectivities can make public apologies.[11] Once an apology has been issued, wronged parties can reconcile themselves to sharing life with those who harmed them. As Rigby maintains, through apology "opinion leaders can open up the symbolic space where victims and survivors can begin to cast the past in a new light, relinquishing the quest to settle old scores, and begin to focus on the future."[12]

In the case of African-Western relations, apologies appear to be a necessary but not sufficient first step to open up symbolic space and focus on the future, at least according to our respondents. Apology is necessary, most of our respondents argued, but must be accompanied by material compensation. Otherwise, it would be meaningless, a whitewash of past injustice. Thus, the apologies that various Western actors have offered Africa in the last few years risk seeming insincere, insofar as they are not accompanied by material compensation.

Some Western Apologies to Africa

In the late 1990s and the first few years of the twenty-first century, some Western states, individual political leaders, churches, and other entities acknowledged some of the damage they had caused in Africa, although they did not always formally apologize. In addition to the apologies mentioned earlier in this volume, states, through their representatives, offered several acknowledgments of or apologies for past harms to Africa, although in some cases requested apologies were withheld.

In 1999, during a visit to South Africa, Queen Elizabeth II spoke of the suffering endured by both whites and blacks during the Anglo-Boer War. "We should remember with sadness the loss of life and suffering, not only of British or Boer soldiers, but of all those caught up in the war—black and white, men, women and children."[13] This speech was noted in the press as "regret," but there was no explicit apology.[14] Moreover, it cannot have been lost on black South Africans that despite the nod in their direction, the Queen's speech primarily concerned a war between two white settler groups in South Africa. Indeed, at the time of her visit, South Africa's Xhosa King unsuccessfully called on her to apologize for British conquest of his people in the nineteenth century.[15]

Also in 1999, the city of Liverpool, noted in Chapter 5 as a major slave-trading port, apologized for its role in the slave trade, although some citizens complained that the apology took place in Liverpool's Town Hall, which had images of black slaves on its walls.[16] In 2007, the two hundredth anniversary of abolition of the British slave trade, London's Mayor Ken Livingston issued a formal apology for London's role in the trade.[17] In Bristol, there was a formal debate in 2006 as to whether that city ought also to apologize.[18] The debate proved so contentious that Nelson Mandela, the former president of South Africa, declined to visit Bristol during the commemoration of abolition; some representatives of Bristol's black community had suggested that by so doing, he would legitimize continued racist practices there.[19]

In 2006, as the United Kingdom began preparations to commemorate the two hundredth anniversary of abolition, Prime Minister Tony Blair issued a statement, strategically released in the black British newspaper, *New Nation*, expressing "sorrow" about British participation in the slave trade, but he did not apologize.

> It is hard to believe that what would now be a crime against humanity was legal at the time. Personally I believe the bicentenary offers us a chance not just to say how profoundly shameful the slave trade was—how we condemn its existence utterly and praise those who fought for its abolition, but also to express our deep sorrow that it ever happened.[20]

In this statement, Blair also noted the contributions of British abolitionists, led by William Wilberforce, to the ending of the slave trade. Blair's statement, however, was not enough for one British activist. Esther Stanford of the Pan African Reparation Coalition was reported to have said, "An apology is just the start—words mean nothing. . . . We're talking about an apology of substance which would then be followed by various reparative measures including financial compensation."[21] On March 25, 2007, the two hundredth anniversary of abolition, Blair made a videotaped statement for a ceremony at Elmina Castle, a former slave-trading center in Ghana. In this statement he said the anniversary was "an opportunity for the United Kingdom to express our deep sorrow and regret for our nation's role in this inhumanity and for the unbearable suffering, individually and collectively, the slave trade caused"; but he still did not issue a direct apology.[22]

Christians in the United Kingdom and elsewhere also issued apologies in the early twenty-first century. In September 2006 Christian leaders from Britain, Germany, France, Portugal, Spain, and the Netherlands traveled to Zimbabwe to apologize for ills committed during the slave trade.[23] Their ceremonial apology was witnessed by several ministers in Mugabe's government, leading one Zimbabwean commentator to note that "an apology for sins committed a century ago means absolutely nothing to oppressed, displaced, diseased, impoverished and starving Africans who are unnecessarily subjected to these ills by erstwhile liberation heroes," a reference to President Mugabe.[24] Those Westerners who apologize ought perhaps to consider the consequences of their choice of venue. Blair's videotaped comment was relayed to Ghana, a country whose government was encouraging civil liberties and democracy (discussed in Chapter 8). By contrast, Zimbabwe in 2006 was under the iron fist of a ruler who might easily be accused of crimes against humanity (discussed in Chapter 9). The Christian apology in Zimbabwe might well have lent credibility to Mugabe's campaign to blame all of Zimbabwe's ills on a Western, imperialist attempt to displace him.

In the United Kingdom itself, Christian apologies might have had more meaning. In February 2006 the Church of England at its official synod apologized for having profited from slavery. "This Synod," it said, "in the light of our involvement in the Slave Trade and of the Christian demands of repentance and sorrow, resolve[s] to . . . recogniz[e] the damage done to those who are the heirs of those who were enslaved, [and] offer an apology to them."[25] The church had held slaves in Barbados and had received £8,823 compensation for its loss of these slaves when slavery was abolished in British colonies in 1933; in today's currency, the compensation amounts to £500,000.[26] Moreover, bishops sitting in the House of Lords during the abolition campaign had voted against abolition.[27]

In 2007 the Archbishop of Canterbury, Rowan Williams, led a Walk of Witness through London to commemorate the two hundredth anniversary of abolition and then delivered a sermon in Westminster Cathedral, in the presence of the queen and other dignitaries, in which he said:

> We who are the heirs of the slave-owning and slave-trading nations of the past have to face the fact that our historic prosperity was built in large part on this atrocity [the slave trade]; those who are the heirs of the communities ravaged by the slave trade know very well that much of their present suffering and struggling is the result of centuries of abuse. It is true that other nations . . . share something of the same inheritance. . . . But today it is for us to face our history; the Atlantic trade was our contribution to this universal sinfulness.[28]

Outside Europe, both President Bill Clinton (1993–2001) and President George W. Bush (2001–2009) of the United States acknowledged that slavery and the slave trade had been wrong. In a speech in Uganda in 1998, Clinton said, "Going back to the time before we were even a nation, European Americans received the fruits of the slave trade. And we were wrong in that."[29] But he did not explicitly apologize. Similarly, at a visit to Gorée Island in Senegal in 2003, Bush stated that slavery had been a "crime," and quoted President John Adams, who called it "an evil of colossal magnitude." Again, however, Bush did not apologize.[30] Pope John Paul II was also reported to have apologized for the role of Catholic missionaries in the slave trade when he visited Gorée in 1992.[31] Lord Gifford, the advocate for reparations who spoke in their favor in the British House of Lords in 1996, quoted the pope as praying, "From this African sanctuary of black pain, we implore forgiveness from Heaven."[32]

At Durban in 2001, the representative from Senegal stated that both the pope's and Clinton's acknowledgment had been insufficient and that they "should be accompanied by acknowledgment by the international community of slavery as a crime against humanity."[33] Yet the very visit to Gorée by the pope and the earlier visit by President Bush were problematic. While a building called the *Maison des esclaves* (House of Slaves), mentioned in Chapter 4, had been designated a World Heritage Site by UNESCO in 1980 because allegedly millions of slaves had been deported through its "Door of No Return,"[34] historians questioned whether it had ever been a site from which slaves were shipped; it was likely that it had been built at the end of the slave trade period in the 1770s.[35] Nor was the island itself a major site for the export of slaves, although perhaps 200 to 300 per year were forcibly removed from Gorée.[36] If the choice of venue is symbolic of the acknowledgment of a crime, then it was unfortunate that Bush and the pope both chose one that was hotly contested.

In the early twenty-first century, apologies were sought for colonial and postcolonial actions, as well as for the slave trade. In 2000 President Jacques Chirac of France rejected calls to apologize for France's use of torture during Algeria's war of independence from 1954 to 1962. These calls for apology came from French citizens who were horrified by evidence of massive, systematic torture, which resurfaced in 2000–2001, although plenty of evidence of torture had been available in France during the war.[37] Chirac claimed that to apologize would simply "reopen old wounds"; moreover, he would not do anything that would "detract from the honor of those French soldiers who'd fought in the conflict."[38] The incident that sparked the call for apologies was the publication of a memoir by General Paul Aussaresses, who had approved of torture in Algeria and was still unrepentant that he had done so. In an interview, he said "I express regrets, regrets, regrets. But I cannot express remorse. That implies guilt. I consider I did my difficult duty of a soldier implicated in a difficult mission."[39] The French government eventually stripped General Aussaresses of his right to wear a military uniform and forced him to take compulsory retirement but otherwise did not condemn him.[40] Nor did the government act on suggestions for a truth commission to determine what its predecessors' policies had been during the war.[41]

The situation of the *harkis*, Algerians who fought on the French side during the war, complicated the matter of a possible apology to Algerian victims of torture. Many tens of thousands of *harkis* were slaughtered after Algeria became independent because France withdrew from its colony without affording them any protection, and those who migrated to France were not well treated.[42] An apology to the Algerians for torture without a simultaneous apology to the *harkis* might have been seen by the French political right as a betrayal of its own allies.[43]

In 2005 President Abdelaziz Bouteflika of Algeria demanded an apology for the French massacre in 1945 of Algerians in the city of Setif, who had turned a celebration of the end of World War II into a pro-independence protest. "French and international public opinion must know that France committed a real act of genocide in May 1945," he said.[44] The official Algerian version was that 45,000 people were murdered, although French historians put the figure at 15,000 to 20,000.[45] In late November 2006 Prime Minister Abdelaziz Belkhadem demanded that the French government admit the crimes it had committed in Algeria throughout the colonial period, including looting and "the deletion of national identity."[46] Then French Interior Minister (later President) Nicolas Sarkozy refused to apologize, arguing, "If we want to have a joint future, there must be no new humiliations added to so many humiliations on both sides. . . . Suffering is not just on one side. . . . There is suffering on both sides."[47]

While France was recalcitrant in its refusal to apologize for colonialism, massacres, and torture in Algeria, other European countries followed a different path. As discussed in Chapter 7, Germany apologized in 2004 for the genocide of the Herero people of Namibia. In 2000 the Prime Minister of Belgium, the former colonial power in Rwanda, asked Rwanda to forgive Belgium for its role in the international failure to prevent the 1994 genocide.[48] In 2002 the Belgian government issued an apology for the murder of Patrice Lumumba, first president of independent Congo.[49] A parliamentary committee had concluded that some Belgian officials did plan to kidnap and kill Lumumba; however, Belgians were not consulted by the Congolese who eventually executed him, and no Belgian took part in the execution. Nevertheless, four Belgian officials were present at the execution and took no action to protect Lumumba.[50] Belgium's apology was to be followed by an annual contribution of $500,000 to a fund to help finance democracy in Congo.[51] However, as of early 2007 Belgium had yet to apologize for the greatest atrocity with which it was connected, the slaughter of millions of Africans in the Congo under the reign of King Leopold II.

While the Belgians had asked for forgiveness for not acting to prevent the Rwanda genocide, no such request emanated from the United States. In 1998 President Clinton went to Kigali, Rwanda's capital, to "pay the respects of my nation to all who suffered" and to announce various aid initiatives.[52] Disingenuously, he claimed that "all over the world there were people like me sitting in offices, day after day after day, who did not fully appreciate the depth and the speed with which you were being engulfed by this unimaginable terror."[53] Thus, he avoided responsibility for the United States' deliberate decision not to intervene to stop the genocide.[54] In March 2004 Secretary-General of the United Nations Kofi Annan accepted responsibility for that organization's inaction during the genocide.[55]

It is unclear whether these small, tentative steps to acknowledge and regret the harms perpetrated against Africa by Western powers will have any real impact on Western-African relations, especially when some leaders acknowledge crimes but stop short of apologizing for them. Nor is it altogether certain that apologies will have any real effect on Africans if our respondents are any guide to African opinion.

African Voices

We asked our respondents whether they thought an apology was due to Africa from the West. The consensus among them was clear: without actions, words are meaningless. An apology that is merely symbolic is useless: it must be followed by some form of material compensation. The consensus was based to a great extent on perceptions of the massive material harm perpetrated upon Africa by the West and on Africa's urgent need for material assistance now. In part, though, it was also based on the cultural rituals of apology in the home societies of the people with whom we spoke.

Although we asked about acknowledgment and apology as separate processes, most respondents did not distinguish between the two, viewing both as important aspects of reparations. Acknowledgment and apology were not merely symbolic: they had real moral and practical significance. It is important to acknowledge that wrongs were committed in the past, according to Matthew, "because if it was not wrong, that means it might happen again." Dawn said, "It would be very hard to pay back what we have lost over all those years. I think that they [the West] should acknowledge that, yes, this happened and probably apologize." Dalia, a civil servant from South Africa, said simply that reparations in general would be "a gesture of kindness beyond monetary value. . . . As [a] way of admitting their mistake, admitting their transgressions."

Yet although apologies include acknowledgment, the reverse does not necessarily hold. One can stipulate that he or she was responsible for a wrong but stop short of showing regret for it. As Timothy said, "Acknowledgment does not necessarily mean an apology. Someone may acknowledge that I have done wrong [to] you [but] may not apologize. So, I think the first stage should be acknowledging. From acknowledging then there should be apology and then the last area is how to start to resolve that, how to reconcile the problem."

Our respondents believed that the symbolic processes of acknowledgment and apology had various pragmatic consequences. One of their most important functions was that through them, facts about the wrongs committed against Africa could be set straight on the public record. Pierre spoke of the West's "debt of acknowledgment, a debt of gratitude for the fact that thanks to Africa, the West had its first industrial revolution." Speaking with regard to colonialism, Philip said, "They [responsible nations] should not look at colonialism as an accident; they should not look at it as a small grief that they cost . . . [those] they colonized, but they should acknowledge that . . . those were wrong policies because of the harm that they cost to people who fell victim."

Many respondents stressed the need to make acknowledgments and apologies public. They wanted statements from government leaders, such as the prime minister of Great Britain and the president of the United States or from the British Parliament or American Congress. Through public acknowledgment and apology, governments could accept their historic responsibility for the ill-treatment of Africa by their predecessors. To have an apology on the public record, hoped our respondents, would also mean future relations between the West and Africa would be more equitable.

Respondents also believed that acknowledgments of and apologies for past wrongdoing should be widely publicized within Africa. Without publicity, there would be no positive psychological effect on Africans who were not among the elite. "Somebody has to take a moral responsibility, and that will contribute to a psychological redress for the people who suffered," said Masoud. Through public apology and acknowledgment, Africans could also gain a better understanding of their own history. Justin, a South African academic, noted that apology might help change the "basic results of [the] colonial project . . . [which was] installing in the subject the . . . idea of them being inferior."

For some individuals, public acknowledgment and apology brought hope that past injuries could never be repeated. As discussed in Chapter 1, guarantees of nonrepetition of harm are central to definitions of reparations. For Indira, acknowledgment meant that an offending nation could no longer ignore its past misdeeds: "If you behave as though you don't recognize . . . that your actions . . . had consequences in the past, then you can continue to disregard and behave as though there aren't consequences or as if you don't care about those consequences." Nevertheless, while the majority of our respondents agreed that apologies and acknowledgment were symbolic reparations, a few demonstrated some hesitancy about them. Political reality made some doubt that they would occur. Charles said, "When you hit somebody, you need to apologize. It is a natural relations. But, because of the politics, maybe the African continent would be asking for too much."

A few respondents believed that apology without material compensation was sufficient reparation. Geoffrey advanced his country's position:

> If you feel that you have been wronged and someone says sorry, even if there's . . . nothing that follows . . . somehow it does help to feel like the person doesn't think, "Oh well, you know, we were just smarter than they were and we continue to be," . . . and, "To hell with them, you can suffer: I don't care." You feel like the person realizes . . . we're all human and what happened we shouldn't ignore; it was wrong and we wouldn't want that [to] happen again.

Yet the majority of our respondents strongly disagreed with Geoffrey: for them, apologies must be accompanied by some form of material compensation; such compensation would be a visible atonement for injury to Africa. As Dudley Thompson put it, "We say, yes, of course we forgive you, but we will not forget. After confession comes atonement."[56] Ronald said, "I am not interested in a verbal apology. I am interested in the economic apology." Haleema believed that the West definitely owed Africa material compensation. "How much did they benefit from each country? . . . It's very easy to be calculated. . . . [It] is their duty [to compensate Africa]. They are not just giving us a favor; this is a duty. . . . They just want to say, 'Let the history be in history and let's start from today.' No, it can't be like this."

In our respondents' eyes, then, true reparations must encompass acknowledgment, apology, and compensation. Alain posited, "For the West, an apology would be to take concrete actions that could return Africans to their lost dignity." Viable and acceptable reparations required measures to address contemporary African deprivation. Absent such measures, it would seem, most respondents might see Western apology as a "politics of gesture,"[57] a method of assuaging Western guilt without providing a concrete remedy. Some respondents were doubtful, however, about the likelihood of an apology because of possible consequences for the apologizers. As Ajayi observed, speaking of the United States, "Americans are always very wary of acknowledging because there's so much [to] leave them open to litigation and therefore they are not willing to acknowledge [wrongdoing]."[58] Yet in much of Africa, according to our respondents, apology required material compensation.

The Cultural Practice of Apology in Africa

One might question whether apologies can withstand intercultural differences; different cultures may have different ways to offer apologies. With this in mind, we asked our respondents how an apology might be offered within their own traditional societies. Usually, we framed this discussion by asking how a "big man," or chief, might apologize to a "small man" for an incident such as accidentally killing his goat or running over his bicycle (these are examples that some of our first respondents introduced). According to our respondents, within traditional African societies apologies tended to be public, often involved a reversal of social roles, and frequently involved material compensation.

Sometimes, we were told, a big man or chief would not apologize personally but through an emissary. "If the chief destroys my bicycle, the chief may send somebody in his council . . . to maybe pacify, maybe tell me what the chief did, it was a mistake, it was not intentional," said David. The chief might also visit the wronged individual at his hut without actually making a verbal apology; this would be a reversal of traditional protocol, which would have required the individual to visit the chief. In other cases, though, a big man or chief would indeed apologize personally. If there were witnesses to his misdeed, he might apologize in front of them, in front of village elders, or in front of the entire community. As Basil explained, "There is a committee in our village. . . . [It] meets . . . during evening or Sunday times or Saturday. . . . Then some people raise their voices and . . . they stand up and [say] 'Mr. So-and-so had these problems, please apologize to him.' Then they force that person to acknowledge that wrongdoing . . . and then publicly apologize."

In almost all cases, the wrongdoer would also offer material compensation. Sometimes this was merely token: a particular item might stand for the apology. In one Togolese community, said Marc, "There are symbolic things to give. . . . A white ram . . . First, there is talking, and then the chief undertakes not to repeat [the wrong], before everyone. And then he presents . . . a white ram to the assemblage." Here, the wrongdoer offers the gift to the entire village as an act of public expiation.

Ordinary people, too, would be expected to offer compensation for a wrong, as Frederick told us.

> Yes, in Malawi, when somebody has wronged you . . . both of you . . . are taken before a chief, when a chief is settling that particular matter, and somebody has agreed that "Indeed, I happened to wrong this particular person, and I would like to apologize"; it is not only by word of mouth. The chief will say a little something. . . . He would say that maybe you should take maybe one goat . . . or one cow and give [it to] this particular person for the wrongdoing that you did.

Although some of the rituals and symbolic goods described by our respondents may be new to readers of this chapter, the underlying premise of rectification should not be. Personal apologies are often considered hollow in Western society, without some form of follow-up gesture. Thus, there are no insurmountable cultural differences between what Westerners and Africans understand as a sincere apology. Respondents' desire for financial compensation from the West, rather than only for "hollow words," is not outside Westerners' own realm of meaning. Actions beyond words were imperative: apologies must be accompanied by compensation that would have real, pragmatic effect.

Material Compensation as a Condition of Sincerity

Our respondents viewed reparations as a means not only to generate moral equality between Africa and the West but also to help develop the very continent that the West, in their view, had underdeveloped. "No apology is acceptable unless it is accompanied by development measures . . . to feed our people," said Stéphane.

We asked our respondents what kind of material compensation they envisaged. The most common request was for funds for education and health care services. Many also wanted help with African infrastructure, including money to build and repair roads and railways and efforts to help communication within and from Africa. For example, Benedict associated communication difficulties with unfair competition in the global economy: "We do not tread on an equal footing. . . . In Kenya to surf the Internet you pay a lot of money. . . . Therefore you limit the time that you surf the Internet, but when I came to Canada it takes me a second to surf the Internet [very inexpensively]. . . . The use of the telephone in Africa is very expensive . . . but here [Canada] [it is] very easy, very cheap."

Respondents also rooted their discussion of material reparations in the need to change the way Africa participates in the global economy. They were particularly interested in more equitable international trade. "Does France trade with these [French-speaking African] countries truly as equal countries . . . ? Are they equal? I think not. . . . There's a kind of colonialism that continues," said Michel. To make trade equitable meant eliminating tariffs charged on African goods by Western countries and reducing subsidies to Western farmers for products that Africans could sell. Some respondents also wanted less foreign influence on prices of African exports. Without changes to the world economy, Geetu explained, "We're just going to continue on the current framework, which is unequal and very biased in favor of the West." Another aspect of international financial relations that concerned our respondents was the imposition of structural adjustment programs (SAPs). Among other measures (discussed in Chapter 8), SAPs required that African countries devalue their currency to make the prices of their exports more competitive on the world market.

Anne-Marie, a teacher, spoke of how she and her colleagues had been given a choice as a result of currency devaluations imposed in Cameroon: either accept that half the staff would lose their jobs or accept a 50 percent cut in pay. She and her colleagues chose the latter option. "So you find, at the end of the month, that you don't even have enough to feed your children. You work and you can't even buy a radio or a television. Why work? You can't even send your children to university." This middle-class woman, part of a new professional African class, saw her hopes dashed by requirements for national fiscal discipline. As she saw it, this discipline had been arbitrarily imposed by foreigners for their own benefit, not for the benefit of Africans.

Most respondents supported debt relief (discussed in Chapter 8) as a form of reparation. Theresa said, "We are indebted to the very people that colonized us. If anything at all, let them keep their money but we say, whatever we are owing, we bring it to zero. . . . Then . . . we start from level ground." At minimum, said Dominic, "Erase the debt that Africa owes . . . to the countries that were colonizers, because not all European countries colonized." Luke argued:

> After all the injustices, and after African people . . . fought for their independence, that the West still has the audacity to claim that Africa owes them so much in terms of debts. . . . It is inhuman . . . if that person owes you money, and you went to ask for your money back and you found the person went without food, it is inhuman and immoral to insist that you must be paid for your money. So I see the reparations in terms of debts cancellations.

A few people noted that it was unfair that Africans should be expected to repay loans obtained by corrupt officials. Pamela, a scholar from Nigeria, revealed, "I don't trust any of the authorities to handle the money well. They have shown over and over that they are not to be trusted." Given their experience with governmental and administrative corruption, respondents also worried about how any financial reparations would be administered. While a few trusted governments to administer reparations funds, others were concerned money would be wasted on weapons, unnecessary commissions, and "white elephant" infrastructure projects.

Thus, some individuals wanted debt cancellation to have conditions attached in order to prevent a recurrence of government corruption or mismanagement. Isaac argued that creditor nations should "scratch out [outstanding debts] but at the same time you might . . . put conditionality . . . [on] what we're going to spend the money with. . . . If Ethiopia owed 20 billion dollars you might want them to invest it not in armaments, which they've been doing the last few years." In response to these concerns, some respondents suggested an independent body to administer financial compensation, which would include input from civil society organizations and which therefore would, they hoped, avoid maladministration and corruption.

Almost all our respondents believed that Western powers and interests had caused both Africa's historic underdevelopment and its current economic weakness. These were reasonable and responsible people, many engaged in the struggle for human rights within their own societies and well aware of the injustices that their political and social systems had generated. They did not blame all African problems on the West. Yet they could not understand why, even when hundreds of millions of lives were at stake, the West, and often the international community as a whole, cared so little for them. Thus, most viewed apologies without material compensation as hypocritical gestures.

Apologies and Political Reality

The German-Israeli precedent suggests that in international relations, as in internal political affairs, apologies for past wrongs generate long-term good will.[59] If this is the case, then even if financial reparations from the Western world to Africa might be incalculable or impractical, perhaps an apology from the Western world, or from certain Western states and other Western actors, might have some value in reconciling the two sides. Perhaps apologies might reduce Africans' feelings of abandonment, the lack of recognition of the "dailyness of [their] enduring,"[60] thus contributing to an international community in which there is moral equality among different regions and less likelihood of political resentment. Lazare contends that "the apology process holds out a promise to us that is well worth the effort it requires: the prospect of restored respect, of healed relationships, of civility, and of a clearer sense of morality among individuals and nations who inhabit an ever-shrinking world."[61]

Lazare compiled a list of "common situations that create a high risk of causing offense." On the nation-to-nation level, this list includes "receiving unfair trade restrictions."[62] As noted, our respondents did believe that Africa was the victim of unfair trade restrictions. Some of the common causes of offense on the person-to-person level compiled by Lazare also apply to Africa as a collectivity of individuals. These include being "overlooked or taken for granted," being "denied basic social amenities," and being "reduced in status or role."[63] Our respondents complained frequently that Africans did not seem to figure at all in the West's moral universe: they were an overlooked group of people whose status was of no significance, it seemed, to Western decision makers. Proof of this was that the West not only, in their view, did not supply basic social amenities to Africa, but it actually went out of its way to reduce the extant social amenities through programs for financial reform. In short, our respondents viewed many Western policies as an assault on human dignity.

Despite the psychological reasons for apology offered by Lazare, in political terms there is little reason for the West to apologize to Africa. Tavuchis argues that "an apology is emblematic of the offender's socially liminal, ambiguous status that places him precariously between exclusion (actual or threatened) and rehabilitation. . . . The crucial concern of an apology is . . . with the reclamation and revalidation of [the rights and obligations] enjoyed prior to the discreditable transgression."[64] This definition implies the offending party's desire to apologize so that the offended party will re-admit the offender to its moral universe. Thus, it implies that the offended has more power than the offender, an implication that does not accurately reflect political reality regarding reparations to Africa, in which the offending parties, Western countries, possess power while the offended party, Africa, does not. The offended party seeks inclusion, not the other way around. Given the extreme political and power differences between the West and Africa, there is far less desire on the part of the West to effect reconciliation with Africa than is normal in a personal apology.

Moreover, an apology by an offending country might open it to legal obligation. One remedy for this problem might be to include acknowledgment and apology as part of a negotiated reparations settlement. If there were separate agreement on material compensation, an apology could be offered without threat of further legal obligation. This, however, is very unlikely. The most that Western apologies to Africa can accomplish is recognition of past injustices, as in the French law on the slave trade discussed in Chapter 5, and aspirations for more concern in the future, as in President Clinton's acknowledgment of American neglect of Rwanda in 1994. Yet, as our respondents' answers show, acknowledgment of and even apologies for the evils of the far distant past are weak measures without material restitution. It is perhaps better not to engage in the breast-beating of international apologies than to make gestures that recipients might regard as hypocritical empty words.

Although an apology is sometimes thought to constitute the "final form of reparation"; sometimes it is seen as "the first component of a more comprehensive (including financial) reparations process."[65] Yet so far, apologies by Western powers to Africa have rarely been accompanied by material compensation. Neither the United States, nor Britain, nor France has linked acknowledgment of the destruction they wrought in Africa to material reparations. Germany did not offer material compensation to the Herero, although Namibia's opposition to financial compensation for the genocide of the Herero might have influenced that decision. The half-million dollars per year that Belgium decided to pay to a democracy fund for Congo in compensation for its part in the murder of Lumumba was a minuscule amount. These Western actors appeared to believe that their apologies were sufficient indication of regret for past actions. By contrast, our interviews suggest that without material compensation, these acknowledgments and apologies indicate only hypocrisy to Africans.

Many Western governments refused to apologize at Durban because they feared the legal consequences of apology.[66] Thus, the Durban participants decided to note in the Conference's final declaration that "some States have taken the initiative to apologize and have paid reparations, where appropriate." But instead of calling on all states to apologize, the final declaration instead called on other countries "who have not yet contributed to restoring the dignity of the victims to find appropriate ways to do so."[67]

The world still consists of legally sovereign states, whose foreign policies will continue to be driven by national interest, not by retrospective or any other form of justice. As Masoud put it, "If you apologize to me and you still practice unfair trade practices which continue to submerge me and become underdeveloped further, then where am I going?" The conditions causing Africans offense and violating their dignity are severe and have profound material consequences. For our respondents, then, it is not enough to issue apologies, however sincere, as long as these conditions continue and the West does not try to ameliorate them. But others might disagree with our respondents about the causes of and appropriate remedies for Africans' poor material conditions. Perhaps a truth commission for Africa might sort out these disagreements, as discussed in Chapter 11. And perhaps more attention to Africans' economic rights might satisfy the desire for material compensation, as recommended in Chapter 12.

Chapter 11
Remedies
A Truth Commission for Africa?

Since the 1980s, many countries have established truth commissions during periods of transition from dictatorial to democratic rule.[1] Some truth commissions are "historic": their goal is to "clarify historical truths and pay respect to previously unrecognized victims or their descendants."[2] This chapter considers the feasibility of establishing a historical truth commission for Africa (TCA). A TCA would assess past damages to Africa, analyze who or what was responsible for them, and, where necessary, acknowledge the damage. Such acknowledgment might contribute to reconciliation between Africa and the West based on agreement on a narrative "truth" about historical relations between the regions. The West, or its representatives, might be more willing to acknowledge its own ill-treatment of Africa if the responsibility of other actors, such as Muslim slave traders and the African political elite, were also acknowledged.

Most past truth commissions focused on violations of civil and political rights, such as torture, disappearances, and arbitrary execution. By contrast, a major aspect of the TCA's mandate would be its focus on violations of economic rights. African reparationists assert that the transatlantic slave trade, colonialism, and postcolonial relations are the causes of Africa's current underdevelopment, that is, its incapacity to fulfill its citizens' economic rights. A TCA might clarify how much responsibility for African underdevelopment is borne by the West, and how much is borne by non-Western actors, and by Africans themselves.

Unfortunately, we neglected to ask our respondents about a possible TCA; thus, there is no section in this chapter featuring African voices.

Justification of a Truth Commission for Africa

Those who call for reparations also call for the truth. At Durban, for example, the president of the Republic of Congo stated:

> Numerous voices have been raised to say that Africa should forgive. Of course, Africa should forgive. But for Africa's forgiveness to be real and sincere, the dam-

age that was caused must be acknowledged. There must be repentance. More than a century after the end of slavery, sorrow about this tragedy remains in the collective memory of Black people, because the truth, all the truth has not yet been told about the millions of Blacks who died in the course of their deportation, or on the plantations.[3]

In his interview with us, Dudley Thompson said, "We Africans have a very great problem in reparations and that is to make all [African] people . . . understand the truth of their situation, to understand the facts of history. . . . It is their own doubt . . . that is our greatest obstacle to its success."

The final declaration of the Durban Conference notes the need to teach "about the facts and truth of . . . history," arguing that "remembering the crimes or wrongs of the past . . . and telling the truth about history are essential elements for international reconciliation."[4] Before the conference, Human Rights Watch proposed something akin to a truth commission. "We propose . . . the establishment of national and international panels to examine racist practices. These would include . . . panels for specific countries that would examine the degree to which the slave trade and colonialism . . . have contributed to the destitution of the country's population."[5] In 2001, the UN Sub-Commission on the Promotion and Protection of Human Rights also asserted that the "historic responsibility" of the powers responsible for slavery and colonialism should be "the subject of solemn and formal recognition and repair." One method of such recognition and repair would be debate and reflection "on the basis of accurate information."[6]

Following these several suggestions, a TCA might contribute to reparations between Africa and the West.

There are three justifications for considering a TCA. The first is rooted in political pragmatism and refers to the "civilizational" conflict affecting current international relations. One does not need to believe in immutable cultures unaffected by economics, politics, or history to accept that there is a great deal of resentment against the West in the less wealthy parts of the world. In Africa much of this resentment stems from the continent's long history of unequal relations with the West. Already this has had political consequences, as in the manner in which some Africans cheered the "triumph" of Al-Qaeda over the United States in September 2001. At least one of the individuals implicated in the bombing of the U.S. embassy in Tanzania in 1998 was African, a Tanzanian national.[7] Resentment could have more consequences. As Ali Mazrui contends "better the music of reparations than the drums of terror."[8]

There are also more prosaic political reasons for a TCA. In countries where citizens have suffered violations of their human rights, civil society and democracy are more likely to be sustained if some form of reconciliation has taken place among the perpetrators and the victims of human rights abuses. In international relations, perhaps this prosaic argument carries less weight since African and Western diplomats are skilled in negotiation and diplomacy and may be able to overcome political disagreements by coming to pragmatic agreements about aid or political relations. On the other hand, if Africa's rulers are influenced by their own or their citizens' resentment of the West, such resentment may affect bilateral negotiations, votes in the UN Security Council and General Assembly, and decision making in multilateral fora such as the World Trade Organization.

The second justification for a TCA is legal. In the late twentieth century, international law began to insist on transnational state responsibility for human rights. No longer was states' responsibility confined to the promotion and protection of human rights within their own domestic jurisdiction: states were also increasingly responsible for their actions and the actions of their agents outside their borders.[9] This evolution of international law is both reflected in and a consequence of the opinions of learned jurists as to what the law ought to be, as reflected in the 2001 resolution on slavery and colonialism of the UN Sub-Commission on the Promotion and Protection of Human Rights. The argument to apply these legal principles retroactively, however, is primarily moral, despite the arguments for retroactive application of the law considered in earlier chapters.

Finally, there is a general moral argument for a TCA, rooted in the emerging international view that there is a "right to the truth." This right derives from Article 19 of the Universal Declaration of Human Rights, which guarantees the right to "seek, receive and impart information and ideas." Article 9(1) of the African Charter on Human and Peoples' Rights also guarantees the "right to receive information."[10]

Perhaps no reconciliation is possible without the disclosure of truth. Mazrui argues that the African reparations movement is inspired by "the continuity of suffering and the persistence of deprivation and anguish in the Black world arising directly out of the legacies of slavery and colonialism."[11] Representations of political relations, such as offered by Mazrui, can be as important as the relations themselves. Many of our respondents believed that the West was responsible for their poverty: such a belief may well affect how these Africans view the entire gamut of their continent's relations with Western powers. Certainly many Africans are suspicious of the West's motives and of Western-dominated international institutions. But there are also serious Western efforts to assist Africa to develop. These efforts may well be stymied by rhetorical representations of both historical and current Western-African relations that are uniformly negative.

The Search for "Truth"

The "truth" about relations between Africa and the West is complex, affected by both the large number of actors involved and the difficulty of establishing causal links between the distant past and the present. Unless properly established and conducted, therefore, a TCA might do more harm than good. A partial, incomplete, or biased truth could adversely affect not only individual Africans' attitudes to the West but also relations between their governments and Western powers.

The concluding statements of the Durban Conference reveal a taken-for-granted assumption that relations with the West have harmed and continue to harm Africa. This assumption suggests the need to clear the air. At least one Western country, the Netherlands, takes seriously the call for truth. Its government commissioned an official study on reparations by its Advisory Council on International Affairs. The council considered nonmonetary forms of reparation such as "revealing and verifying facts . . . and full and public disclosure of the truth."[12] As discussed in Chapter 3, the Netherlands expressed remorse at Durban for its slave trading and colonial past. Other European states at Durban did not specifically advocate a search for the truth about Western-African relations, but they did discuss a duty to remember. Vice-Prime Minister and Minister of Foreign Affairs and External Trade of Luxembourg Lydia Polfer stated that "we have responsibility for the past. It is our duty to identify in our past the mechanisms which led to racism. . . . The duty to remember . . . helps to become aware of the guilt of all of us."[13] Prior to Durban, the European Union also acknowledged the need to remember the sufferings caused by past wrongs and, especially, to educate young people about them.[14]

These European statements suggest that a TCA dedicated to investigation of the slave trade and colonialism might be considered partial reparation to Africa. Nevertheless, two serious problems arise. One is how to establish the historical link between past Western activities and the current situation in Africa. The other is how to sort out the relative responsibilities of the West, other non-African actors (especially the Arab world and the Soviet/Socialist bloc), and Africans themselves. Whether these matters can be sorted out depends in part on what type of "truth" is sought.

South Africa established its Truth and Reconciliation Commission (TRC), after apartheid ended, to reveal the truth about gross violations of human rights, such as murder and torture, during the apartheid era. In the view of the TRC, there was no single "truth." No matter by what means it is derived, truth is not factual: it is a representation of history, not the history itself. Alex Boraine, one of the TRC commissioners, differentiated four types of truth. The first is "factual or forensic truth," which lays out the facts of what happened but also tries to put them in context. The second is "personal or narrative truth," in which individuals give meaning to their experiences through their personal testimony. The third type is "social or 'dialogic' truth," in which democratic and transparent dialogue results in a narrative agreed to by various social actors. The final type is "healing and restorative truth." This is not a truth so much as a social act of acknowledgment and "acceptance of accountability" for past acts.[15]

Two scholarly commentators on truth commissions, Audrey Chapman and Patrick Ball, were concerned about the multiple definitions of truth proposed by the TRC. Narrative, social, and restorative truths, they argued, were "subjective, not objective . . . [and] are process goals, not forms of truth." They agreed, however, that truth commissions were a good vehicle for establishing this type of "macro" truth, as opposed to the "micro" forensic (legal) truth that is required to determine which individuals are responsible for specific acts. Macro-truth, they argued, requires a social scientific rather than a legal approach. Micro-truth, on the other hand, must be carefully adjudged according to evidence. Otherwise, "the conflation of the subjective with objective truth-finding weakens the political and moral importance of truth by making truth a matter of personal opinion."[16]

A TCA might focus on macro-truth, supplemented by personal, narrative truths, with the aim of eventually reaching the social, dialogic truth that might result in acknowledgment and acceptance of accountability. The TCA could take seriously the personal testimonies of Africans who narrate the suffering they contend they or their ancestors endured as a result of relations with the West. To listen to such narratives would constitute a form of acknowledgment. As the TRC concludes, "Acknowledgment is an affirmation that a person's pain is real and worthy of attention. It is thus central to the restoration of the dignity of the victims."[17]

But, no matter how compelling, personal narrative testimonies might not reveal the central "truth" of African suffering, which is that structural and institutional processes rather than individual perpetrators have caused most of it. From the slave trade to globalization, Africans have been and are affected by macro-political and macroeconomic policies and practices emanating in large part, but not entirely, from the West. The Nuremberg trials set the precedent that individuals could not be absolved of responsibility for harming others merely because they had followed military or government orders. But even if specific individuals could be identified as responsible for the harms Africa now suffers, Nuremberg set no precedent that individuals who formulate or enact economic policy could be indicted for crimes. Although one industrialist, Alfried Krupp, was convicted at Nuremberg, his crimes were not that he formulated economic policies that undermined individuals' economic rights; rather, they were crimes such as plunder, torture, and exploitation of slave laborers.[18] As discussed in Chapter 9, private citizens can sue corporations (in some jurisdictions) for harming their interests, and there is an emerging international law of corporate responsibility, but there are no international laws or procedures that can effectively judge and punish individual violators of others' economic rights.

One might argue that just as Nuremberg and its successors, the International Criminal Tribunals for Yugoslavia and for Rwanda and the International Criminal Court (ICC), were set up to judge individuals responsible for genocide, war crimes, and crimes against humanity, so there ought to be a vehicle to judge individuals for gross violations of economic rights. The Universal Declaration of Human Rights was proclaimed in 1948. Many Africans are convinced that some of the economic policies of the post–1948 period have detrimentally affected their economic rights, and they focus far more on these internationally generated policies than on the policies of their own governments. Yet a TCA that addressed institutional causes of violations of Africans' economic rights would be obliged to focus on the responsibilities of Africa's own political leaders as much as on the responsibilities of Westerners or international organizations.

In so doing, the TCA would not be able to follow the example either of international criminal tribunals or of the growing number of national truth commissions in Africa that have dealt with individuals' abuses of others' civil and political rights during periods of dictatorial rule, such as the reign of Jerry Rawlings in Ghana. To address institutional causes of human rights violations, the TCA would have to rely on factual or "forensic" truth. But such factual truth would depend upon academic interpretation of the historical, political, and economic context of African underdevelopment. Such a forensic exercise might result in an agreed-upon social or dialogic truth, at least among those experts who might be the commissioners. But such a dialogic truth might well not satisfy African activists or those who might already harbor resentment against the West. The "facts" ascertained by a TCA might contradict individual Africans' personal or narrative truths. As such, they might undermine attempts to generate a healing or restorative truth. To summarize five centuries of history and international relations and to add to it a satisfactory explanation of economic policy might be too daunting a chore for any commissioners.

Different "truths" offered by a TCA, then, would have different political effects. Historical truth would reveal a complicated picture, one attributing responsibility for Africa's economic underdevelopment to diverse actors. A narrative truth, on the other hand, would tell stories that could profoundly influence citizens' emotional reactions to African-Western relations. Altruistic Westerners, in dialogue with Africans, might well agree to a narrative truth to which scholars might object. Such a narrative might then affect interpretations of present-day international relations. These potential incompatibilities among the various kinds of truth imply different policy outcomes.

Organization of the TCA would also affect the kind of truth discovered and the consequent public policy outcome.

Organizing a Truth Commission for Africa

If any serious attempt were made to set up a TCA, several problems would have to be solved. Organizers would have to determine the TCA's terms of reference, find sponsors for it, appoint commissioners, and decide how and to whom it would issue its report.

The choice of time period covered by the TCA would be crucial. A minimum option would cover only the slave trade. A medium option would confine the terms of reference to the slave trade and colonialism. The maximum option would require the TCA to cover the entire history of Africa's relations with the West, including the present. In the first two cases, there are historical end points. In the last case, there is no end point, and persons testifying before the commission could refer to events occurring as they spoke.

Probably most people interested in establishing a TCA would want to investigate the slave trade and colonialism. Both Western and African actors might prefer to leave the postcolonial period alone. To ignore the postcolonial period would absolve the TCA of responsibility to investigate possible exploitive relations between Western and African states or between international organizations or transnational corporations and Africa since independence. To ignore the postcolonial period would also absolve the TCA of any obligation to investigate African responsibility for African problems since independence.

Organizers of a TCA would also need to determine which actors to investigate. The TCA might investigate only Western countries or Western private entities in Africa, or it might also investigate the role of non-Western outsiders. As a historical truth commission, it might be interested in the Muslim as well as the transatlantic slave trade. Turning to the postcolonial period, it might take into account Soviet interest in Africa during the Cold War, as well as Western interest. The TCA could also address the roles of African elites in undermining both civil and political and economic rights, debating the extent to which Africans were responsible for their own decisions.

The commission's terms of reference would undoubtedly influence its final report. A commission looking only at Western-African relations during the slave trade and colonialism might present a much more negative picture than one that included non-Western actors or dealt with the postcolonial period. The former option might well reinforce the politics of resentment against the West, while the latter might also cause resentment for calling to Africans' attention that their continent had produced perpetrators as well as victims. Western actors would be unlikely to take seriously a report that ignored African and Muslim participation in the slave trade or Soviet and Chinese interference in postcolonial Africa.

Accompanying the question of mandate is the question of who would sponsor a TCA. It could be sponsored by private actors, public officials, or scholars. Private actors would have to be completely unbiased because any tribunal established by actors seen to be biased would suffer from lack of credibility. Indeed, the Durban Conference functioned as a kind of informal truth commission but suffered from just such perceived bias, especially insofar as NGO activists made statements incompatible with the final official declaration, which was negotiated by diplomats. Nevertheless, trusted private actors, enjoying respect in the international community, could put on the international agenda matters that representatives of the former slave-trading or colonizing powers might wish to ignore. Theo Van Boven argues that "many Europeans feel vulnerable and uncomfortable when they are taken to task on issues of racism and racial discrimination."[19] Such a feeling might be overcome if respected organizations sponsored a TCA and if Westerners as well as Africans were appointed commissioners.

As Klinghoffer and Klinghoffer state, "International citizens' tribunals can . . . serve as a corrective mechanism through which public intellectuals mobilize world opinion."[20] The knowledge they generate would then be "officially sanctioned" and become "part of the public cognitive scene."[21] But such knowledge must be unbiased, and the outcome not prejudged. The Bertrand Russell Tribunal on U.S. involvement in Viet Nam in the 1960s was established by private activists, but the members of the tribunal were known opponents of the Viet Nam War. This drastically undermined their credibility, especially when they claimed the United States was perpetrating genocide.[22]

In late 2006, a citizens' tribunal concerned with Africa took place in New York, but it focused on internal African affairs, not Western-African relations. Wole Soyinka presided over a "trial" *in absentia* of Omar Hasan Ahmad al-Bashir, the president of Sudan since 1989. Al-Bashir was charged with war crimes, crimes again humanity, genocide, and other crimes, which, it was alleged, had taken place since 1989 in several areas of Sudan, including Darfur.[23] This citizens' court was established by human rights activists in California, and numerous private individuals possessing legal expertise took part, including lawyers acting for Al-Bashir's defense.[24] The five judges found Al-Bashir guilty.[25] This verdict had no force in law;

rather, it was meant to publicize the charges against Al-Bashir, especially because the ICC planned to charge some Sudanese officials and members of the Arab militias in Darfur. In February 2007 the prosecutor at the ICC brought charges against its first two Sudanese suspects, Ahmad Harun, a Sudanese government minister, and Ali Kushayb, a leader of the Arab militias.[26]

That Soyinka presided over this citizens' tribunal was not surprising. Soyinka insists that everyone take responsibility for his or her actions. He has little patience for a movement for reparations to Africa from the West when so many Africans are still enslaved, in his words, by their own rulers. Thus, the judgment in the Sudan citizens' trial implicated both the Arab League and the African Union (AU) for their neglect of Sudan's suffering citizens. "The Arab family has steadfastly refused to call Sudan to order," said the judgment. "Nor has the African family, represented by the African Union, taken a seriously critical stance."[27]

A privately organized TCA could follow the Sudan tribunal model, relying on elite actors to establish it. The option of a "people's" tribunal of some sort, a TCA established by ordinary citizens, from among whom commissioners could be chosen, also exists. People's tribunals are sometimes thought to be an exercise in democracy. More commonly, however, they are manipulated by government elites. Such was the case in Africa during the 1970s, when some countries established "people's courts" as an alternative to the complex, mysterious, and lengthy legal processes of British common law. In Malawi, these courts were simply manipulated by the dictator H. Kamuzu Banda for his own ends. In Ghana the original intent may have been sincerely to find a judicial alternative to British law, but the people's courts were also manipulated by the ruling military-populist regime of Jerry Rawlings.[28]

Alternatively, a truth commission could be established by public authorities, for example, by a group of non-Western or ex-colonial Western states such as Canada or the Netherlands. Such a gesture might be a means to ingratiate such Western powers with Africa, perhaps in order to reap the benefits of trade. Canada, for example, attempts to reap such benefits through its self-presentation as a sympathetic "middle power" in its relations with African countries. On the other hand, the establishment of a TCA might be seen merely as a form of hypocritical expiation by a Western country that has benefited by exploiting Africa. While never a slave-trading or colonial power, Canada was part of the British Empire, and imperial relations favored white settler colonies.

Finally, a scholarly commission could be established, either by private or public actors or perhaps by the United Nations. UNESCO, for example, attempted to disseminate the "truth" about the Atlantic slave trade when it commissioned a report on it.[29] Assuming it was staffed by unbiased scholars, such a commission would be the most likely to ascertain the factual, or forensic, truth about historical Western-African relations, but it would be least likely to have substantial social impact. It would undoubtedly report a degree of complexity unpalatable to reparationists seeking the "truth"; for example, scholarly estimates of the number of slaves taken in the transatlantic trade are much lower than the numbers quoted by some activists and official representatives at Durban. Some of these activists and officials might be unhappy with a TCA that told them that "only" 11.3 million slaves were taken across the Atlantic.

Finally, organizers of a TCA would have to consider whether reconciliation was one of its specific goals, as was the case with South Africa's TRC. Most commentators agree that Bishop Desmond Tutu, the TRC's chairperson, influenced its orientation to reconciliation and forgiveness. Tutu favored the creation of a collective narrative that would bring together all significant parties in South Africa, even at the expense of a forensic truth about what had happened during apartheid. Jacob Ajayi shares Tutu's Christian approach. He would like the Christian world to recognize slavery as a sin. "There is still the need for the Christian churches to appreciate the uniqueness of the trans-Atlantic [slave] trade and American slavery. They should stop comparing . . . [it] with slavery in the Old or New Testament, and condemn it and American slavery not only as [a] crime against humanity, but also a sin against the majesty of God, requiring confession and restitution."[30] Ajayi's Christian approach suggests creation of a social or dialogic truth that could result in an official narrative of healing or restoration.

Some activists and scholars might disagree that the final purpose of a TCA should be reconciliation. Reconciliation might be seen as a distant goal, to be effected only after Western countries and intergovernmental actors had shown concrete signs of remorse. As discussed in Chapter 10, almost all our respondents insisted that acknowledgment of or apology for past wrongs was meaningless without concrete restorative action. Activists and victims might also reject the focus on forgiveness that was part of the South African approach.

While clerics, activists, and other private individuals appointed as commissioners might have a social goal in mind, academics and lawyers might be more interested in factual truth. Unfortunately, however, factual truths to do with centuries-long processes are hard to come by. All facts are interpreted by the academics who consider them; facts can also be affected by the subjectivity of the scholars seeking agreement. On the other hand, it might be precisely these scholars' willingness to debate the truth in an open fashion, recognizing that their perceptions and interpretations could never be fully objective, that would result in an agreed narrative. This narrative would not be perfectly objective, and it would not reveal all the facts of Western-African relations, but it would provide a broad-brush interpretation on which truth commissioners could agree. Such an interpretation might contribute to a "moral reconstruction" of Western-African relations, "by producing a social judgment and moral account of the historical record."[31]

In order to produce a report that all sides could agree on, organizers of a TCA would need to ensure that the commissioners included both Africans and Westerners. The outcomes of the various truth commissions established in the 1980s and 1990s were influenced by their compositions, especially by whether insiders (from the state being investigated), outsiders, or a combination of both were appointed as commissioners. Thus, it would be imperative to have African commissioners on a TCA, but if the results were to be acceptable to Westerners, the TCA would also have to include Western commissioners.

Just as important as all the above concerns are the questions of who would produce the TCA report, how it would be written, to whom it would be presented, and how it would be received. Without an authoritative report accepted by the relevant governments, as well as by the general population, a TCA would have little impact. If the report were to circulate only among the elite, it might be a useful tool in diplomatic negotiation, but it would have no wider effect. A report meant to reduce tensions between Africa and the West would have to be widely distributed among both Africans and Westerners and publicized on radio, television, and the Internet. Moreover, its contents would have to be incorporated into education programs in both Africa and the West. Without the report's widespread distribution, the past would continue to impinge on the present in ways that might impede understanding and exacerbate resentment.

Political Consequences of a TCA

The Durban Conference's final declaration, Human Rights Watch, and the UN Sub-Commission on the Promotion and Protection of Human Rights all called for truth-telling about slavery and colonialism in Africa. A historical truth commission would seem to be the ideal venue to discover and disseminate this truth. Yet there would be so many difficulties in setting up a TCA that perhaps the idea should be aborted before it bears fruit. Whatever a TCA would do, it would not establish an unadulterated factual truth, nor would dialogic, narrative, or restorative interpretations of the truth be uncontroversial. It might be better simply to concentrate on the present. Whatever the facts about the past, and whatever type of truth is sought, justice still requires institutional, political, and legal change within Africa, as well as devotion of more of the world's resources to African development.

Perhaps a different mechanism to establish trust between Africa and the West should be found. There is a risk that a TCA might be a sort of show trial that could be organized or hijacked by those interested in blaming the West for all aspects of Africa's current situation. Such a show trial might paint an unmediated picture of Western-African relations, which could detrimentally affect possibilities for political compromise and economic change.

Africa is currently, and is likely to be for the foreseeable future, the weakest continental player in the world political and economic system. Thus, a political realist might argue that whether the West acknowledges the "truth" of its historic and current relations with Africa is of no great consequence; in its dealings with Africa, the West can continue to act in its own interest without risk to itself. Moreover, we ought not to be seduced by the current popular notion that truth is always a path to reconciliation. Truth might also be a path to revenge: victims, buttressed at last by the truth, might seek retribution previously denied them. Even a forensic truth, agreed to by historians and lawyers, might be so inflammatory as to stir up a desire for revenge, if not against the West as a political entity, then against individual Westerners who might venture into Africa.

Yet establishment of responsibility for their situation appears to be important to Africans, if our respondents' views are any indication. To argue that only material assistance is necessary might be to leave Africans floundering in an uncertain moral universe, where patronizing Westerners attempt to assist them without taking responsibility for the actions of their own governments, whether such actions adversely affected Africans in the distant or the recent past.

Truth commissions are usually established in order to restore relationships between citizens and the state that violated their original trust. In the case of Western-African relations, such trust may never have existed. But the search for truth can be one way of establishing relationships of moral equality between Africans and Westerners. Perhaps a TCA might modify hostile and racist images on both sides of the Western-African divide. Ajayi writes that "to end . . . colonialism without Reparation is to leave an open sore unattended."[32] Part of that open sore is the feeling among some Africans that the truth is buried by Western powers uninterested in the consequences of their forebears' actions.

One should certainly not assume that all Africans are angry with the West or that all wish for acknowledgment of the West's detrimental effects on Africa. Many are probably more preoccupied with the day-to-day necessities of survival. Many are undoubtedly grateful for the assistance of Christian churches and Western nongovernmental organizations, as were some of our respondents. On the other hand, in the post–September 11 world, the politics of resentment has real political and military consequences. The moral imperative for truth—the right of both Africans and Westerners to a truthful account of their past and present relations—is therefore supplemented by a pragmatic reason for truth. Such a truth might also have practical consequences, influencing, for example, the politics of African relations with international financial institutions, aid donors, and private investors.

The entire history of African relations with the West might be considered a moral injury to Africans. Nevertheless, too much memory can be a disease. To establish a TCA might merely be an exercise in the politics of representation. A TCA that merely reiterated the many reasons some Africans already have to resent the West might do more harm than good. If a TCA creates, or resurrects, a "memory" of the slave trade, that memory could result in increased bitterness, fear, and resentment of Westerners. What happened to Africans hundreds of years ago, one might argue, is finished. To "remember" is to neglect the business of life today and to deflect from the many worthwhile aspects of international attempts to assist Africa.

But not to remember—or to remember an ideological, divisive truth—may be equally detrimental. Africans are entitled to know what happened to their continent and who is responsible for their current situation. To be treated with dignity requires acknowledgment of one's suffering and access to the truth about why that suffering occurs. This is the best argument, in my view, for a carefully constructed TCA. Its commissioners should be respected and unbiased scholars, lawyers, and activists, from both the West and Africa. Its mandate should be to construct a historically based social truth based in large part on scholarly research but also based on the narrative voices of individual Africans. The mandate should cover not only Western but also non-Western relations with Africa: it should also assess African responsibility for African problems. It should be sponsored by an official international organization, such as the United Nations or the AU. Its report should be accessible to the lay public, widely distributed in Africa and the West, and incorporated into educational curricula. Such a TCA might result in reconciliation and might result in forgiveness, where necessary; but these should not be among its formal aims.

Chapter 12

Remedies

Economic Rights and Universal Obligations

Chapters 10 and 11 present the case for symbolic reparations to Africa by the West. They address acknowledgment of and apology for some specific harms caused by the West and examine the difficulties that might be experienced were a truth commission set up for Africa.

Symbolic reparations are relatively costless. Those who call for reparations to Africa, however, want financial compensation, not merely symbolic reparations, for past injuries. But justifying such calls for financial compensation is difficult. Chapter 1 discusses the difficulties that attend any attempt at transgenerational justice. Chapters 3 and 4 show how these difficulties affect the social movement for reparations to Africa. Chapters 5 through 9 discuss calls for reparations for the slave trade, colonialism, and postcolonial relations, and they address the difficulty of attributing responsibility for and calculating the costs of the historical and contemporary events that have harmed Africa.

Nevertheless, the question of how to remedy the severe poverty that exists in Africa today remains, as does the question of who is responsible for that remedy. Even if calls for reparative justice are unlikely to be persuasive, the West is obliged as a matter of distributive justice to assist Africa. This obligation is taken for granted by many members of the Western elite, as well as by many Western nongovernmental organizations, civil society activists, and private citizens. These Westerners take this obligation for granted, even though they recognize that the West is far from the only outside actor to have harmed Africa.

This Western sense of obligation is not rooted in the belief that the West owes reparations to Africa for past injuries, although some Westerners may hold such a view. Rather, many in the West believe that the rich are obliged to assist the poor. This obligation extends not only to the poor in one's own society but also to the poor in distant societies. It exists regardless of whether one has personally caused that poverty, or one's ancestors, or one's country, caused it. Poverty is an economic condition, but it is also a morally degrading condition. It is undignified; it erodes the sense of self-worth of those who endure it.

Moral Integrity and the Case for Reparations

The international human rights regime is based on the principle of human dignity. It is difficult for any individual to function effectively without a sense of moral worth, a sense of self-respect. This is all the more so for individuals suffering from poverty, without any sense that the future might bring some relief. As Didjob Divungui Di-Ndinge, vice-president of Gabon, said at the Durban Conference, "What Africa is asking for is not compassion, pity or charity. We are asking for recognition . . . of the dignity of its sons and daughters."[1] Robert, one of our respondents, said, "Reparations means a change of mentalities. . . . It's from the moment . . . that a young African can discuss as an equal with his Western colleague. Without that, we'll keep on creating monsters, and Africa won't develop." Yet we found in our interviews a massive sense that the rest of the world did not recognize the dignity of Africans. Our respondents felt neglected and abandoned. I found it saddening and frightening when some of the people I spoke with thanked me for listening to them, in effect, for treating them as human beings.

For many years, I have been concerned that Westerners have not recognized Africans' moral integrity. In early debates about human rights in postcolonial Africa, a common contention was that civil and political rights were unnecessary for Africans, if they did not yet enjoy basic material security. I call this argument the "full-belly thesis" and criticize it, among other reasons, for not recognizing Africans' human needs. I argue that Africans, like Westerners, value personal freedom, personal happiness, and the chance to participate in collective decision-making.[2] Since the late 1980s, the international community has rejected the full-belly, "food first" view of African needs. It has called for increased accountability, rule of law, transparency, and good governance as keys to African development. These changes permit ordinary Africans to participate in making political decisions, not only decisions that determine whether they can lift themselves out of poverty but also decisions that determine whether they can lead dignified lives. The changes also mean that African political leaders must take responsibility for their citizens' human rights.

But any approach that stresses African responsibility for African political and institutional arrangements must also recognize that African states cannot provide for their citizens' basic needs without changes in international policies and governance, nor without sustained international assistance. International respect for Africans' moral integrity requires assurance that they are not deprived of their basic economic rights. During the last twenty years, Western governments and international financial institutions (IFIs), such as the World Bank (WB) and the International Monetary Fund (IMF), have urged African states to adopt market economies, institute the rule of law, and hold democratic, multiparty elections. Yet, even in countries that have completely followed these prescriptions, many citizens are still extremely poor. It is difficult, although certainly not impossible, for those Africans who live in dire poverty to maintain their sense of self-worth or exercise their moral agency and integrity as citizens of the wider polity.

The moral integrity of Africans requires serious Western consideration of its obligations to Africa. Moral integrity implies Africans' moral value and competence. The moral value of each individual African is equal to the moral value of any other human being, rich or poor. Moral competence is the capacity of any—or most (allowing for various forms of disability)—human beings to distinguish right from wrong and to make active decisions about matters of morality. Acknowledgment of moral competence implies respect for the judgment of others, even when the observer disagrees with their conclusions. Thus, even if the idea of financial compensation to Africa for the injuries of the past five centuries seems outlandish or unattainable, Westerners are obliged to think carefully about why so many Africans favor reparations.

Acknowledgment of moral integrity requires that outsiders listen carefully to insiders' accounts of the wrongs they have suffered. In the case of Africa, this requires careful attention to accounts of wrongs, both to individuals and to communities, endured as a consequence of the slave trade, colonialism, and various postcolonial Western incursions into the continent. Westerners need to know and to respect the personal and collective stories of Africans: to acknowledge their moral integrity requires acts by Westerners of empathic imagination. Only with attention to personal and collective narratives can there be a real basis for collective empathy.

However, the requirement to respect Africans' accounts of their history does not require that the outsider suspend judgment. Govier argues that we do not always have to believe others' claims; rather, we can "take an interest, listen respectfully, and reflectively consider claims made by other people *without believing or accepting them*."[3] When acknowledgment, apology, or financial compensation is at issue, it is legitimate to apply a careful lawyer's or historian's consideration to the "facts." Historical evidence for charges of collective or individual injury should be pursued.

The outsider is not required automatically to accept narratives and claims for reparations as truths; thus, I disagree with some accounts and explanations offered by the Africans quoted in this volume. Nor is the outsider obliged to absolve those from within the claiming community who are responsible for ill-treatment of one another. If Africans are responsible for harming one another, that must be acknowledged. If Africans blame the West without blaming other actors who harmed their continent, that must also be taken into account. Claims for reparations for past wrongs require a sympathetic and respectful hearing but no automatic reparatory action, especially if some of the entities that caused past injuries are not called upon to participate in programs for reparative justice.

Moreover, Westerners also possess moral integrity. Their historical and their present relations with Africa were and are not influenced only by racist perceptions or policies, despite the statements emanating from Durban, especially from the NGO Forum. Particularly in the postcolonial era, many Westerners involved in the social movements for economic development, human rights, ecological protection, international feminism, children's rights, and other causes have been trying very hard to rectify the results of past policies, racist or otherwise, and to remedy current economic inequities. These Westerners are engaged in building the international moral community that is required if Africa is to overcome its severe disadvantages.

Thus, just as Westerners ought to listen to Africans' narratives, so Africans must listen to Westerners'. Both groups, moreover, must take seriously scholarly and scientific evidence of past wrongs and of present proposals to remedy their consequences. Resorting to feelings of guilt on the part of Westerners or to feelings of resentment on the part of Africans will not solve the human rights difficulties of Africa today, unless social divisions based on perceived identities and analytical divisions based on rhetoric are overcome.

The Global Responsibility Stretch

Academic literature and the popular press often refer to the "international community." I define a community as a set of people who interact with each other, take one another as their reference group (those whom they esteem and whose opinions they value), and feel a sense of obligation to one another.[4] There is an international community that exhibits these characteristics and that takes Africa as its object of concern. Members of this community include officials of the United Nations and its affiliated or connected organizations (including the WB and the IMF), officials of various states, activists in numerous nongovernmental organizations (NGOs), and innumerable private individuals.

Within this international community, there is a global responsibility stretch: states, organizations, and individuals stretch their sense of responsibility to encompass the entire world. A social movement to ameliorate global suffering has swept the planet since the Universal Declaration of Human Rights (UDHR) was proclaimed by the United Nations in 1948. This social movement refers to global history and focuses on the adverse effects of the slave trade, imperialism and colonialism, and postcolonial relations upon the poorer countries of the world. Moreover, it identifies both states and other actors such as private corporations as responsible for past wrongs. Not only governments but also private corporations, social organizations, civil society, and individuals are actors in the global responsibility stretch. They often consider themselves responsible for the policies of their institutional ancestors and consider that, accordingly, they must make amends for policies that have harmed others, including Africans. The call for reparative justice thus appeals to many members of this international community.

Yet reparative justice is not enough; it may contribute to but cannot substitute for distributive justice. But there is no concrete responsibility in international law for richer states to redistribute wealth to or otherwise assist poorer states. As noted in Chapter 1, article 28 of the UDHR states that "everyone is entitled to a social and international order in which the rights and freedoms set forth in this Declaration can be fully realized." Insofar as the West is responsible for much of that social and international order, it might be thought, it has a special duty to protect the rights and freedoms of everyone in the world. But the UDHR is, at best, a normative, standard-setting statement. Only those articles that have since 1948 been written more concretely into conventions that states can sign and ratify have the potential to become domestic law and thus influence state behavior.

The closest that international law comes to mandating a responsibility for richer states to redistribute wealth to poorer states or to otherwise assist them to realize their citizens' economic rights is the 1986 Declaration on the Right to Development. In several of its articles, this declaration refers to responsibilities of states to cooperate, most notably in article 3(3), which mandates that "states have the duty to cooperate with each other in ensuring development and eliminating obstacles to development."[5] But this is very soft, unenforceable law. Foreign aid is a public policy option, not a legal imperative.

One might reply to this that the emerging law of the right to reparations suggests that the wealthier countries must provide resources to poorer countries. But this law mandates reparations to individuals, not to collectivities such as states, and certainly not to an entire continent. It also applies to living victims or, in the case of those murdered, to their immediate surviving families, not to victims long dead.

One is left, then, with a moral, not a legal, imperative for the West to assist Africa. To some, this moral imperative is overwhelming. Thomas Pogge suggests that the West's willingness to ignore its moral responsibility to help the poorest countries renders political authorities and managers of the international economy "hunger's willing executioners."[6] The reference is to Goldhagen's discussion of Germans as "Hitler's Willing Executioners."[7] Recognizing the West's moral obligation, in early 2005

Prime Minister Tony Blair of the United Kingdom said, "There can be no excuse, no defence, no justification for the plight of millions of our fellow beings in Africa today. . . . I fear my own conscience on Africa. I fear the judgment of future generations, where history properly calculates the gravity of the suffering."[8]

That Blair urges the West to acknowledge its responsibility to Africa does not mean, however, that African states, elites, and citizens do not have the same responsibility as their counterparts in the West. Postcolonial African political leaders have much to answer for, from ill-conceived economic policies to intentional imprisonment and persecution of their critics, to large-scale personal corruption. If the world community, a community inhabited by Africans as well as others, does not require that Africans take responsibility for their actions, then in a backhanded way it denies them their own moral integrity. Africans, like Westerners, must accept their duties to others. Nor is it a "Western" imposition to argue this moral perspective. The indigenous moral systems of Africa do not permit blatant disregard of others' rights.[9]

Thus, to urge more ethical responsibility upon the West is not to suggest lesser responsibility for African or other states, even if the slave trade and colonialism set the stage for the emergence of vicious political leaders in post-1960 Africa. The slave trade from the west coast of Africa was conducted by individuals from European and North and South American countries, while colonialism was an entirely European affair. After independence, Western states at various times and in various places supported political rulers whom they knew to be rapacious, cruel, and murderous. Western states, corporations, and institutions are implicated in many of the human rights abuses of postcolonial Africa. That Muslim traders also took slaves from Africa and that other states, most notably the Soviet Union during the Cold War and China today, also harmed Africa does not absolve Westerners of their own responsibilities.

Theoretical Bases for Western Responsibility

Philosophers work hard to enunciate theories of obligation, as discussed in Chapter 1 in the section on transgenerational justice. This section, though, focuses on ways that citizens and policy makers might think about their obligations. I suggest there are three common ways we do this.

The first way we think about responsibility is to believe that individuals, states, and other entities should take responsibility for what they caused. This is the model implicit in the call for reparations both by the Group of Eminent Persons and by our Africans respondents. Insofar as Western states, corporations, institutions, or individuals caused or contributed to African poverty and its other ills, reparationists believe, they should make amends. Those who harmed Africa, or their personal or institutional descendants, should now undo that harm.

Henry Shue argues that everyone has three sets of duties: to avoid depriving others of their human rights, to protect others from deprivation, and to aid the deprived.[10] Most private individuals in the West can show that they do not deliberately harm others. Many aid the deprived through their work in NGOs or by donating to charities. And some hope that they can protect others from deprivation, perhaps by urging their governments to intervene in situations that seem likely to result in mass starvation. Yet many individuals still feel uncomfortable, knowing that they do much less for others far away than they do for their families or fellow citizens.

Contradicting this urge to assist distant others, however, is the concentric-circle theory of obligation, the second way that citizens and policy makers often think about their responsibilities. This theory posits that our greatest obligation is to those nearest us. Most individuals' strongest sense of obligation is to their kin. Perhaps this is for sociobiological reasons: if we are programmed to reproduce, then investment in our own offspring makes sense.[11] Perhaps we feel obligations closest to home because of our human capacity to respond directly to body language and verbal expression, so that the suffering of those with whom we are in most direct contact affects us most deeply. Whatever the reasons may be, if parents do not feel primary obligation to their children, and children in turn to their parents, then the institutional and state-controlled organization of care will have to be much more complex and all-pervasive. Societies ought to be organized so that most individuals can take care of themselves and their families. This is what we hope will someday be the case in Africa.

Once they have cared for their families, individuals tend to look to their community. Communities can be those into which they are born, such as religious or ethnically based communities, or communities of choice. For many individuals, the community of choice becomes the nation. National boundaries are morally arbitrary in their creation, yet they make practical ethical sense. Nations are units to which individuals can feel attached, within which they have social interactions, and in which, in consequence, they feel a sense of belonging and sometimes of efficacy. "Compatriot favouritism," to use Charles Jones's term, is a common way for individuals to think through their obligations to distant others.[12] Thus, obligation radiates out in a concentric circle from family, to community, to nation, to the wider world.

Orend argues that duties to others must be "fair and readily absorbable."[13] This contention makes sociological sense. The closer to home the duties, the more likely are ordinary citizens to feel that their obligation is fair. Citizens are also more likely to think their obligations are fair if they can absorb their costs without depriving themselves or their families, or indeed, lowering their own standard of living.[14] This commonsense view of morality is also one that guides the behavior of states. For some years the United Nations' target for Official Development Assistance from richer to poorer countries has been 0.7 percent of each country's gross national product. Yet despite much rhetoric about this goal, few countries give this much. In real terms, 0.7 percent of gross national product is a very large amount, on which citizens of a state have first claim. In 2005 this figure (using gross national income, substituted for gross national product by the WB in 1993) was $7.7 billion for Canada, $15.0 billion for France, $15.7 billion for the United Kingdom, and $87.1 billion for the United States.[15]

A third view of responsibility suggests that you should do what you can, regardless of who caused what when and regardless of your relationship to the persons you are helping. This is Karl Jaspers's view: "Help wherever there is distress, no matter what the cause."[16] In this view, everyone has equal obligations to everyone else: universal, individual human rights require a universal sense of obligation by all human beings to all other human beings. This principle reflects the Golden Rule, "Do unto others as you would have them do unto you," a fundamental principle of Judaism, Christianity, and Islam,[17] as well as, presumably, of numerous other religions. In secular terms, one might find the Golden Rule in Immanuel Kant's categorical imperative, "Act only according to that maxim whereby you can at the same time will that it should become a universal law."[18] Whatever you need to make your life worthwhile, Kant implies, is what others also need to make their lives worthwhile.

How would adherents of these different approaches to obligation deal with the claim that the West ought to pay financial reparations to Africa? Those who base their reply on the theory of causation might argue that since the West caused Africa's poverty, it should pay reparations for causing that poverty. Yet it is impossible to determine the extent to which Western, non-Western, and African actors caused Africa's current state of severe economic crisis. If the West assumes historical or contemporary responsibilities for injustices for which it is not actually responsible, it might risk absolving African and other actors of responsibility for their actions. If these other actors, especially African political leaders and elites, do not pay attention to their responsibilities, then the internal institutional changes necessary for development in Africa will be less likely to occur.

Nevertheless, if one bases one's views on the causative theory, it is possible to sort out different levels of responsibility by different actors. Some of these actors can be shown to bear direct responsibility for depriving Africans of their human rights and might therefore be shown to bear a moral responsibility to compensate some Africans. Chapter 9 discusses core, contributory, and circumstantial responsibility. Core causes of poverty in Africa are decisions that are not inevitable, that are caused by human agency, and that further the interests of the actors—states, corporations, institutions, or private persons—who make them. Corrupt expropriation of state funds by African politicians, for example, is a core cause of African poverty; so is criminal engagement by Western, African, or other private individuals in drug trafficking or diamond smuggling. Contributory factors are short-term prior events that inadvertently worsen the economic situation of many Africans. Structural adjustment programs exemplify such contributory factors. Circumstantial factors are those that are part of the underlying economic or political scene and that often reflect historical events. Circumstantial factors in Africa include the legacy of political, economic, and social disruption caused by the slave trade and colonialism. Responsibility can be attributed to human actors, individual or collective, for contributory and circumstantial causes, but it does not bear the same weight as responsibility for core causes. Nevertheless, particular Western states may well have obligations to particular African countries as a result of damaging them in the past.

The concentric-circle theory of responsibility suggests that even if their prior responsibilities are to their families, communities, and nations, citizens of Western democracies are also capable of a sense of responsibility to distant others. Such citizens can choose to pressure their governments to assist Africa or they can choose to ignore suffering outside their borders. In practice, there are many Western-based NGOs working in or for Africa that are supported by voluntary donations from Western citizens. Thousands of Western volunteers work for these NGOs.

Thus, there is a widespread sense of concern among Westerners for distant others, even if their first concern is for those closer to themselves. These Westerners incorporate distant others into their personal universe of obligation, to use a term coined by Helen Fein.[19] Like rescuers of Jews during the Holocaust, they are capable of independent thought, able to follow their consciences even when they have little or nothing in common with the people for whom they are concerned.[20] By acts of empathic imagination, they reduce the social distance between themselves and Africans. This social distance is also reduced by the realities of globalization. Many more Westerners than in earlier decades travel to Africa; many more Africans travel to the West; knowledge is obtained far more easily via the Internet; and communications between Westerners and Africans are also intensified by the Internet and electronic mail.

Thus, many Westerners feel responsible to remedy past injuries, even if they did not cause them, and even if they have no personal ties to those who suffer their consequences. In so doing, they follow Jaspers's injunction to help wherever there is distress, regardless of the cause. The Jewish teacher Hillel, who lived around the time of Christ, asked, "If not now, when? If not us, who?"[21] In one sense, it does not matter who caused Africa's problems; everyone is responsible for solving them. This is especially so in Western democracies, where every private citizen has access to government and can pressure it to take responsibility to assist Africa.

But this does not absolve other states of responsibility to help Africa. Global ethics require global responsibility. This is, in effect, both the Golden Rule and the Kantian imperative. All who are responsible for causing underdevelopment, corruption, genocide, famine, or any other of Africa's tragically myriad ills must take responsibility. But those who did not in any way cause these problems are also responsible. The "when" is now and the "who" is everyone. The global responsibility stretch encompasses all actors and allows no region of the world, no government, no institution, and no individual to deny responsibility.

Economic Human Rights

Jaspers's view of responsibility reflects the principles of international human rights law, in which the obligation to assist Africa does not rest on any calculation of the harm caused by any individual, state, or region to that continent. All members of the world community are obliged to respect universal economic rights. This principle focuses on distributive rather than reparative justice.

As explained in Chapter 1, internationally acknowledged economic rights are enunciated in the United Nations' 1976 International Covenant on Economic, Social and Cultural Rights. They include rights to food, health care, education, shelter, clean water, and social welfare. Everyone in the world is entitled to economic rights. Whatever has happened to an individual, a group, or a nation in the past is irrelevant to the imperative to fulfill economic rights: the only relevant matter is the current need for them. A world economic order based on individual economic rights would require all economic actors—whether states, private corporations, international institutions, civil society organizations, or individuals—to consider the effects of their actions on everyone's economic rights, such as their rights to food, shelter, and health care. Economic human rights provide a standard of accountability by all actors to those affected by their policies. Economic human rights, moreover, mandate that no one should be born or fall into a degrading or humiliating standard of living. Human dignity demands respect for everyone's basic economic rights. This is all the more so for individuals suffering from such abject poverty that there is no hope that the future might bring some relief.

If deprivation of economic rights is both dangerous to the individual and degrading to human dignity, why not advocate world redistribution of wealth? Indeed, world distributive justice figures prominently in the debate about how to alleviate poverty. But we should separate analysis of how to guarantee economic rights from the assumption that the only way to achieve this goal is through redistribution of the wealth that already exists. The actual distribution of wealth may be a function not of *re*distribution but of economic, political, legal, and institutional arrangements.

Proponents of world redistribution point to the oft-cited contention that redistribution of only 1 percent of aggregate global income would "eradicate severe poverty worldwide."[22] But it is unrealistic to suppose that in the present world configuration of wealth and power, the richer countries would agree to redistribution of such an enormous amount of money: 1 percent of aggregate global income was estimated as about $312 billion in 2002.[23] Most states respond to the concentric-circle theory of obligation; their first obligation is to their own citizens, whose claims on 1 percent of the state's revenues—a smaller amount than 1 percent of the aggregate income in their state—take precedence over the claims of outsiders. If redistribution of 1 percent of aggregate global income did occur, moreover, it would have to take place on an annual basis. Redistribution would entail extremely high organizational and administrative costs and much discussion about avoiding corruption and waste, analogous to past discussions of foreign aid.

In practical terms, far more important than redistribution is the creation of a political, social, legal, and economic system that allows people to use their own resources and capacities to support themselves (discussed in Chapter 8). Better institutional organization will undoubtedly assist in realizing economic rights, as Pogge argues.[24] At minimum, these institutions must include democratic government, the rule of law, effective protection of private property, and a regulated market economy. They must also include civil and political rights. Economic justice means allowing individuals both the political and the economic freedoms that will enable them to stand on their own two feet. Some redistribution of the world's wealth, whether in the form of debt relief, foreign aid, or reparations, might assist to bring about the changes that Africa needs so that most Africans can stand on their own two feet, but it will not be the primary means of realizing this goal. Such redistribution, moreover, will face the same obstacles as has foreign aid if Africans cannot reform their own governments to eliminate corruption, maladministration, and waste.

When the focus is on institutional reform, Western governments and their citizens can more easily consider their obligations to assist Africa to protect economic rights than if the only proposed mechanism is redistribution of their wealth. Any plan for massive material redistribution attacks most individuals' innate sense that obligations start from the family and move outward in a concentric circle to the community, the nation, and the world. Most Westerners, like most people elsewhere, do not believe they should sacrifice their own well-being for others. Westerners are unlikely to give up more than a small portion of their wealth to help citizens of other countries, even when they feel a sense of empathy and obligation toward distant others.

Thus, it is more realistic to promote Africans' economic human rights through institutional, political, legal, and economic reform than to urge either world redistribution of wealth or financial compensation to Africa for past injuries. As Richard Vernon notes, "Intuition strongly suggests that restitutive claims would . . . be very much less compelling in a distributively more just world."[25] Were economic goods more justly distributed, Africans would not need to make arguments for reparation based on sometimes shaky historical evidence. The claim for financial compensation is based on the assumption that responsibilities for historical deprivations can be accurately and quantifiably attributed to activities of external actors. It is also based on the assumption that without such historical deprivations, Africa would be more developed (wealthy) than it is presently. While this is undoubtedly partially correct, it requires a degree of accuracy in attribution of responsibility that is impossible to attain. It is impossible to calculate the financial cost of such injury in any realistic sense, as opposed to the absurdly large figures some reparationists have proposed.

Any realistic policy that urges Western states, institutions, organizations, and individuals to accept responsibility for Africa must accept the limitations of ordinary citizens' moral perspectives. On the one hand, Western citizens are unlikely to be swayed by demands for huge amounts of money based on unavoidably partial readings of the history of relations between Africa and the West, especially if such readings ignore the responsibility of other external actors, and of internal African actors, for the economic ills that plague Africa today. On the other hand, significant numbers of Westerners are swayed by the principle that even if one's first responsibility is to those to whom one is closest, one also bears some responsibility to distant others. Jaspers's dictum to "help wherever there is distress, no matter what the cause" is already fully integrated into the moral perspective of many influential and activist Westerners. But there remains the problem of sorting out a reasonable level of responsibility.

Who Bears What Obligations?

In general, obligations may be distributed among individuals, families, communities, states, and international actors. In the case of Africa, as elsewhere, states bear the principal responsibilities to promote economic rights, both states within that continent and states in the international community. Despite globalization of governance and economies, African states are sovereign over their own resources and bear principal responsibility for their citizens' welfare. Within the limits of their international treaty obligations, Western states are responsible for their own foreign and aid policies. But international organizations, nongovernmental organizations, and individuals also bear responsibilities.

In some parts of the world, such as Canada, the United States, and Western Europe, most individuals are able to take care of their own economic needs. Such is not the case in sub-Saharan Africa, with its tragically high levels of poverty, social disorder, and disease. Although I have advocated that policies be designed that permit Africans to support themselves as much as possible, we cannot expect individual Africans merely, or even primarily, to fend for themselves. Nor can individual Africans rely for assistance as much as they used to on their extended families. As a consequence of HIV/AIDS, as well as other diseases, some countries have extremely high numbers of orphaned children, many of whose extended family members are ill, poverty-stricken, or overburdened by trying to care for many people.[26]

Moreover, Africans cannot rely as much as they used to on their own communities. The villages, clans, and ethnic groups in which African social relations were once embedded are breaking down, not only because of disease but also as a consequence of more than a hundred years of urbanization, migration, and other social changes. Community in Africa is a much thinner entity than it once was. Communities are increasingly embodied in local, regional, and national governments. Only governments can create and manage the social institutions necessary to ensure economic rights.

In international law, the obligation on states in Africa and elsewhere is not to immediately implement the entire range of economic human rights but rather to ensure their progressive realization.[27] In the 1960s, when this law was written, decolonization and post–World War II prosperity suggested that development was a progressive and incremental process and that all poor countries would gradually catch up with the prosperous West. But Africa has not managed to develop, in part because many African leaders made policy errors, and some deliberately distorted, and even stole from, their national economies.

Even though early postcolonial African governments were responsible for many of their countries' economic misfortunes, rectifying their policy mistakes requires considerable outside assistance, as well as internal institutional change. This is not a matter of reparations, even though some Africans, desperate for any ideological tool they might find to assist their cause, frame their claims for justice as reparative. Western governments have long accepted some responsibility to assist Africa, having donated foreign aid for many decades. Recently, they have also introduced debt relief. Another responsibility of non-African states is to support the institutional changes that might assist Africans. This requires a fair, regulated international trade system, but it also requires both support and pressure for legal, political, and institutional changes within Africa.

Western governments are aware of some of the constraints on Africa's abilities to export its products. These constraints include high tariffs on goods that Africa can produce and subsidies to European and North American farmers that reduce the prices at which consumers can buy European, as opposed to African, products. For example, Calderisi estimated in 2006 that Europe spent some $350 billion subsidizing its farmers to produce crops, including some that Africans could produce.[28] Again and again in our interviews, we heard complaints that if there really were free trade, Western countries would eliminate both tariffs on African goods and subsidies to their own producers. This would permit African exports such as textiles, leather goods, and agricultural products to enter Western markets at prices competitive with goods from other regions.

The World Trade Organization (WTO), much reviled by many poverty activists, was in fact organized to free international trade by reducing subsidies and tariffs, although so far it has not had complete success.[29] Reduction in tariffs and subsides is not in the interests of some influential voting lobbies in the United States and the European Union, both of which have used their superior negotiating power in the WTO to block these changes, to Africa's detriment. Yet, Africa is a net food-importing continent, and some African countries rely heavily on subsidized wheat and maize from Europe. If subsidies to European wheat and maize producers are removed, food imports to Africa will be more expensive.[30] As with debt relief, remedies to Africa's poverty that in the popular mind seem obvious are in fact likely to have complex and contradictory effects. There is no magic recipe—aid, freer trade, debt relief, or reparations—to solve Africa's problems.

Aside from states and international organizations, NGOs outside Africa also play a role in promoting economic human rights. Nongovernmental organizations are part of international civil society, networks of voluntary organizations below the level of the nation-state. Such networks have mixed impact in Africa. They often support programs that are dedicated to economic rights, such as education and health care. But they are also criticized for following donors' rather than recipients' programs for change and for spending the bulk of their funds on foreign and local salaries and equipment. These difficulties, however, do not mean NGOs are useless. The elite Africans we interviewed, many of whom were human rights activists, had been influenced and supported by contact with international civil society.

Another type of nonstate organization that affects Africans' economic rights is transnational corporations (TNCs). Insofar as they are interested in Africa, their primary purpose is profit, not promotion of Africans' human rights. Nevertheless, when they trade with or invest in Africa, the resultant economic growth may well promote poverty reduction and thus economic rights.[31] One could, therefore, argue that TNCs have no particular human rights obligations to Africa; their normal profit-seeking activities will assist African development. Unfortunately, however, as noted in Chapter 8, as of 2005 only 1.7 percent of the world's foreign direct investment went to sub-Saharan Africa.[32] Moreover, much transnational corporate activity in Africa focuses on resource extraction, not industrial production, and much takes place in a context of corrupt dealings with government officials or criminal agreements with warlords. These alliances diminish the likelihood that TNCs will contribute to growth, development, or economic human rights in Africa.

In this mix of levels of obligation, many private individuals in the West also feel a sense of obligation to Africans, even though they are distant others. Many citizens donate funds to development projects or to support the civil and political freedoms that are absolutely essential to economic progress. Just as important is Western citizens' attention to the policies of their own governments and commitments to participate in an informed manner when they observe that such policies do not promote economic rights elsewhere.

There is, therefore, a strong case for Westerners to ensure distributive justice for Africa. The case for reparative justice is weaker, although not entirely unpersuasive. Having reviewed the many complicated aspects of the call for reparative justice for Africa, I conclude by presenting my own views of the legitimacy of the movement for reparations to Africa.

Legitimacy of Calls for Reparations to Africa

I support calls for acknowledgment of the harm the West—or some Western countries and institutions—has caused Africa. Victims of genocide, such as the Herero, ought to have that genocide acknowledged, as the German government has done; the Belgian government ought also to acknowledge the terrible treatment of Congolese under Leopold II. However historically distant the events, contemporary governments of countries that participated in the slave trade and colonialism ought to acknowledge that the acts of their predecessor governments were immoral at the time and should have been illegal. Symbolic reparative justice can have positive effects. Africans' sense of human dignity might improve if the West acknowledges and apologizes for the harm it caused.

I also support financial compensation for harm caused to specific groups of Africans in the recent past. These include the *anciens combattants* in the French army who suffered discriminatory pensions; the Mau Mau prisoners abused by their British captors; and Algerians tortured during the war of independence from France. I do not support these financial reparations solely on the grounds of feasibility, despite my analysis in Chapter 4 of when social movements for reparations are likely to succeed. Rather, I believe that when victims or their children (victimized by the loss or suffering of their parents) are still alive, when they suffered death or physical injury, or when they were clearly victims of discriminatory policies, they deserve compensation. They also deserve financial compensation if they were victims of violations of the law of the day, as may be the case in several of the suits against corporations that operated in South Africa during apartheid or against other corporations in other parts of Africa.

Turning to the postcolonial period, I believe that IFIs, and the Western governments that supported them, ought to have been guided in policy making by the principles of distributive justice. They ought to have paid more attention to the detrimental effects of the structural adjustment programs required of African states since the mid 1980s as a condition of continued financial assistance. To cushion the blows against individuals—such as the quarter million people dismissed from Ghana's civil service who lost their incomes—ought to have been possible in the past, and is so today. Under no circumstances should IFIs have urged or tolerated reductions in state provision of basic economic rights, such as health care or primary education, as a means to reign in state spending. Clean water, adequate sewage, primary health care, and primary education are, in my view, absolute minimum criteria of economic human rights, which African states, international organizations, and Western donors must always respect. Societies that respect these human rights also, as it happens, promote economic growth because a healthy and educated work force is better able to participate in the national and international economy.[33]

Similarly, I believe that if African states are to be expected to participate in the international free market economy, forgoing earlier protectionist policies, they should have access to adjustment funds to assist those enterprises that are accordingly undermined. Bhagwati believes that international organizations, such as the WB, should provide the financing necessary to cushion these enterprises' adjustment shocks.[34] I also believe that the Western powers that support the changes instituted by the WTO should practice what they preach: they should be far more willing than they presently are to reduce their own tariffs and subsidies. None of these, however, is a reparative measure. Rather, these are measures of international fairness, fitting better with an approach to justice that is distributive rather than reparative.

I also support debt relief, although not debt relief without conditionality. Conditionality should be related to human rights; it should promote democracy, the rule of law, and eradication of corruption. The conditions of debt relief should not be that African states should introduce free market economies, unless it can be reasonably predicted that free market economies will not undermine, and might improve, extant economic rights. Free markets are not human rights ends; they are merely one means to possibly attain economic human rights, if there is also political liberalization, and if social welfare guarantees accompany creation of freer markets.

Much of Africa's debt was incurred by corrupt, brutal leaders who manipulated Cold War interests to enrich themselves with the willing connivance of Western powers and the Soviet Union. Western nations, private banks, and IFIs lent the money, knowing that much of it would go into the pockets of private individuals, who would deposit it in their own names in Western banks. Africans today ought not to have to pay the debts these leaders incurred. The international community could have instituted rules decades ago to prevent Western financial institutions from accepting these deposits: it chose not to do so. Morally speaking, I would prefer that the debt be completely wiped out, for the whole of Africa, immediately. But practically speaking, this would leave more funds in the hands of current leaders, some of whom might use them for personal purposes, for military enlargement, or other illegitimate reasons. Debt relief cannot be a blanket invitation to wasteful expenditure. Countries with democratically elected leaders, who respect civil and political rights and the rule of law, should have first priority in debt relief programs.

Along with debt relief, I support the increased use of international criminal law to prosecute all those—Western, African, and others—whose activities deliberately impoverish or otherwise harm Africans in a manner contrary to the law. I also support the innovative use of tort law to sue private corporations whose activities may exploit or harm some Africans. Reparations obtained through criminal and civil law refer to contemporary wrongful acts. Such reparations, entrenched in legal practice, do not require rhetoric about past historic wrongs to legitimate them.

In this book, I focus on the demand for reparations to Africa from the Western world. The West, however, is not the only international actor to have harmed Africa. Thus, I disagree with the sanguine manner in which Ali Mazrui dismisses the Muslim slave trade and its effects on Africa. I also disagree with his easy dismissal of African political elites' own responsibilities for African suffering. Finally, I disagree with his focus on Western states to the exclusion of others. During the Cold War, the

Soviet Union sold arms to Africa, participated by proxy in some African wars, and supported some highly abusive political regimes.[35] In the early twenty-first century, China entered Africa as a major buyer of its resources, especially oil, and bears responsibility for its actions, for example, in Sudan.

Political action that calls for reparations for acts that occurred in the distant past while ignoring the causes of current African suffering is irresponsible. Whatever history teaches us about the sufferings of those long dead, the sufferings of those who are alive should take precedence in any discussion of moral responsibility for that suffering and appropriate remedial policies for it. The slave trade and colonialism were great injustices that cannot be undone. Africa cannot be restored to the state it enjoyed—or endured—seven centuries ago. Nor can Africa be restored to the hypothetical state it might have reached had there been no slave trade or colonialism. Thus, the call for reparative economic justice to Africa for long-past historical events, or for international policies that some activists and many of our respondents believe harmed Africa, should not take precedence over other policies or activities that might ameliorate the violations of their human rights that so many Africans now endure.

The greater justice now is distributive, not restorative. Wealth must be created within Africa and distributed in such a manner that all Africans enjoy their economic rights. Economic justice is promoted better through economic human rights than through the call for financial compensation for past harms perpetrated by the West (but not by other regions of the world) against Africa. Africans deserve respect for their economic human rights, regardless of who or what is responsible for the situation in which they currently find themselves. Indeed, the argument for present-day distributive justice for Africa is much stronger than the argument for restorative justice. It does not rely on counterfactual interpretations of or controversial debates about history. It relies merely on demonstration of living Africans' actual need for economic rights.

In an ideal world, all states, institutions, organizations, and individuals would examine their actions through a human rights filter: this filter would include economic rights. The economic rights of individuals now alive would be the key preoccupation of distributive justice. Financial compensation for past harms might contribute to economic rights in some limited instances, but the claim for reparation is not necessary to the principle of economic rights. Reparative justice can supplement distributive justice, but it should not substitute for it. Whether or not reparationists can prove their case, Westerners, international organizations, and Africans themselves are all responsible to ensure that every African individual enjoys his or her economic human rights.

Notes

Chapter 1. Reparations to Africa: A New Kind of Justice

1. Malyn D. Newitt, *Portugal in Africa: The Last Hundred Years* (London: C. Hurst & Co., 1981).

2. Nancy Fraser, "From Redistribution to Recognition? Dilemmas of Justice in a 'Post-Socialist' Age," *New Left Review* 212 (1995): 68–93.

3. John Torpey, "Making Whole What Has Been Smashed: Reflections on Reparations," *Journal of Modern History* 73, no. 2 (2001): 338.

4. Elazar Barkan, *The Guilt of Nations: Restitution and Negotiating Historical Injustices* (New York: W. W. Norton, 2000), 30–45; John Torpey, *Making Whole What Has Been Smashed: On Reparations Politics* (Cambridge, Mass.: Harvard University Press, 2006), 78–106.

5. Barkan, *The Guilt of Nations*, 46–64.

6. United Nations Development Programme, *Human Development Report 2006: Beyond Scarcity: Power, Poverty and the Global Water Crisis* (New York: Palgrave Macmillan, 2006), 286, Table 1, "Human Development Index."

7. Ibid., 292–94, Table 3, "Human and Income Poverty: Developing Countries."

8. World Bank, "World Bank Development Indicators" (World Bank, 2007).

9. Torpey, "Making Whole What Has Been Smashed," 337.

10. Dinah Shelton, "Righting Wrongs: Reparations in the Articles on State Responsibility," *American Journal of International Law* 96, no. 4 (2002): 833–56.

11. Dinah Shelton, "The World of Atonement: Reparations for Historical Injustices," *Miskolc Journal of International Law* 1, no. 2 (2004): 279.

12. International Criminal Court, "Rome Statute of the International Criminal Court" (1998), article 75 (1), "Reparations to Victims," http://www.un.org/law/icc/statute/99_corr/cstatute.htm, accessed August 7, 2007.

13. Office of the High Commission for Human Rights (OHCHR), *Basic Principles and Guidelines on the Right to a Remedy and Reparations for Victims of Gross Violations of International Human Rights Law and Serious Violations of International Humanitarian Law*, C.H.R. Res. 2005/35 U.N. Doc. E/Cn.4/2005/L.10/ Add.11: Office of the High Commission for Human Rights (OHCHR), 2005. For a legal history of these principles, see Marten Zwanenburg, "The Van Boven/Bassiouni Principles: An Appraisal," *Netherlands Quarterly of Human Rights* 24, no.4 (2006): 641–68.

14. United Nations General Assembly, "Basic Principles and Guidelines on the Right to a Remedy and Reparations for Victims of Gross Violations of International Human Rights Law and Serious Violations of International Humanitarian Law," A/Res/60/147, December 21, 2005.

15. Ibid., section IV, par. 8.

16. Ibid., preamble.

17. Ibid., section IX.

18. Ibid., section IX, par. 19.

19. Ibid., section IX, par. 20.

20. Ibid., section IX, par. 21.

21. Ibid., section IX, par. 22 (a), (b), (e), (g), and (h).

22. Louis Henkin, Gerald L. Neuman, David W. Leebron, and Diane F. Orentlicher, eds., *Human Rights* (New York: Foundation Press, 1999), 657.

23. Human Rights Watch, "The Pinochet Precedent: How Victims Can Pursue Human Rights Criminals Abroad" (New York: Human Rights Watch, 2000) section 2, "What Is Universal Jurisdiction?"

24. Richard Alan White, *Breaking the Silence: The Case That Changed the Face of Human Rights* (Washington, D.C.: Georgetown University Press, 2004).

25. William J. Aceves, "Affirming the Law of Nations in U.S. Courts: An Overview of Transnational Law Litigation," *The Federal Lawyer* 49, no. 5 (2002): 35.

26. Michael J. Bazyler, *Holocaust Justice: The Battle for Restitution in America's Courts* (New York: New York University Press, 2003).

27. Ibid., 317–20.

28. Jeremy Sarkin, "Reparations for Past Wrongs: Using Domestic Courts Around the World, Especially the United States, to Pursue African Human Rights Claims," *International Journal of Legal Information* 32, no. 2 (2004): 452–54.

29. Barkan, *The Guilt of Nations*, 159–282.

30. Aceves, "Affirming the Law of Nations in U.S. Courts," 37. See also Sarkin, "Reparation for Past Wrongs," 442.

31. Mark Gibney, *Five Uneasy Pieces: American Ethics in a Globalized World* (New York: Rowman and Littlefield, 2005), 23.

32. Sarkin, "Reparation for Past Wrongs," 457.

33. Ibid., 431, fn. 17.

34. Jan Narveson, "Collective Responsibility," *The Journal of Ethics* 6, no. 2 (2002): 179–98.

35. Barry O'Neill, *Honor, Symbols, and War* (Ann Arbor: University of Michigan Press, 1999), 189.

36. Alasdair MacIntyre, *After Virtue: A Study in Moral Theory*, 2nd ed. (London: Duckworth, 1981), 220, quoted in Janna Thompson, *Taking Responsibility for the Past: Reparation and Historical Justice* (Cambridge, UK: Polity Press, 2002), 11.

37. Kok-Chor Tan, "Colonialism, Reparations and Global Justice," in *Reparations: Interdisciplinary Inquiries*, ed. Jon Miller and Rahul Kumar (Oxford: Oxford University Press, 2007), 298.

38. Joel Feinberg, "Collective Responsibility," *Journal of Philosophy* 65, no. 21 (1968): 677.

39. Ton van den Beld, "Can Collective Responsibility for Perpetrated Evil Persist over Generations?" *Ethical Theory and Moral Practice* 5, no. 2 (2002): 198.

40. Margaret Gilbert, "Group Wrongs and Guilt Feelings," *Journal of Ethics* 1, no. 1 (1997): 79–81.

41. Nava Löwenheim, "Asking Forgiveness for Wrongdoing in International Relations," working paper, website on Political Apologies and Reparations, Wil-

frid Laurier University, Waterloo, Canada, 2007, http://political-apologies.wlu.ca/documents/working/Lowenheim_Nava, accessed August 7, 2007.

42. George Sher, "Transgenerational Compensation," *Philosophy and Public Affairs* 33, no. 2 (2005): 181–200.

43. Jeremy Waldron, "Superseding Historic Injustice," *Ethics* 103, no. 1 (1992): 11.

44. Thompson, *Taking Responsibility for the Past*, 139.

45. Tyler Cowen, "How Far Back Should We Go? Why Restitution Should Be Small," in *Retribution and Reparation in the Transition to Democracy*, ed. Jon Elster (Cambridge, UK: Cambridge University Press, 2006), 21.

46. Ibid., 23.

47. Michael Cunningham, "Saying Sorry: The Politics of Apology," *Political Quarterly* 70, no. 3 (1999): 289.

48. Doron Shulnitzer, "Human Dignity: Functions and Meanings," *Global Jurist Topics* 3, no. 3 (2003): 1–4.

49. Organization of African Unity, "African Charter on Human and Peoples' Rights," *Organization of African Unity*, June 27, 1981, preamble.

50. Rhoda E. Howard, *Human Rights and the Search for Community* (Boulder, Colo.: Westview, 1995), 16.

51. Charles Taylor, "The Politics of Recognition," in *Multiculturalism*, ed. Amy Gutmann (Princeton, N.J.: Princeton University Press, 1994), 25.

52. Trudy Govier, "Trust and Testimony: Nine Arguments on Testimonial Knowledge," *International Journal of Moral and Social Studies* 8, no. 1 (1993): 31.

53. Oscar Schachter, "Human Dignity as a Normative Concept," *American Journal of International Law* 77, no. 4 (1983): 848.

54. Aaron Lazare, *On Apology* (New York: Oxford University Press, 2004), 45.

55. Schachter, "Human Dignity as a Normative Concept," 851.

56. Centre for Human Rights, *Compendium of Key Human Rights Documents of the African Union* (Pretoria, South Africa: Pretoria University Law Press, 2005).

57. Abdullahi Ahmed An-Na'im, ed., *Human Rights Under African Constitutions: Realizing the Promise for Ourselves* (Philadelphia: University of Pennsylvania Press, 2003).

58. Makau Mutua, *Human Rights: A Political and Cultural Critique* (Philadelphia: University of Pennsylvania Press, 2002).

59. Rachel Murray, *Human Rights in Africa: From the OAU to the African Union* (Cambridge, UK: Cambridge University Press, 2004).

60. Trudy Govier, *Social Trust and Human Communities* (Montréal, Québec: McGill-Queen's University Press, 1997), 210–36.

61. Trudy Govier, "An Epistemology of Trust," *International Journal of Moral and Social Studies* 8, no. 2 (1993): 156.

62. Ibid., 157.

63. Janna Thompson, "Reparative Justice and International Relations," unpublished manuscript, 2007, 6.

64. Löwenheim, "Asking Forgiveness for Wrongdoing in International Relations," 27.

65. Thompson, "Reparative Justice and International Relations," 24.

66. Samuel P. Huntington, *The Clash of Civilizations and the Remaking of World Order* (New York: Simon & Schuster, 1996).

67. Omofolabo Ajayi-Soyinka, "The Fashion of Democracy: September 11 and Africa," *Signs: Journal of Women in Culture and Society* 29, no. 2 (2003): 604.

68. Rita Abrahamsen, "A Breeding Ground for Terrorists? Africa & Britain's 'War on Terrorism'" *Review of African Political Economy* 31, no. 102 (2004): 680.

69. James Samuel Coleman, *Foundations of Social Theory* (Cambridge, Mass.: Harvard University Press, 1990), 91–116.

70. "Policing the Undergoverned Spaces: Africa and the 'War on Terror,'" *The Economist*, June 16, 2007, 55.

Chapter 2. African Voices

1. Michael Quinn Patton, *Qualitative Evaluation and Research Methods*, 2nd ed. (Newbury Park, Calif.: Sage Publications, 1990), 177.

2. Ibid., 169.

3. Anthony Peter Lombardo, "Reparations to Africa: Examining the African Viewpoint," master's thesis, McMaster University (2004).

4. I am grateful to Bogumil Jewsiewicki, Canada Research Chair in the History of Memory at Université Laval, for permitting Ms. Bergeron to attend this colloquium.

Chapter 3. Genesis of the Reparations Movement

1. Interview with Jacob Ade Ajayi, December 6, 2002.

2. Bashorun M. K. O. Abiola, "Why Reparations?" *West Africa*, June 1–7, 1992.

3. Bola Makanjuola, "Cost of Suffering: Africans Demand Compensation for Slavery and Exploitation," *West Africa*, February 4–10, 1991.

4. Ali A. Mazrui, Albert Luthuli, and Andrew D. White, "The Campaign for Black Reparations: An African Initiative," website no longer available, 2002.

5. Interview with Dudley Thompson, December 5, 2002.

6. Interview with Ali A. Mazrui, December 7, 2002.

7. Interview with Jacob Ajayi, December 6, 2002.

8. "ECOWAS Defence Commission," *West Africa*, February 11–17, 1991.

9. Civil Liberties Organization, *Annual Report on Human Rights in Nigeria, 1990* (Lagos: Civil Liberties Organization, 1990).

10. Ali A. Mazrui, *Black Reparations in the Era of Globalization* (Binghamton, N.Y.: Institute of Global Cultural Studies, 2002), 135.

11. Ibid., 135–38, "The Abuja Proclamation," quotations from 136.

12. Ibid., 137–38.

13. United Nations Department of Public Information, "General Assembly Seeks to End 15-Year Stalemate over Security Council Reform," United Nations General Assembly, GA/10552, December 11, 2006.

14. Mazrui, *Black Reparations in the Era of Globalization*, 139, "The Accra Declaration on Reparations and Repatriation."

15. Ibid., 139–43, quotation from 140.

16. World Bank, "World Development Indicators" (World Bank, 2007).

17. Interview with Dudley Thompson, December 5, 2002.

18. Mazrui, *Black Reparations in the Era of Globalization*, 60. Italics in original.

19. Anthony Gifford, "The Legal Basis of the Claim for Reparations," First Pan-African Congress on Reparations, Abuja, April 27–29, 1993, http://www.arm.arc .co.uk/legalBasis.html, accessed August 7, 2007.

20. Ron Eyerman, *Cultural Trauma: Slavery and the Formation of African American Identity* (New York: Cambridge University Press, 2001), 91.

21. Dudley Thompson, "The Debt Has Not Been Paid, the Accounts Have Not Been Settled," *African Studies Quarterly* 2, no. 4 (1999).
22. Interview with Dudley Thompson, December 5, 2002.
23. Darshana Soni, "The British and the Benin Bronzes (ARM Information Sheet 4)," African Reparations Movement (ARM), n.d., http://www.arm.arc.co.uk/CRBBinfo4.html, accessed August 7, 2007.
24. According to ARM's website, the death of the Rt. Honourable Bernie Grant, M.P., has resulted in the website's no longer being maintained. http://www.arm.arc.co.uk/, accessed August 7, 2007.
25. Alamin M. Mazrui, "Introduction: The Struggle for Black Reparations: From Emancipation to the Age of Globalization," in Mazrui, *Black Reparations in the Era of Globalization*, 14–15.
26. Jamaica Reparations Movement, "Reparations Document," *Jamaica Reparations Movement*, February 28, 2003, http://www.geocities.com/i_makeda/draftdocument.html, accessed August 7, 2007.
27. Interview with Dudley Thompson, December 5, 2002.
28. Interim Steering Committee of the Africans and African Descendants Caucus, "Proposal for a Permanent Organizational Structure of the African and African Descendants Caucus," n.d., http://www.geocities.com/i_makeda/permanentstructure.htm, accessed August 7, 2007.
29. Commission of the African Union, "Strategic Plan of the Commission of the African Union, Volume 3: 2004–2007 Plan of Action" (Addis Ababa: African Union, 2004).
30. African Union, "Report of the First Conference of Intellectuals of Africa and the Diaspora," First Conference of Intellectuals of Africa and the Diaspora, Rapt/Rpt/CAID(I), Dakar, Senegal, October 6–9, 2004.
31. N'Cobra, "Global Pan-African Reparations Conference," n.d., http://www.ncobra-intl-affairs.org/conference.html, accessed August 7, 2007.
32. Global Afrikan Congress, news release, Toronto, Canada, n.d.
33. Global Afrikan Congress, "Background to the GAC," 2003, http://www.globalafrikancongress.com/aboutus.html, accessed August 7, 2007.
34. Vernellia R. Randall, "The Vienna Declaration and Program of Action with Background Information," *Washington and Lee Race and Ethnic Ancestry Law Journal* 8 (2002).
35. Email message from Dorothy Lewis to Gregory Eady (research assistant to Rhoda Howard-Hassmann), February 1, 2007.
36. Free Zim-Youth, "We Need to Change Strategy to Oust Mugabe Says [*sic*] Zim-Youth," *Free Zim-Youth*, September 18, 2006, http://www.zimbabwejournalists.com/story.php?art_id=1000&cat=4, accessed August 7, 2007.
37. Interview with Ali A. Mazrui, December 7, 2002.
38. Mazrui, *Black Reparations in the Era of Globalization*, 67.
39. Abiola, "Why Reparations?" 910.
40. Walter Rodney, *How Europe Underdeveloped Africa* (London: Bogle-L'Ouverture Publications, 1972), 149.
41. Rupert Charles Lewis, *Walter Rodney's Intellectual and Political Thought* (Detroit, Mich.: Wayne State University Press, 1998), 243–48.
42. Interim Steering Committee of the Africans and African Descendants Caucus, "Proposal for a Permanent Organizational Structure of the African and African Descendant Caucus."
43. Interview with Dudley Thompson, December 5, 2002.
44. Ali A. Mazrui, "From Slave Ship to Space Ship: Africa Between Marginalization and Globalization," *African Studies Quarterly* 2, no. 4 (1999): 1.

45. Interview with Ali A. Mazrui, December 7, 2002.
46. Ibid.
47. Interview with Dudley Thompson, December 6, 2002.
48. Ibid.
49. Mazrui, *Black Reparations in the Era of Globalization*, 136, "The Abuja Proclamation."
50. African Regional Preparatory Conference for the World Conference Against Racism, Racial Discrimination, Xenophobia, and Related Intolerance, "Draft Declaration of the African Regional Preparatory Conference for the World Conference Against Racism, Racial Discrimination, Xenophobia, and Related Intolerance," WCR/RCONF/DAKAR/2001/L.1 Rev. 3, January 24, 2001, http://www.africapolicy.org/docs01/wcar0101.htm, accessed August 7, 2007.
51. Dudley Thompson, "The Debt Has Not Been Paid, the Accounts Have Not Been Settled."
52. Mazrui, *Black Reparations in the Era of Globalization*, 88. Italics in original.
53. Interview with Ali A. Mazrui, December 7, 2002.
54. Interview with Dudley Thompson, December 5, 2002.
55. J. A. Lindgren Alves, "The Durban Conference Against Racism and Everyone's Responsibility," *Netherlands Quarterly of Human Rights* 21, no. 3 (2003): 369.
56. World Conference Against Racism, Racial Discrimination, Xenophobia, and Related Intolerance, "Declaration," 2001, www.unhchr.ch/pdf/Durban.pdf, accessed August 7, 2007, pars. 13 and 14.
57. Ibid., par. 104.
58. United Nations Department of Public Information, "Acknowledgement of Past, Compensation Urged by Many Leaders in Continuing Debate at Racism Conference," United Nations, September 2, 2001, http://www.un.org/WCAR/pressreleases/rd-d24.html, accessed August 7, 2007.
59. Ibid.
60. Olusegun Obasanjo, "Nigeria: Statement by President Olusegun Obasanjo," World Conference Against Racism, Racial Discrimination, Xenophobia, and Related Intolerance, Durban, South Africa, August 31, 2001, http://www.un.org/WCAR/ statements/nigeriaE.htm, accessed August 7, 2007.
61. World Conference Against Racism, Racial Discrimination, Xenophobia, and Related Intolerance Preparatory Committee, "Report of the Regional Conference for Africa," United Nations, Dakar, January 22–24, 2001, A/CONF.189/PC.2/8, http://www.unhchr.ch/Huridocda/Huridoca.nsf/A.CONF.189.PC.2.8.En?Opendocument, accessed August 7, 2007, article 10.
62. Ibid., article 11.
63. Agence France-Presse, "Slavery Should Be Declared a 'Crime Against Humanity': OAU Head," Agence France-Presse, September 1, 2001.
64. Fode M. Dabor, "Republic of Sierra Leone: Statement by Fode M. Dabor," World Conference Against Racism, Racial Discrimination, Xenophobia, and Related Intolerance, September 4, 2001, Durban, South Africa, http://www.un.org/ WCAR/statements/sierraE.htm, accessed August 7, 2007.
65. Mariama Cisse, "République du Niger, communication de la commission nationale des droits de l'homme et des libertés fondamentales," World Conference Against Racism, Racial Discrimination, Xenophobia, and Related Intolerance, September 3, 2001, Durban, South Africa, http://www.un.org/WCAR/

statements/ niger_hrF.htm, accessed August 7, 2007. This and all subsequent quotations in French translated by the author.

66. Abdoulaye Wade, "Sénégal: conférence mondiale contre le racisme, la discrimination raciale, la xénophobie, et l'intolérance qui y est associé, intervention de maître Abdoulaye Wade, président de la République du Sénégal," World Conference Against Racism, Racial Discrimination, Xenophobia, and Related Intolerance, September 1, 2001, Durban, South Africa, http://www.un.org/WCAR/ statements/senegalF.htm, accessed August 7, 2007.

67. See, for example, Joint Statement by African and Other NGOs, "Oral Intervention at the Informal Consultation of the Preparatory Committee for the World Conference Against Racism, Racial Discrimination, Xenophobia, and Related Intolerance," January 15–16, 2001, Geneva 200. Website no longer available.

68. WCAR NGO Forum, "WCAR NGO Forum Declaration," September 3, 2001, http://www.liberationafrique.org/IMG/article_PDF/article_384.pdf, accessed August 7, 2007, par. 71.

69. U.S. Department of State, "2000 Country Reports on Human Rights Practices," 2000, http://www.state.gov/g/drl/rls/hrrpt/2000/, accessed August 7, 2007, cited in Christopher N. Camponovo, "Disaster in Durban: The United Nations World Conference Against Racism, Racial Discrimination, Xenophobia, and Related Intolerance," *George Washington International Law Review* 34, no. 4 (2003): 671, fn. 66.

70. Camponovo, "Disaster in Durban," 671–73.

71. Ibid., 672–73.

72. Alhaji Mustapha Idris, "Republic of Ghana: Statement by Alhaji Mustapha Idris," World Conference on Racism, Racial Discrimination, Xenophobia, and Related Intolerance, Durban, South Africa, September 3, 2001, http://www.un.org/WCAR/ statements/ghanaE.htm, accessed August 7, 2007.

73. Both quotations from United Nations Department of Public Information, "Acknowledgement of Past, Compensation Urged by Many Leaders in Continuing Debate at Racism Conference."

74. United Nations General Assembly, "Commemoration of the Two-Hundredth Anniversary of the Abolition of the Trans-Atlantic Slave Trade." United Nations General Assembly, 59th Plenary Meeting, Draft Resolution A/61/L.28, November 28, 2006, statement by Finnish representative Janne Jokinen to agenda item 155.

75. Ibid., 11–13, 15.

76. Camponovo, "Disaster in Durban," 703.

77. Marc Bossuyt and Stef Vandeginste, "The Issue of Reparation for Slavery and Colonialism and the Durban World Conference Against Racism," *Human Rights Law Journal* 22, nos. 9–12 (2001): 349.

78. Michelle E. Lyons, "World Conference Against Racism: New Avenues for Slavery Reparations?" *Vanderbilt Journal of Transnational Law* 35 no. 4 (2002): 1249.

79. Nadine Gordimer, "Purge This Evil," *Sunday Observer*, London, September 23, 2001.

80. Alves, "The Durban Conference Against Racism," 361.

81. Camponovo, "Disaster in Durban," 660.

82. Michael Banton, "Lessons from the 2001 World Conference Against Racism," *Journal of Ethnic and Migration Studies* 28, no. 2 (2002): 360.

Chapter 4. The Social Movement for Reparations to Africa: Comparison to Holocaust Reparations

1. Part of this chapter is drawn from Rhoda E. Howard-Hassmann and Anthony P. Lombardo, "Framing Reparations Claims: Differences Between the African and Jewish Social Movements for Reparations," *African Studies Review* 50, no. 1 (2007): 27–48.
2. David S. Meyer and Nancy Whittier, "Social Movement Spillover," *Social Problems* 41, no. 2, (1994): 281.
3. Ali A. Mazrui, *Black Reparations in the Era of Globalization* (Binghamton, N.Y.: Institute of Global Cultural Studies, 2002), 87–88.
4. Interview with Ali A. Mazrui, December 7, 2002.
5. Bashorun M. K. O. Abiola, "Why Reparations?" *West Africa*, June 1–7, 1992, 910.
6. Quoted in Howard W. French, "The Atlantic Slave Trade: On Both Sides, Reason for Remorse," *New York Times*, April 5, 1998, reprinted in Roy L. Brooks, *When Sorry Isn't Enough: The Controversy over Apologies and Reparations for Human Injustice* (New York: New York University Press, 1999), 355–57.
7. African Regional Preparatory Conference for the World Conference Against Racism, Racial Discrimination, Xenophobia, and Related Intolerance, "Draft Declaration of the African Regional Preparatory Conference for the World Conference Against Racism, Racial Discrimination, Xenophobia, and Related Intolerance," WCR/RCONF/DAKAR/2001/L.1 Rev. 3, January 24, 2001, http://www.africapolicy.org/docs01/wcar0101.htm, pars. 19, 20, and 38, accessed August 7, 2007.
8. United Nations Department of Public Information, "Acknowledgement of Past, Compensation Urged by Many Leaders in Continuing Debate at Racism Conference," United Nations, September 2, 2001, http://www.un.org/WCAR/pressreleases/rd-d24.html, accessed August 7, 2007.
9. P. A. Chinamasa, "Zimbabwe: Statement Delivered by the Hon. P. A. Chinamasa, M.P., Minister of Justice, Legal and Parliamentary Affairs and Head of the Zimbabwe Delegation to the World Conference Against Racism, Racial Discrimination, Xenophobia, and Related Intolerances," World Conference Against Racism, Racial Discrimination, Xenophobia, and Related Intolerance, September 3, 2001, Durban, South Africa, http://www.un.org/WCAR/statements/zimbE.htm, accessed August 7, 2007.
10. Michael Bazyler, *Holocaust Justice: The Battle for Restitution in America's Courts* (New York: New York University Press, 2003), 297.
11. Bill Clinton, "Remarks in Apology to African Americans on the Tuskegee Experiment," *Weekly Compilation of Presidential Documents* 33, no. 20 (1997): 695–724.
12. Bazyler, *Holocaust Justice*, figures from 101.
13. Meyer and Whittier, "Social Movement Spillover," 277.
14. John D. McCarthy, "Pro-Life and Pro-Choice Mobilization: Infrastructure Deficits and New Technologies," in *Social Movements in an Organizational Society: Collected Essays*, ed. Meyer N. Zald and John D. McCarthy (New Brunswick, N.J.: Transaction Books, 1987), 59.
15. David A. Snow and Robert D. Benford, "Ideology, Frame Resonance, and Participant Mobilization," *International Social Movement Research* 1 (1988): 198.
16. Alison Brysk, "'Hearts and Minds': Bringing Symbolic Politics Back In," *Polity* 27, no. 4 (1995): 560–61.

17. Myra Marx Ferree and Frederick D. Miller, "Mobilization and Meaning: Toward an Integration of Social Psychological and Resource Perspectives on Social Movements," *Sociological Inquiry* 55, no. 1 (1985): 50.
18. Martha Finnemore, "International Organizations as Teachers of Norms: The United Nations Educational, Scientific, and Cultural Organization and Science Policy," *International Organization* 47, no. 4 (1993): 566, fn.1.
19. Frank R. Baumgartner and Bryan D. Jones, "Agenda Dynamics and Policy Subsystems," *Journal of Politics* 53, no. 4 (1991): 1050.
20. Finnemore, "International Organizations as Teachers of Norms," 594.
21. United Nations Sub-Commission on the Promotion and Protection of Human Rights, "Recognition of Responsibility and Reparation for Massive and Flagrant Violations of Human Rights Which Constitute Crimes Against Humanity and Which Took Place During the Period of Slavery, of Colonialism and Wars of Conquest," United Nations High Commission for Human Rights, E/CN.4/Sub.2/2001/L/11, August 6, 2001.
22. Meyer and Whittier, "Social Movement Spillover," 280.
23. Peter M. Haas, "Introduction: Epistemic Communities and International Policy Coordination," *International Organization* 46, no. 1 (1992): 29–30.
24. Ibid., 2, and fn. 4.
25. Ibid., 27.
26. Baumgartner and Jones, "Agenda Dynamics and Policy Subsystems," 1045.
27. Haas, "Introduction," 1.
28. Snow and Benford, "Ideology, Frame Resonance, and Participant Mobilization," 200.
29. Margaret E. Keck and Kathryn Sikkink, *Activists Beyond Borders: Advocacy Networks in International Politics* (Ithaca, N.Y.: Cornell University Press, 1998), 204.
30. Ibid., 195.
31. Ibid., 181.
32. Brysk, "'Hearts and Minds,'" 561.
33. Pierre Bourdieu, "The Forms of Capital," in *Handbook of Theory and Research for the Sociology of Education*, ed. John G. Richardson (New York: Greenwood Press, 1986), 245.
34. David A. Snow, E. Burke Rochford, Jr., Steven K. Worden, and Robert D. Benford, "Frame Alignment Processes, Micromobilization, and Movement Participation," *American Sociological Review* 51, no. 4 (1986): 472–73.
35. The following section draws in part on Elazar Barkan, *The Guilt of Nations: Restitution and Negotiating Historical Injustices* (New York: W. W. Norton, 2000), 3–29, 88–111.
36. United Nations General Assembly, "Convention on the Prevention and Punishment of the Crime of Genocide," Resolution 260 A (III), December 9, 1948, entry into force January 12, 1951.
37. Bazyler, *Holocaust Justice*, 202–68.
38. Ricardo René Laremont, "Jewish and Japanese American Reparations: Political Lessons for the Africana Community," *Journal of Asian American Studies* 4, no. 3 (2001): 238, endnote 4.
39. Ibid., 237.
40. Christian Pross, *Paying for the Past: The Struggle over Reparations for Surviving Victims of Nazi Terror* (Baltimore, Md.: Johns Hopkins University Press, 1998), 173. This figure is converted to dollars in Laremont, "Jewish and Japanese Reparations," 241.

41. Edwin Black, *IBM and the Holocaust: The Strategic Alliance Between Nazi Germany and America's Most Powerful Corporation* (New York: Crown Publishing, 2001).
42. Norman G. Finkelstein, *The Holocaust Industry: Reflections on the Exploitation of Jewish Suffering*, 2nd ed. (New York: Verso, 2001), 3.
43. Ronald J. Berger, *Fathoming the Holocaust: A Social Problems Approach* (New York: Aldine de Gruyter, 2002), 175–96.
44. Ibid., 141–42, 146–48.
45. Personal communication from Paul Kerstens, a researcher for Belgium's Lumumba Commission, October 2004.
46. BBC News, "France Gives Overseas Veterans More," November 21, 2002, http://news.bbc.co.uk/2/hi/europe/2498521.stm, accessed August 7, 2007. Several respondents from francophone countries mentioned this issue during our interviews in 2002.
47. Christine Ollivier, "France Boosts Pensions for Colonial Vets," Associated Press, September 28, 2006.
48. Ibid.
49. Carol Elkins, *Imperial Reckoning: The Untold Story of Britain's Gulag in Kenya* (New York: Henry Holt and Company, 2005).
50. Pascal James Imperato, "Differing Perspectives on Mau Mau," *African Studies Review* 48, no. 3 (2005):148, 150; Bethwell A. Ogot, "Britain's Gulag," *Journal of African History* 46, no. 3 (2005): 494.
51. David Anderson, *Histories of the Hanged: The Dirty War in Kenya and the End of Empire* (New York: W. W. Norton, 2005).
52. Elkins, *Imperial Reckoning*, 96, 129–30, 194, 304, 314.
53. Ibid., 275–310.
54. George Mwangi, "Kenya's Mau Mau Rebels Celebrate 50th Anniversary with Plea for Legalization," Associated Press, August 12, 2000.
55. Mikewa Ogada, Program Officer, Coordinator of the Mau Mau Advocacy Project, "NGOs/Organizations in Partnership with the Kenya Human Rights Commission (KHRC)," November 24, 2006, email sent to Gregory Eady; Associated Press, "Lawyers for Kenyan Veterans Demand Apology from Britain for Alleged Atrocities," October 16, 2006.
56. Leigh Day and Co. Solicitors, "Mau Mau Claims," Clerkenwell, UK. Letter sent by mail. Cited with permission of Mikewa Ogada, Program Officer, Research, Mau Mau Reparations and Recognition Project, April 2, 2007.
57. Henry Rousso, "Justice, History and Memory in France: Reflections on the Papon Trial," in *Politics and the Past: On Repairing Historical Injustices*, ed. John Torpey (New York: Rowman and Littlefield, 2003), 277–93; Robert O. Paxton, "The Trial of Maurice Papon," *New York Review of Books* 46, no. 2 (December 16, 1999): 32–37.
58. Geoffrey Robertson, *Crimes Against Humanity: The Struggle for Global Justice* (New York: New Press, 1999), 368–400.
59. Elkins, *Imperial Reckoning*, 361.
60. Bethwell, "Britain's Gulag," 504.

Chapter 5. Reparations for the Slave Trade: Law and Rhetoric

1. "Slavers," in *Slavers and Privateers: Liverpool Packet No. 5, Collections of Local History Materials*, ed. Fritz Spiegl (Liverpool, UK: Scouse Press, n.d.). Given to me at the Liverpool Library in 1973 or 1974.

2. "An Accurate Account of the Slave Trade," in *Slavers and Privateers*.
3. "Exploitation of Forced Labor," Dodd Archives (Nuremberg Trial), University of Connecticut, Box 288, folder 7349, December 11–13, 1945.
4. "The Slave Labour Program and the Special Responsibility of the Defendant Speer for the Planning and Execution of That Program," in Dodd Archives (Nuremberg Trial), University of Connecticut, Box 310, File 7926. Memo to Alfred Rosenberg, August 18, 1942.
5. Frantz Fanon, *The Wretched of the Earth* (New York: Grove Press, 1963).
6. Frantz Fanon, *Black Skins, White Masks* (New York: Grove Press, 1967), 226, 228, 230.
7. Paul Lovejoy, *Transformations in Slavery: A History of Slavery in Africa*, 2nd ed. (New York: Cambridge University Press, 2000), 19, 49.
8. Anthony Gifford, "Slavery: Legacy," *Hansard: Debate Initiated by Lord Gifford QC in the House of Lords of the British Parliament*, March 14, 1996, http://www.arm.arc.co.uk/LordsHansard.html, accessed August 12, 2007.
9. George Pavlu, "The First Slavers," *New African* 379 (1999): 17.
10. Tseliso Thipanyane, "Current Claims, Regional Experiences, Pressing Problems: Identification of the Salient Issues and Pressing Problems in an African Post-colonial Perspective," in *Human Rights in Development: Reparations; Redressing Past Wrongs*, ed. George Ulrich and Louise Krabbe Boserup (The Hague, Netherlands: Kluwer Law International, 2003), 36.
11. République du Niger, "Communication de la commission nationale des droits de l'homme et des libertés fondamentales, à la conférence mondiale contre le racisme, la discrimination raciale, la xénophobie, et l'intolérance qui y est associé," World Conference Against Racism, Racial Discrimination, Xenophobia, and Related Intolerance, Durban, South Africa, September 3, 2001, http://www.un.org/WCAR/statements/niger_hrF.htm, accessed August 7, 2007.
12. Georges Chikoti, "Statement by Dr. Georges Chikoti, Angolan Deputy Minister of Foreign Affairs," World Conference Against Racism, Racial Discrimination, Xenophobia, and Related Intolerance, Durban, South Africa, September 2, 2001, http://www.un.org/WCAR/statements/angolaE.htm, accessed August 7, 2007.
13. WCAR NGO Forum, "WCAR NGO Forum Declaration," September 3, 2001, http://www.liberationafrique.org/IMG/article_PDF/article_384.pdf, accessed August 7, 2007.
14. United Nations Department of Public Information, "Acknowledgement of Past, Compensation Urged by Many Leaders in Continuing Debate at Racism Conference," United Nations, September 2, 2001, http://www.un.org/WCAR/pressreleases/rd-d24.html, accessed August 7, 2007.
15. Deborah Scroggins, *Emma's War: Love, Betrayal and Death in the Sudan* (London: HarperCollins, 2003), 43.
16. Gabriel R. Warburg, "Ideological and Practical Considerations Regarding Slavery in the Mahdist State and the Anglo-Egyptian Sudan: 1881–1918," in *The Ideology of Slavery in Africa*, ed. Paul Lovejoy (Beverly Hills, Calif.: Sage Publications, 1981), 246.
17. Suzanne Miers, *Slavery in the Twentieth Century: The Evolution of a Global Problem* (New York: Rowman and Littlefield, 2003), 91.
18. Ibid., 153.
19. Fatima Babiker Mahmoud, *The Sudanese Bourgeoisie: Vanguard of Development?* (London: Zed Books, 1984), 81.

20. There is some dispute whether one should use the term "Arab" or "Muslim" slave trade, which I cannot resolve here. Not all Muslims who captured or sold African slaves were Arabs, although the term "Arab slave trade" is frequently used to refer to export of slaves to the Arabian peninsula. Many Muslim slave traders and buyers were Africans. Nor, of course, were all Muslims slave traders. Paul Lovejoy, personal communication, August 4, 2006.

21. Michelle E. Lyons, "World Conference Against Racism: New Avenues for Slavery Reparations?" *Vanderbilt Journal of Transnational Law* 35, no. 4 (2002): 1249.

22. Miers, *Slavery in the Twentieth Century*, 421–23.

23. League of Nations, "Convention to Suppress the Slave Trade and Slavery," September 25, 1926, article 1 (1).

24. Miers, *Slavery in the Twentieth Century*, 130.

25. Hilary McDonald Beckles, "Slave Voyages: The Transatlantic Trade in Enslaved Africans," UNESCO, ED-2002/WS/37 (2002), 4.

26. Dinah Shelton, "The World of Atonement: Reparations for Historical Injustices," *Miskolc Journal of International Law* 1, no. 2 (2004): 284.

27. Personal communication from Paul Lovejoy, August 4, 2006.

28. Shelton, "World of Atonement," 284.

29. Roger T. Anstey, "Capitalism and Slavery: A Critique," *Economic History Review* 21, no. 2 (1968): 319.

30. Lovejoy, *Transformations in Slavery*, 290–91.

31. Ibid., 291.

32. Shelton, "World of Atonement," 284.

33. Ibid., 284.

34. Max du Plessis, "Historical Injustice and International Law: An Exploratory Discussion of Reparation for Slavery," *Human Rights Quarterly* 25, no. 3 (2003): 635.

35. Geoffrey Robertson, *Crimes Against Humanity: The Struggle for Global Justice* (New York: New Press, 1999), 209.

36. Lovejoy, *Transformations in Slavery*, 291.

37. Paul Lovejoy, personal communication; Lovejoy, *Transformations in Slavery*, 294.

38. Lovejoy, *Transformations in Slavery*, 292–93.

39. Ibid., 292.

40. Shelton, "World of Atonement," 285.

41. Ibid., 284.

42. Lovejoy, *Transformations in Slavery*, 293.

43. Christopher N. Camponovo, "Disaster in Durban: The United Nations World Conference Against Racism, Racial Discrimination, Xenophobia, and Related Intolerance," *George Washington International Law Review* 34, no. 4 (2003): 675.

44. Robertson, *Crimes Against Humanity*, 13.

45. Ryan Michael Spitzer, "The African Holocaust: Should Europe Pay Reparations to Africa for Colonialism and Slavery?" *Vanderbilt Journal of Transnational Law* 35, no. 4 (2002): 1319.

46. Ibid., 1320.

47. Miers, *Slavery in the Twentieth Century*, 19.

48. David Brion Davis, *Slavery and Human Progress* (New York: Oxford University Press, 1984), 305.

49. Shelton, "The World of Atonement," 276.

50. Dinah Shelton, "Righting Wrongs: Reparations in the Articles on State Responsibility, *American Journal of International Law* 96, no. 4 (2002): 846.

51. Gifford, "Slavery: Legacy."

52. Paul M. Kennedy, *The Rise and Fall of British Naval Mastery* (London: The Ashfield Press, 1986), 165–66.

53. United Nations General Assembly. "Commemoration of the Two-Hundredth Anniversary of the Abolition of the Trans-Atlantic Slave Trade." United Nations General Assembly, 59th Plenary Meeting, Draft Resolution A/61/L.28, November 28, 2006, statement by Richard Miller (United States) to agenda item 155.

54. Ricardo René Laremont, "Political Versus Legal Strategies for the African Slavery Reparations Movement," *African Studies Quarterly: The Online Journal for African Studies* 2, no. 4 (1999).

55. United Nations General Assembly, "Convention on the Prevention and Punishment of the Crime of Genocide," Resolution 260 A (III), December 12, 1948, entry into force January 12, 1951, article II.

56. Robert Dibie and Johnston Njoku, "Cultural Perceptions of Africans in Diaspora and in Africa on Atlantic Slave Trade and Reparations," *African and Asian Studies* 4, no. 3 (2005): 410.

57. Marc Bossuyt and Stef Vandeginste, "The Issue of Reparation for Slavery and Colonialism and the Durban World Conference Against Racism," *Human Rights Law Journal* 22, no. 9–12 (2001): 345.

58. I am grateful to Adrian L. Jones, LLB, for explaining the law of unjust enrichment to me, March 10, 2006.

59. George E. Brooks and Bruce L. Mouser, "An 1804 Slaving Contract Signed in Arabic Script from the Upper Guinea Coast," *History in Africa* 14 (1987): 341–48.

60. Henry Campbell Black, *Black's Law Dictionary*, 5th ed. (St. Paul, Minn.: West Publishing, 1979), 1377.

61. I am grateful to Keith Calow, LLB, for his suggestion of this use of the concept of unjust enrichment.

62. World Conference Against Racism, Racial Discrimination, Xenophobia, and Related Intolerance, "Declaration" (2001), http://www.unhchr.ch/pdf/Durban.pdf, par. 13, accessed August 7, 2007,

63. Bossuyt and Vandeginste, "The Issue of Reparation for Slavery and Colonialism and the Durban World Conference Against Racism," 350.

64. World Conference Against Racism, Racial Discrimination, Xenophobia, and Related Intolerance, "Declaration," par. 99.

65. Ibid.

66. Légifrance: Le service public de la diffusion du droit, "Loi no 2001-2434 du 21 mai 2001 Tendant à la reconnaissance de la traite et de l'esclavage en tant que crime contre l'humanité" (2001), http://www.legifrance.gouv.fr/WAspad/UnTexteDeJorf?numjo=JUSX9903435L, accessed August 7, 2007. The exact wording is "La République française reconnaît que la traite négrière transatlantique . . . constituent un crime contre l'humanité."

67. Michel Giraud, "Le passé comme blessure et le passé comme masque: la réparation de la traite négrière et de l'esclavage pour les peuples des départements français d'Outre-Mer," *Cahiers d'études africaines* 44 (1–2), no. 173–174 (2004): 71, fn. 9.

68. BBC News, "France Remembers Slavery Victims," May 10, 2006.

69. Anthony J. Sebok, "Slavery, Reparations and Potential Legal Liability: The Hidden Legal Issue Behind the U.N. Racism Conference," *Findlaw: Legal News*

and Commentary, September 10, 2001, http://writ.findlaw.com/sebok/20010910.html, accessed August 7, 2007.

70. Camponovo, "Disaster in Durban," 705.

71. Thipanyane, "Current Claims, Regional Experiences, Pressing Problems," 47–48, quotations from 48.

72. Theodor van Boven, "Study Concerning the Right to Restitution, Compensation and Rehabilitation for Victims of Gross Violations of Human Rights and Fundamental Freedoms," Sub-Commission on Prevention of Discrimination and Protection of Minorities, United Nations Document E.CN.4/sub.2/1993/8, July 2, 1993, 12.

73. Roger Wareham, "The Popularization of the International Demand for Reparations for African People," in *Should America Pay? Slavery and the Raging Debate on Reparations*, ed. Raymond A. Winbush (New York: HarperCollins, 2003), 228.

74. Walter Rodney, *How Europe Underdeveloped Africa* (London: Bogle-l'Ouverture Publications, 1972), 86.

75. Robertson, *Crimes Against Humanity*, 86.

76. Spitzer, "The African Holocaust," 1342.

77. Shelton, "The World of Atonement," 279.

Chapter 6. Reparations for the Slave Trade: Historical Debates

1. Paul Lovejoy, *Transformations in Slavery: A History of Slavery in Africa*, 2nd ed. (New York: Cambridge University Press, 2000), 26, 62, 156.

2. Patrick Manning, "The Slave Trade: The Formal Demography of a Global System," in *The Atlantic Slave Trade: Effects on Economies, Societies and Peoples in Africa, the Americas, and Europe*, ed. Joseph E. Inikori and Stanley L. Engerman (Durham, N.C.: Duke University Press, 1992), 119–20.

3. Ali A. Mazrui, *Black Reparations in the Era of Globalization* (Binghamton, N.Y.: Institute of Global Cultural Studies, 2002), 33–46, quotation from 41.

4. Interview with Ali A. Mazrui, December 7, 2002.

5. David Brion Davis, *Slavery and Human Progress* (New York: Oxford University Press, 1984), 18.

6. Paul Lovejoy, "Slavery in the Context of Ideology," in *The Ideology of Slavery in Africa*, ed. Paul Lovejoy (Beverly Hills, Calif.: Sage Publications, 1981), 17.

7. Davis, *Slavery and Human Progress*, 39.

8. Martin Klein, "The Impact of the Atlantic Slave Trade on the Societies of the Western Sudan," in *The Atlantic Slave Trade: Effects on Economies, Societies and Peoples in Africa, the Americas, and Europe*, ed. Joseph E. Inikori and Stanley L. Engerman (Durham, N.C.: Duke University Press, 1992), 35.

9. Jacob Ade Ajayi, "The Politics of Reparation in the Context of Globalisation," Distinguished Abiola Lecture, African Studies Association, Washington, D.C., December 7, 2002, 8.

10. Davis, *Slavery and Human Progress*, 8.

11. Ibid., 42.

12. Ibid., 5.

13. Edward A. Alpers, "Slave Trade: Eastern Africa," in *Encyclopedia of Africa*, ed. John Middleton (New York: Charles Scribner's Sons, vol. 4, 1997), 95.

14. Frederick Cooper, "Islam and Cultural Hegemony: The Ideology of Slaveowners on the East African Coast," in *The Ideology of Slavery in Africa*, ed. Paul Lovejoy (Beverly Hills, Calif.: Sage Publications, 1981), 280.

15. Suzanne Miers, *Slavery in the Twentieth Century: The Evolution of a Global Problem* (New York: Rowman and Littlefield, 2003), 25.
16. Ibid., 348.
17. Geoffrey Robertson, *Crimes Against Humanity: The Struggle for Global Justice* (New York: New Press, 1999), 13.
18. Ajayi, "The Politics of Reparation in the Context of Globalisation," 7.
19. Paul Edwards, ed., *Equiano's Travels* (London: Heinemann Educational Books, 1967).
20. Lovejoy, *Transformations in Slavery*, 278.
21. Ibid., 281–82.
22. Igor Kopytoff and Suzanne Miers, "African 'Slavery' as an Institution of Marginality," in *Slavery in Africa: Historical and Anthropological Perspectives*, ed. Suzanne Miers and Igor Kopytoff (Madison: University of Wisconsin Press, 1977), 30–32.
23. Victor Uchendu, "Slaves and Slavery in Igboland, Nigeria," in *Slavery in Africa: Historical and Anthropological Perspectives*, ed. Igor Kopytoff and Suzanne Miers (Madison: University of Wisconsin Press, 1977), 123.
24. Joseph E. Inikori, "Slavery in Africa and the Transatlantic Slave Trade," in *The African Diaspora*, ed. Alusine Jalloh and Stephen E. Maizlish (Arlington: Texas A&M University Press, 1996), 41.
25. Lovejoy, "Slavery in the Context of Ideology," 15.
26. Kopytoff and Miers, "African 'Slavery' as an Institution of Marginality," 52.
27. Lovejoy, "Slavery in the Context of Ideology," 23.
28. A. Norma Klein, "The Two Asantes: Competing Interpretations of 'Slavery' in Akan-Asante Culture and Society," in *The Ideology of Slavery in Africa,* ed. Paul Lovejoy (Beverly Hills, Calif.: Sage Publications, 1981), 150.
29. Lovejoy, "Slavery in the Context of Ideology," 32.
30. Ibid., 11.
31. Kwame Anthony Appiah, "A Slow Emancipation," *New York Times Magazine*, March 18, 2007, 15–17.
32. U.S. Department of State, "Country Reports on Human Rights Practices: 2005," http://www.state.gov/g/drl/rls/hrrpt/2005/, accessed August 11, 2007.
33. Supplementary Convention on the Abolition of Slavery, the Slave Trade, and Institutions and Practices Similar to Slavery. September 7, 1956, 266 United Nations Treaty Series 3.
34. République du Niger, "Communication de la commission nationale des droits de l'homme et des libertés fondamentales, à la conférence mondiale contre le racisme, la discrimination raciale, la xénophobie, et l'intolérance qui y est associé," World Conference Against Racism, Racial Discrimination, Xenophobia, and Related Intolerance, Durban, South Africa, September 3, 2001, http://www.un.org/WCAR/statements/niger_hrF.htm, accessed August 7, 2007.
35. Miers, *Slavery in the Twentieth Century*, 418–20.
36. Christopher N. Camponovo, "Disaster in Durban: The United Nations World Conference Against Racism, Racial Discrimination, Xenophobia, and Related Intolerance," *George Washington International Law Review* 34, no. 4 (2003): 684, fn. 145.
37. Ajayi, "The Politics of Reparation in the Context of Globalisation," 9.
38. Ibid., 9.
39. Ronald Segal, *Islam's Black Slaves: The Other Black Diaspora* (New York: Farrar, Straus and Giroux, 2001), 40–41, 80, 95, 109, 170–71.
40. Joseph E. Inikori, "Slave Trade: Western Africa," in *Encyclopedia of Africa,* ed. John Middleton (New York: Charles Scribner's Sons, vol. 4, 1997), 89.

41. Martin A. Klein, *Slavery and Colonial Rule in French West Africa* (New York: Cambridge University Press, 1998), 37–58.

42. Klein, "The Impact of the Atlantic Slave Trade on the Societies of the Western Sudan," 34.

43. Manning, "The Slave Trade," 121.

44. Inikori, "Slave Trade: Western Africa," 89.

45. Lovejoy, *Transformations in Slavery*, 277.

46. Interview with Dudley Thompson, December 5, 2002.

47. Nick Mathiason, "Barclays Admits Possible Link to Slavery After Reparation Call," *The Observer*, London, April 1, 2007. I am grateful to Nicola Jagers for this reference.

48. Walter Rodney, *How Europe Underdeveloped Africa* (London: Bogle-l'Ouverture Publications, 1972), 85.

49. Ibid., 93.

50. Ibid., 90.

51. Ibid., 95.

52. Ibid., 96.

53. Eric Williams, *Capitalism and Slavery* (New York: Capricorn Books, 1966), 65–84, 126–34, 154–68.

54. Joseph E. Inikori, "Slavery and the Revolution in Cotton Textile Production in England," in *The Atlantic Slave Trade: Effects on Economies, Societies and Peoples in Africa, the Americas, and Europe*, ed. Joseph E. Inikori and Stanley L. Engerman (Durham, N.C.: Duke University Press, 1992), 145–81.

55. Ronald Bailey, "The Slave(ry) Trade and the Development of Capitalism in the United States," in *The Atlantic Slave Trade: Effects on Economies, Societies and Peoples in Africa, the Americas, and Europe*, ed. Joseph E. Inikori and Stanley L. Engerman (Durham, N.C.: Duke University Press, 1992), 205–46.

56. Stanley L. Engerman, "The Slave Trade and British Capital Formation in the Eighteenth Century: A Comment on the Williams Thesis," *Business History Review* 46, no. 4 (1972): 442.

57. David S. Landes, *The Wealth and Poverty of Nations: Why Some Are So Rich and Some So Poor* (New York: W. W. Norton, 1998), 119–20.

58. Ibid., 121.

59. Nathan Rosenberg and L. E. Birdzell, Jr., *How the West Grew Rich: The Economic Transformation of the Industrial World* (New York: Basic Books, 1986), 19.

60. Landes, *Wealth and Poverty of Nations*, 171.

61. Bailey, "The Slave(ry) Trade of Capitalism in the United States," 222–25.

62. Ibid., 216.

63. James Walvin, "The Colonial Origins of English Wealth: The Harewoods of Yorkshire," *Journal of Caribbean History* 39, no. 1 (2005): 38–53.

64. S. D. Smith, *Slavery, Family and Gentry Capitalism in the British Atlantic: The World of the Lascelles, 1648–1834* (New York: Cambridge University Press, 2006), 6–7.

65. James Walvin, public lecture, Wilfrid Laurier University, Waterloo, Canada, February 8, 2006.

66. Landes, *The Wealth and Poverty of Nations*, 121–22.

67. Wole Soyinka, *The Burden of Memory, the Muse of Forgiveness* (New York: Oxford University Press, 1999), 73.

68. Ibid., 86.

69. Paul D. Ocheje, "Refocusing International Law on the Quest for Accountability in Africa: The Case Against the 'Other' Impunity," *Leiden Journal of International Law* 15, no. 4 (2002): 753.

70. Soyinka, *The Burden of Memory*, 53–55.

71. Quoted in Bola Makanjuola, "Cost of Suffering: Africans Demand Compensation for Slavery and Exploitation," *West Africa*, February 4–10, 1991, 143.

72. Kwame Anthony Appiah, "Comprendre les réparations: une réflexion préliminaire," *Cahiers d'études africaines* 44, no. 1–2 (2004): 25–40. English manuscript provided to the author by Dr. Appiah, entitled "Understanding Reparations: A Preliminary Reflection."

73. Diadie Ba, "Senegal's Wade Calls Slave Reparations Absurd," *Independent Online*, August 11, 2001, http://www.iol.co.za/general/news/newsprint.php?art_id=qw997554422285B252&sf=68, accessed August 11, 2007.

74. Abdoulaye Wade, "Sénégal: conférence mondiale contre le racisme, la discrimination raciale, la xénophobie, et l'intolérance qui y est associé, intervention de maître Abdoulaye Wade, président de la république du Sénégal," World Conference Against Racism, Racial Discrimination, Xenophobia, and Related Intolerance, Durban, South Africa, September 1, 2001, http://www.un.org/WCAR/ statements/senegalF.htm, accessed August 11, 2007.

75. Ba, "Senegal's Wade Calls Slave Reparations Absurd."

76. Wade, "Sénégal."

77. Edward Ball, *Slaves in the Family* (New York: Ballantine Books, 1998), 441.

78. Ibid., 443.

Chapter 7. Reparations for Colonialism

1. Daniel Leblanc, "Mandela Tells West to Pay Colonial Debt," *Globe and Mail* (Toronto), April 9, 2002.

2. Preparatory Committee, "Report of the Regional Conference for Africa (Dakar, January 22–24, 2001)." United Nations, A/CONF.189/PC.2/8, March 27, 2001. Section B, "Recommendations," par. 3, 8.

3. English manuscript provided to the author by Dr. Appiah, entitled "Understanding Reparations: A Preliminary Reflection," p. 13. French original published as Kwame Anthony Appiah, "Comprendre les réparations: une réflexion préliminaire," *Cahiers d'études africaines* 44, no. 1–2 (2004): 25–40.

4. Jacob Ade Ajayi, "The Politics of Reparation in the Context of Globalisation," Distinguished Abiola Lecture (Washington, D.C.: African Studies Association, December 7, 2002), 3.

5. Ibid., 5.

6. Geoffrey Robertson, *Crimes Against Humanity: The Struggle for Global Justice* (New York: New Press, 1999), 150–56.

7. United Nations, "Charter of the United Nations," June 26, 1945, quotation from preamble to article 73.

8. Johannes Morsink, *The Universal Declaration of Human Rights: Origins, Drafting, and Intent* (Philadelphia: University of Pennsylvania Press, 1999), 353, fn. 11.

9. Ibid., 96–101.

10. United Nations General Assembly, "Declaration of the Granting of Independence to Colonial Countries and Peoples," United Nations, General Assembly Resolution 1514 (XV), December 14, 1960.

11. Max du Plessis, "Historical Injustices and International Law: An Exploratory Discussion of Reparations for Slavery," *Human Rights Quarterly* 25, no. 3 (2003): 657.

12. Georges Chikoti, "Statement by Dr. Georges Chikoti, Angolan Deputy Minister of Foreign Affairs," World Conference Against Racism, Racial Discrimination, Xenophobia, and Related Intolerance, Durban, South Africa, September 2, 2001, http://www.un.org/WCAR/statements/angolaE.htm, accessed August 7, 2007.

13. Preparatory Committee, "Report of the Regional Conference for Africa (Dakar, January 22–24, 2001)," 6, par. 17, 20.

14. World Conference Against Racism, Racial Discrimination, Xenophobia, and Related Intolerance, "Declaration" (2001), http://www.unhchr.ch/pdf/Durban.pdf, accessed August 7, 2007, par. 14.

15. WCAR NGO Forum, "WCAR NGO Forum Declaration," September 3, 2001, http://www.liberationafrique.org/IMG/article_PDF/article_384.pdf, accessed August 7, 2007, par. 43.

16. African American Policy Forum, "Oral Intervention at the Informal Consultation of the Preparatory Committee for the World Conference Against Racism, Racial Discrimination, Xenophobia, and Related Intolerance," Geneva, Switzerland, January 15–16, 2001, website no longer available.

17. Jacob Zuma, "Statement to the Plenary by Deputy President Jacob Zuma," World Conference Against Racism, Racial Discrimination, Xenophobia, and Related Intolerance, Durban, South Africa, September 2, 2001, http://www.un.org/WCAR/statements/sthafricaE.htm, accessed August 11, 2007.

18. Piet Konings, "The Anglophone Cameroon-Nigeria Boundary: Opportunity and Conflicts," *African Affairs* 104, no. 415 (2005): 275–301.

19. United Nations Department of Public Information, "Acknowledgement of Past, Compensation Urged by Many Leaders in Continuing Debate at Racism Conference," United Nations, September 2, 2001, http://www.un.org/WCAR/pressreleases/rd-d24.html, accessed August 7, 2007.

20. Walter Rodney, *How Europe Underdeveloped Africa* (London: Bogle-l'Ouverture Publications, 1972), 167.

21. Ibid., 171–72.

22. Ibid., 175.

23. Ibid., 176.

24. Ibid., 225.

25. Ibid., 276.

26. Rhoda Howard, *Colonialism and Underdevelopment in Ghana* (London: Croom Helm, 1978), 20, 83, 107–8, 138–39.

27. Ibid., 23, 162, 166, 171, 175.

28. Ibid., 64–66, 68, 73, 77–78.

29. Ali A. Mazrui, *Black Reparations in the Era of Globalization* (Binghamton, N.Y.: Institute of Global Cultural Studies, 2002), 105.

30. Ibid., 64.

31. David S. Landes, *The Wealth and Poverty of Nations: Why Some Are So Rich and Some So Poor* (New York: W. W. Norton, 1998), 505.

32. Ibid., 436.

33. Rodney, *How Europe Underdeveloped Africa*, 195.

34. Barrington Moore, Jr., *Social Origins of Dictatorship and Democracy: Lord and Peasant in the Making of the Modern World* (Boston: Beacon Press, 1966); Max Weber, *The Protestant Ethic and the Spirit of Capitalism* (New York: Charles Scribner's Sons, 1958).

35. Landes, *The Wealth and Poverty of Nations*, 426.

36. Ibid., 429.

37. Nathan Rosenberg and L. E. Birdzell, Jr., *How the West Grew Rich: The Economic Transformation of the Industrial World* (New York: Basic Books, 1986), 18.

38. Landes, *The Wealth and Poverty of Nations*, 431.
39. Rosenberg and Birdzell, *How the West Grew Rich*, 18.
40. Sidney L. Harring, "German Reparations to the Herero Nation: An Assertion of Herero Nationhood in the Path of Namibian Development?" *West Virginia Law Review* 104 (2001–2002): 400.
41. Mark Cocker, *Rivers of Blood, Rivers of Gold: Europe's Conquest of Indigenous Peoples* (New York: Grove Atlantic, Inc. 1998), 267–357; Jon Swan, "The Final Solution in South West Africa," *MHQ: The Quarterly Journal of Military History* 3, no. 4 (1991): 36–55.
42. Max Hamata, "Germany Apologizes for Colonial-Era Genocide of Namibia's Herero People," Associated Press, August 14, 2004; and Brigitte Weidlich, "Germany Admits 'Genocide' in Namibia, But Says No to Reparations," Agence France-Presse, August 14, 2004.
43. Heidemarie Wieczorek-Zeul (Federal Minister for Economic Cooperation and Development [of Germany]), "Speech at the Commemorations of the 100th Anniversary of the Suppression of the Herero Uprising," Okakarara, Namibia, August 14, 2004, http://www.windhuk.diplo.de/Vertretung/windhuk/en/seite_rede_bmz_engl_okakahandja.html, accessed August 11, 2007.
44. Harring, "German Reparations to the Herero Nation," 409.
45. Ibid., 406–7.
46. Ibid., 395.
47. Jeremy Sarkin, "Reparation for Past Wrongs: Using Domestic Courts Around the World, Especially the United States, to Pursue African Human Rights Claims," *International Journal of Legal Information* 32, no. 2 (2004): 453.
48. Harring, "German Reparations to the Herero Nation," 414.
49. John Torpey, *Making Whole What Has Been Smashed: On Reparations Politics* (Cambridge, Mass.: Harvard University Press, 2006), 137.
50. Harring, "German Reparations to the Herero Nation," 93, 395.
51. Warren Buford and Hugo van der Merwe, "Les réparations en Afrique australe," *Cahiers d'études africaines* 44, no.1–2 (2004): 298–305.
52. Harring, "German Reparations to the Herero Nation," 413.
53. Ibid., 415.
54. Adam Hochschild, *King Leopold's Ghost: A Story of Greed, Terror, and Heroism in Colonial Africa* (New York: Houghton Mifflin, 1999), 233.
55. Ibid., 120, 126, 149, 165.
56. Jan-Bart Gewald, "More Than Red Rubber and Figures Alone: A Critical Appraisal of the Memory of the Congo Exhibition at the Royal Museum for Central Africa, Tervuren, Belgium," *International Journal of African Historical Studies* 39, no. 3 (2006): 471–86.

Chapter 8. Neocolonialism and Globalization

1. World Conference Against Racism, Racial Discrimination, Xenophobia, and Related Intolerance, "Declaration" (2001), http://www.unhchr.ch/pdf/Durban.pdf, accessed August 7, 2007, par. 9.
2. Ibid., par. 11.
3. WCAR NGO Forum, "WCAR NGO Forum Declaration," September 3, 2001, http://www.liberationafrique.org/IMG/article_PDF/article_384.pdf, accessed August 7, 2007, par. 24.
4. Ibid., pars. 121, 123, and 124.

5. This section is drawn in part from Rhoda E. Howard-Hassmann, "An Airborne Disease: Globalization Through African Eyes," in *Unsettled Legitimacy: Political Community, Power, and Authority in a Global Era*, ed. Steven Bernstein and William Coleman (under review).

6. Jan Aart Scholte, *Globalization: An Introduction* (Basingstoke, UK: Palgrave, 2002), 44.

7. Gérard's figures are an underestimate. Africa's share of world merchandise exports in 2006 was 3 percent; its share of world merchandise imports in the same year was 2.3 percent. World Trade Organization, "Times Series Statistical Database" (2007). Sub-Saharan Africa's share of foreign direct investment in 2005 was 1.7 percent of the world total. World Bank, "World Development Indicators" (2007).

8. Joseph E. Stiglitz, *Globalization and Its Discontents* (New York: W. W. Norton, 2002), 180–81.

9. World Public Opinion: Global Public Opinion on International Affairs, "Poll of 8 African Nations," 2003–2004, http://www.worldpublicopinion.org/incl/printable_version.php?pnt=138, accessed August 11, 2007.

10. United Nations Department of Public Information, "Opening Session of Conference General Debate Focuses on Addressing Legacy of Slavery, Colonialism," Plenary RD/D/19, 2nd meeting (AM), September 1, 2001, http://www.un.org/WCAR/pressreleases/rdd19.htm, accessed August 11, 2007.

11. Ibid.

12. République du Niger, "Communication de la commission nationale des droits de l'homme et des libertés fondamentales, à la conférence mondiale contre le racisme, la discrimination raciale, la xénophobie, et l'intolérance qui y est associé," World Conference Against Racism, Racial Discrimination, Xenophobia, and Related Intolerance, Durban, South Africa, September 3, 2001, http://www.un.org/WCAR/statements/niger_hrF.htm, accessed August 7, 2007.

13. United Nations, "Sub-Commission Continues Debate on Situation of Human Rights Around the World," United Nations Sub-Commission on the Promotion and Protection of Human Rights, 53rd Session, August 1, 2001.

14. World Bank, *Global Development Finance: The Development Potential of Surging Capital Flows* (Washington, D.C.: World Bank, 2006), 194.

15. George B. N. Ayittey, *Africa Unchained: The Blueprint for Africa's Future* (New York: Palgrave Macmillan, 2004), 299.

16. Organisation for Economic Co-operation and Development. "OECD Annual Estimates of Total External Debt," 2002, http://www.oecd.org/dataoecd/54/53/31604144.xls, accessed August 11, 2007, Table 2; "Debt Outstanding at End-December 2002."

17. Nick Buxton, "Debt Cancellation and Civil Society: A Case Study of Jubilee 2000," in *Fighting for Human Rights*, ed. Paul Gready (New York: Routledge, 2004).

18. Joseph Stiglitz, "Odious Rulers, Odious Debt," *Atlantic Monthly* 292, no. 4 (2003): 39, 42, 45.

19. Jubilee 2000 South Africa, "Founding Declaration of the South African Jubilee 2000 Campaign," Cape Town, South Africa, November 5, 1998.

20. World Bank, "The HIPC Debt Initiative," http://www.worldbank.org/hipc/about/hipcbr/hipcbr.htm, accessed August 11, 2007.

21. World Bank, "Debt Relief," http://web.worldbank.org/WBSITE/EXTERNAL/NEWS/0,contentMDK:20040942~menuPK:34480~pagePK:34370~theSitePK:4607,00.html, accessed August 11, 2007.

22. World Bank, "World Bank Implements Multilateral Debt Relief Initiative," Press Release no. 2006/504/WB, June 29, 2006.
23. Buxton, "Debt Cancellation and Civil Society," 59–60.
24. World Bank, "World Bank Implements Multilateral Debt Relief Initiative."
25. International Monetary Fund and World Bank Development Committee, "Notes on the G8 Debt Relief Proposal: Assessment of Costs, Implementation Issues, and Financing Options," *International Monetary Fund and the World Bank*, DC, 2005-0023, September 21, 2005.
26. Serkan Arslanalp and Peter Henry Blair, "Policy Watch: Debt Relief," *Journal of Economic Perspectives* 20, no. 1 (2006): 213.
27. World Bank, "World Bank Development Indicators."
28. Arslanalp and Blair, "Policy Watch: Debt Relief," 218.
29. Andrew Mwaba, "Beyond HIPC: What Are the Prospects for Debt Sustainability?" *African Development Review* 17, no. 3 (2007): 547.
30. "Jubilee Still Active Two Years Later," Africa News Service, June 13, 2003.
31. Ayittey, *Africa Unchained*, 302–3.
32. "Nigeria's Debt: No Longer Unforgivable," *The Economist*, March 19, 2005, 16.
33. Africa Action, "Critique of the HIPC Initiative," June 2002, http://www.africaaction.org/action/hipc0206.htm, accessed August 11, 2007.
34. "Forgiving Their Debtors," *Wall Street Journal*, October 12, 2000.
35. Gerald Caplan, "The Conspiracy Against Africa," *Walrus Magazine*, November 2006.
36. United Nations General Assembly, "International Covenant on Economic, Social, and Cultural Rights," Resolution 2200A (XXI), December 16, 1966, entry into force January 3, 1976, articles 9, 11(1), 12(1), 13(1).
37. United Nations General Assembly, "Declaration on the Right to Development," Resolution 41/128, December 4, 1986, preamble.
38. Organization of African Unity, "African Charter on Human and Peoples' Rights," June 27, 1981.
39. International Conference on Popular Participation in the Recovery and Development Process in Africa, "African Charter for Popular Participation in Development and Transformation," United Nations, A/45/427, par. 22, August 22, 1990.
40. Organization of African Unity, "Resolution on Environment," CM/Res.281 (XIX), June 5–12, 1972.
41. World Conference Against Racism, Racial Discrimination, Xenophobia, and Related Intolerance, "Declaration," par. 19.
42. Goran Hyden, *African Politics in Comparative Perspective* (New York: Cambridge University Press, 2006), 207–10.
43. Goran Hyden, *No Shortcuts to Progress: African Development Management in Perspective* (Berkeley: University of California Press, 1983), 17–28.
44. Bonny Ibhawoh, "Structural Adjustment, Authoritarianism and Human Rights in Africa," *Comparative Studies of South Asia, Africa and the Middle East* 19, no. 1 (1999): 158–67; Macleans A. Geo-Jaja and Garth Magnum, "Structural Adjustment as an Inadvertent Enemy of Human Development in Africa," *Journal of Black Studies* 32, no. 1 (2001): 30–49.
45. Jagdish Bhagwati, *In Defense of Globalization* (New York: Oxford University Press, 2004), 88–89.
46. The following paragraphs on Ghana are drawn from Susan Dicklitch and Rhoda E. Howard-Hassmann, "Public Policy and Economic Rights in Ghana and Uganda," in *Economic Rights: Conceptual, Measurement and Policy Issues*, ed.

Shareen Hertel and Lanse Minkler (New York: Cambridge University Press, 2007), 325–44.

47. Hyden, *African Politics in Comparative Perspective*, 217.

48. Richard Sandbrook, *Closing the Circle: Democratization and Development in Africa* (London: Zed Books, 2001), 120.

49. Kojo Appiah-Kubi, "State-Owned Enterprises and Privatisation in Ghana," *Journal of Modern African Studies* 39, no. 2 (2001): 227, fn. 34.

50. Jay Oelbaum, "Populist Reform Coalitions in Sub-Saharan Africa: Ghana's Triple Alliance," *Canadian Journal of African Studies* 36, no. 2 (2002): 310–11.

51. Kwame Boafo-Arthur, "Ghana: Structural Adjustment, Democratization, and the Politics of Continuity," *African Studies Review* 42, no. 2 (1999): 51, 53.

52. United Nations Statistics Division, "United Nations Common Database," United Nations, Ghana.

53. Ibid.

54. National Reconciliation Commission [for Ghana], "Report," October 2004, vol. 1, chap. 5, 103–17, 123–55.

55. E. Gyimah-Boadi, "A Peaceful Turnover in Ghana," *Journal of Democracy* 12, no. 2 (2001): 103–117; Tim Hughes, "Ghana: Tarnished Past, Golden Future," in *South African Yearbook of International Affairs 2002/03* (Johannesburg, South Africa: Jan Smuts House, 2003).

56. E. Gyimah-Boadi and Kwabena Amoah Awuah Mensah, "Afrobarometer Paper No. 28: The Growth of Democracy in Ghana Despite Economic Dissatisfaction: A Power Alternation Bonus?" *Afrobarometer*, April 2003, xiii.

57. Amartya Sen, *Development as Freedom* (New York: Alfred A. Knopf, 1999).

58. Mwangi S. Kimenyi, *Ethnic Diversity, Liberty and the State: The African Dilemma* (Cheltenham, UK: Edward Elgar, 1997), 98.

59. Timothy Besley and Robin Burgess, "Halving Global Poverty," *Journal of Economic Perspectives* 17, no. 3 (2003): 3–22.

60. Organization of African Unity, "Constitutive Act of the African Union," July 11, 2000.

61. Ali A. Mazrui, *Black Reparations in the Era of Globalization* (Binghamton, N.Y.: Institute of Global Cultural Studies, 2002), 67–68.

62. Jeffrey D. Sachs, *The End of Poverty: Economic Possibilities for Our Time* (New York: Penguin Press, 2005), 190.

63. United Nations Department of Public Information, "Acknowledgment of Past, Compensation Urged by Many Leaders in Continuing Debate at Racism Conference," September 2, 2001, http://www.un.org/WCAR/pressreleases/rd-d24.html, accessed August 7, 2007.

64. Caplan, "The Conspiracy Against Africa," 15.

Chapter 9. Postcolonial Relations, Postcolonial Crimes

1. Jim Day, "Lawsuit Launched Against Asbestos Companies," *Mail and Guardian* (South Africa), April 18, 1997.

2. Reuters Business News, "UK Court Approves Cape Payment to S. African Miners," June 27, 2003.

3. Ann Eveleth, "New Claim Against Chemical Giant Thor," *Mail and Guardian* (South Africa), February 20, 1998.

4. "Cancer Widows Sue US Petro-Giant," *Mail and Guardian* (South Africa), September 15, 2000.

5. Gail Appleson, "Apartheid Victims Sue Citigroup, Other Banks," Reuters, June 19, 2002; John Torpey, *Making Whole What Has Been Smashed: On Reparations Politics* (Cambridge, Mass.: Harvard University Press, 2006), 147.

6. "South Africa Takes on the Giants," *Mail and Guardian* (South Africa), June 21, 2002.

7. Torpey, *Making Whole What Has Been Smashed*, 151–52.

8. Thabo Mbeki, "Mbeki: Tabling of TRC Report: Statement by President Thabo Mbeki to the National Houses of Parliament and the Nation, on the Occasion of the Tabling of the Report of the Truth and Reconciliation Commission," Office of the Presidency of South Africa, Cape Town, April 15, 2003.

9. Jędrzej George Frynas, "Social and Environmental Litigation Against Transnational Firms in Africa," *Journal of Modern African Studies* 42, no. 3 (2004): 384.

10. Amos Adeoye Idowu, "Human Rights, Environmental Degradation and Oil Multinational Companies in Nigeria: The Ogoniland Episode," *Netherlands Quarterly of Human Rights* 17, no. 2 (1999): 166–67.

11. Ibid., 171.

12. Ibid.

13. Estelle Shirbon, "Insecurity in Nigeria's Oil Delta Here to Stay," Reuters, March 23, 2006.

14. Sigrun I. Skogly, "Complexities in Human Rights Protection: Actors and Rights Involved in the Ogoni Conflict in Nigeria," *Netherlands Quarterly of Human Rights* 15, no. 1 (1997): 48.

15. Claude E. Welch, Jr., *Protecting Human Rights in Africa: Strategies and Roles of Non-Governmental Organizations* (Philadelphia: University of Pennsylvania Press, 1995), 114.

16. Ibid., 113.

17. Rotimi T. Suberu, *Federalism and Ethnic Conflict in Nigeria* (Washington, D.C.: United States Institute of Peace Press, 2001), 65. I am grateful to Boye Ejobowah for this reference.

18. Idowu, "Human Rights, Environmental Degradation and Oil Multinational Companies in Nigeria," 179.

19. David P. Forsythe, *Human Rights in International Relations*, 2nd ed. (Cambridge, UK: Cambridge University Press, 2006), 225; Mahmood Monshipouri, Claude E. Welch, Jr., and Evan T. Kennedy, "Multinational Corporations and the Ethics of Global Responsibility: Problems and Prospects," *Human Rights Quarterly* 25, no. 4 (2003): 977.

20. Hillary Bain Lindsay, "Shell Shocked: People of the Niger Delta Fight Back Against Violence and Corruption," *The Dominion: News from the Grassroots*, March 20, 2006, http://dominionpaper.ca/environment/2006/03/20/shell_shoc .html, accessed August 11, 2007.

21. Alexis Akwagyiram, "Working in a Danger Zone," BBC News, January 20, 2006.

22. "Nigerian Hostage Crisis Continues," *The Star* (South Africa), March 6, 2006.

23. Helen Vesperini, "Kidnappings in Nigeria's Oil Region More Frequent, Bolder," Agence France-Presse, January 25, 2007.

24. These details taken from various issues of BBC News and other new sources available online in 2006.

25. BBC News, "Nigeria Hostages 'in Good Health,'" January 17, 2006; BBC News, "Shell Told to Pay Nigeria's Ijaw," February 24, 2006; Dulue Mbachu, "Shell Misses Nigeria Deadline for Payment," Associated Press, May 22, 2006.

26. Elizabeth Kusta, "Oil Prices Jump Nearly $1.50 After Militant Violence in Nigeria," Associated Press, February 20, 2006.

27. Transparency International, "Corruption Perceptions Index 2006," Berlin, Germany, 2006.

28. Welch, *Protecting Human Rights in Africa*, 114.

29. Pini Jason, "S-East/S-South Professionals and the N-Delta crisis," *Vanguard*, March 7, 2006, http://odili.net/news/source/2006/mar/7/331.html, accessed August 12, 2007.

30. Frynas, "Social and Environmental Litigation Against Transnational Firms in Africa," 371, 375–76.

31. Okey Onwuchekwa, "N/Delta: Militants Threaten Attack on Mobil," *Daily Champion* (Nigeria), April 11, 2006.

32. Energy Information Administration, "Crude Oil and Total Petroleum Imports: Top 15 Countries," *Energy Information Administration: Official Energy Statistics from the U.S. Government*, http://www.eia.doe.gov/pub/oil_gas/petroleum/data_publications/company_level_imports/current/import.html.

33. John Donnelly, "Burdens of Oil Weigh on Nigerians," *Boston Globe*, October 3, 2005.

34. Sandra T. Barnes, "Global Flows: Terror, Oil & Strategic Philanthropy," *Review of African Political Economy* 32, no. 104–5 (2005): 235–52.

35. World Conference Against Racism, Racial Discrimination, Xenophobia, and Related Intolerance, "Declaration," 2001, http://www.unhchr.ch/pdf/Durban.pdf, accessed August 7, 2007, par. 215.

36. Jeremy Sarkin, "Reparation for Past Wrongs: Using Domestic Courts Around the World, Especially the United States, to Pursue African Human Rights Claims," *International Journal of Legal Information* 32, no. 2 (2004): 435.

37. Forsythe, *Human Rights in International Relations*, 238–44; Ralph G. Steinhardt, "Corporate Responsibility and the International Law of Human Rights: The New *Lex Mercatoria*," in *Non-State Actors and Human Rights*, ed. Philip Alston (New York: Oxford University Press, 2005), 180–87.

38. Michael Freeman, *Human Rights: An Interdisciplinary Approach* (Cambridge, UK: Polity Press, 2002), 159.

39. Rory Sullivan, "NGO Influence on the Human Rights Performance of Companies," *Netherlands Quarterly of Human Rights* 24, no. 3 (2006): 418.

40. Debora L. Spar, "The Spotlight and the Bottom Line: How Multinationals Export Human Rights," *Foreign Affairs* (March–April 1998): 11.

41. Ali Mazrui, *Black Reparations in the Era of Globalization* (Binghamton, N.Y.: Institute of Global Cultural Studies, 2002), 69–70.

42. World Conference Against Racism, Racial Discrimination, Xenophobia, and Related Intolerance Preparatory Committee, "Report of the Regional Conference for Africa," United Nations, January 22–24, 2001, A/CONF.189/PC.2/8, http://www.unhchr.ch/Huridocda/Huridoca.nsf/A.CONF.189.PC.2/8.En?Opendocument, par. 7, accessed August 7, 2007.

43. James H. Mittelman and Robert Johnston, "The Globalization of Organized Crime, the Courtesan State, and the Corruption of Civil Society," *Global Governance* 5, no. 1 (1999): 106.

44. Robert I. Rotberg, "Failed States, Collapsed States, Weak States: Causes and Indicators," in *State Failure and State Weakness in a Time of Terror*, ed. Robert I. Rotberg (Cambridge, Mass. and Washington, D.C.: World Peace Foundation and Brookings Institute Press, 2003).

45. Thomas Pogge, *World Poverty and Human Rights: Cosmopolitan Responsibilities and Reforms* (Malden, Mass.: Blackwell Publishing, 2002), 165.
46. Ian Taylor, "Conflict in Central Africa: Clandestine Networks and Regional/Global Configurations," *Review of African Political Economy* 30, no. 95 (2003): 48.
47. J. Anyu Ndumbe and Babalola Cole, "The Illicit Diamond Trade, Civil Conflicts, and Terrorism in Africa," *Mediterranean Quarterly* 16, no. 2 (2005): 61.
48. Rasna Warah, "Illicit Diamonds: Africa's Curse," *UN Chronicle*, September 2004.
49. Paul S. Orogun, "'Blood Diamonds' and Africa's Armed Conflicts in the Post-Cold War Era," *World Affairs* 166, no. 3 (2004): 154.
50. Milan Veseley, "Shadow of the Gun: Who Funds Africa's Wars?" *African Business* (December 1999): 9.
51. Paul S. Orogun, "Plunder, Predation and Profiteering: The Political Economy of Armed Conflicts and Economic Violence in Modern Africa," *Perspectives on Global Development and Technology* 2, no. 2 (2003): 289, 292, 306.
52. Orogun, "Plunder, Predation and Profiteering," 301.
53. Ian Smillie, "Getting to the Heart of the Matter: Sierra Leone, Diamonds, and Human Security," *Social Justice* 27, no. 4 (2000): 24–31.
54. "The Kimberley Process at Risk," *Global Witness*, November 2006.
55. Chris Allen, "Africa & the Drugs Trade," *Review of African Political Economy* 26, no. 79 (1999): 5–11.
56. Milan Veseley, "Cocaine Kings Target Kenya," *African Business*, February 1, 2005.
57. Allen, "Africa & the Drugs Trade," 9.
58. Forsythe, *Human Rights in International Relations*, 237.
59. The following material on Sudan and Zimbabwe is drawn in part from Rhoda E. Howard-Hassmann, "Genocide and State-Induced Famine: Global Ethics and Western Responsibility for Mass Atrocities in Africa," in *Globalization and Political Ethics*, ed. Richard B. Day and Joseph Masciulli (Leiden-Boston: Brill, 2007).
60. Douglas Anglin, "Rwanda Revisited: Search for the Truth," *International Journal* 56, no. 1 (2000–2001): 152.
61. Justice and Equality Movement, "Proposal by the Justice and Equality Movement (JEM) for Peace in Sudan in General and Darfur in Particular," *Justice and Equality Movement*, n.d.; Sudan Liberation Movement and Sudan Liberation Army (SLM/SLA), "Political Declaration," March 13, 2003, http://www.sudan.net/news/press/postedr/214.shtml, accessed August 12, 2007.
62. John Ryle, "Disaster in Darfur," *New York Review of Books* 51, no. 13 (2004): 55–59; Tim Judah, "The Stakes in Darfur," *New York Review of Books* 52, no. 1 (2005): 12–16.
63. Ken Silverstein, "Official Pariah Sudan Valuable to America's War on Terrorism," *Los Angeles Times*, April 29, 2005.
64. George W. Bush, "Remarks by the President in Address to the United Nations General Assembly," September 21, 2004, http://www.state.gov/p/io/rls/rm/2004/36350.htm, accessed August 12, 2007.
65. United Nations Security Council, "Resolution 1556," July 30, 2004, articles 7 and 8, http://www.un.org/Docs/journal/asp/ws.asp?m=S/RES/1556(2004); United Nations Security Council, "Resolution 1591," March 29, 2005, http://www.un.org/Docs/journal/asp/ws.asp?m=S/RES/1591(2005); United Nations Security Council, "Resolution 1593," March 31, 2005, http://www.un.org/Docs/journal/asp/ws.asp?m=S/RES/1593 (2005), accessed August 12, 2007.

66. Nick Grono, "Briefing Darfur: The International Community's Failure to Protect," *African Affairs* 105, no. 421 (2006): 626.

67. Colum Lynch, "Sudan Rejects Request to Allow U.N. Troops," *Washington Post*, September 20, 2006.

68. John Sullivan, "U.N. Security Council Approves Joint Force of Up to 26,000 Peacekeepers for Darfur," *New York Times*, August 1, 2007.

69. "War in Sudan: Don't Forget It," *The Economist*, May 15, 2004; United Nations News Centre, "14 Elected to UN Human Rights Commission," United Nations News Centre, http://www.un.org/apps/news/story.asp?NewsID=10634&Cr=commission&Cr1=rights, accessed August 12, 2007.

70. Mona Salem, "Darfur Mini-Summit Aims to Ward Off UN Sanctions with African Solution," Agence France-Presse, October 18, 2004.

71. Chris McGreal, "Darfur Violence Wrecks Sudan's Attempt to Take AU Leadership," *Guardian* (London), January 30, 2007; Moyiga Nduru, "Sudan Loses AU Chair to Ghana," Inter Press Service, January 29, 2007.

72. "A New Scramble: China's Business Links with Africa," *The Economist*, November 27, 2004.

73. Ryle, "Disaster in Darfur," 58.

74. International Panel of Eminent Persons, "Rwanda: The Preventable Genocide," Organization for African Unity, July 7, 2000. Ch. 16, par. 47; ch. 17, par. 21; and ch. 24, A. I. 12.

75. Samantha Power, "How to Kill a Country," *The Atlantic* 292, no. 5 (2003).

76. "Zimbabwe: Not Eligible: The Politicization of Food in Zimbabwe," *Human Rights Watch* 15, no. 17 (A) (2003): 18.

77. Ibid., 1.

78. "Zimbabwe: Food Used as Political Weapon," *Human Rights Watch*, October 24, 2003, http://www.hrw.org/press/2003/10/zimbabwe102403.htm, accessed August 13, 2007.

79. Regional Bureau for Southern Africa, "Projected Food Needs for 2007," *World Food Programme* (2006).

80. Michael Wines, "In Zimbabwe, Homeless Belie Leader's Claims," *New York Times*, November 12, 2005.

81. Deborah Potts, "Restoring Order: Operation Murambatsvina and the Urban Crisis in Zimbabwe," *Journal of Southern Africa Studies* 12, no. 2 (2006): 276.

82. Kitsepile Nyathi, "Zimbabwe: Refugee Crisis as Citizens Rush to Leave Their Country," *The Nation* (Kenya), March 22, 2007.

83. Neil H. Thomas, "Land Reform in Zimbabwe," *Third World Quarterly* 24, no. 4 (2003): 696–97.

84. Power, "How to Kill a Country," 3.

85. Ibid.

86. Gift Phiri, "Mugabe Faces Class Action Lawsuit over Massacres," *Zimbabwe Independent*, November 3, 2006, http://www.newzimbabwe.com/pages/gukgenocide.1111607.html, accessed August 12, 2007. For background, see Hevina S. Dashwood and Cranford Pratt, "Leadership, Participation and Conflict Management: Zimbabwe and Tanzania," in *Civil Wars in Africa: Roots and Resolutions*, ed. Taisir M. Ali and Robert O. Matthews (Montréal, Canada: McGill-Queen's University Press, 1999).

87. Katawala Sunder, "Zimbabwe and the Commonwealth," *Guardian Unlimited*, March 20, 2002, http://www.guardian.co.uk/theissues/article/0,6512,631253,00.html, accessed August 14, 2007.

88. Richard Dowden, "Zimbabwe's Commonwealth Suspension Extended," *The Independent*, London, December 8, 2003.

89. BBC News, "Zimbabwe Quits Commonwealth," December 8, 2003.

90. United Kingdom Parliament, "Zimbabwe," Column 825W, House of Commons Hansard, Written Answers, March 2, 2004.

91. Fanuel Jongwe, "Pressure Mounts on Mugabe with Blair Sanctions Call," Agence France-Presse, March 21, 2007.

92. Ian Phimister and Brian Raftopoulos, "Mugabe, Mbeki and the Politics of Anti-Imperialism," *Review of African Political Economy* 31, no. 101 (2004): 385–400.

93. Ian Taylor and Paul Williams, "The Limits of Engagement: British Foreign Policy and the Crisis in Zimbabwe," *International Affairs* 78, no. 3 (2002): 558.

94. Padraig O'Malley, "Zimbabwe: South Africa's Failure," *International Herald Tribune*, April 2, 2005.

95. BBC News, "Africa Rejects Action on Zimbabwe," June 24, 2005.

96. IRIN, "AU Suspends Report on Zimbabwe Rights Abuses," July 8, 2006.

97. Associated Press, "African Union Chairman Calls Situation in Zimbabwe 'Embarrassing,'" March 15, 2007.

98. Agence France-Presse, "African Union Denounces EU 'Double Standards' over Zimbabwe," March 21, 2007.

99. Southern African Development Community, "2007 Extra-ordinary SADC Summit of Heads of State and Government," Communiqué, Dar-es-Salaam, Tanzania, March 28–29, 2007.

100. BBC News, "Zimbabwe to Chair Major UN Body," May 12, 2007.

101. Deutsche Presse-Agentur, "Zimbabwe Chair of UN Green Commission 'Destroyed Seized Farm,'" May 13, 2007.

102. Bruce Baker, "Twilight of Impunity for Africa's Presidential Criminals," *Third World Quarterly* 25, no. 8 (2004): 1496.

103. Joshua Eisenman and Joshua Kurlantzick, "China's Africa Strategy," *Current History*, May (2006): 219.

104. Geoffrey York, "China Keeps Bad Company," *Globe and Mail*, March 4, 2006.

105. Max du Plessis, "The Creation of the ICC: Implications for Africa's Despots, Crackpots and Hotspots," *African Security Review* 12, no. 4 (2003): 7.

106. International Criminal Court, "The States Parties to the Rome Statute: African States," http://www.icc-cpi.int/php/show.php?page=region&id=3, accessed August 14, 2007.

107. International Criminal Court, "Rome Statute of the International Criminal Court," 1998, http://www.un.org/law/icc/statute/99_corr/cstatute.htm, accessed August 7, 2007. Article 7, 1(d) and (k).

108. Paul Ocheje, "Refocusing International Law on the Quest for Accountability in Africa: The Case Against the 'Other' Impunity," *Leiden Journal of International Law* 15, no. 4 (2002): 749–79.

109. Rachel Murray, *Human Rights in Africa: From the OAU to the African Union* (Cambridge, UK: Cambridge University Press, 2004), 246.

110. International Criminal Court, "Warrant of Arrest Unsealed Against Five LRA Commanders," October 14, 2005, http://www.icc-cpi.int/pressrelease_details&id=114&l=en.html, accessed August 14, 2007.

111. International Criminal Court, "Pre-Trial Chamber I Commits Thomas Lubanga Dyilo for Trial," January 29, 2007, http://www.icc-cpi.int/pressrelease_details&id=220&l=en.html, accessed August 14, 2007.

Chapter 10. Remedies: Acknowledgment and Apologies

1. This chapter draws in part from Rhoda E. Howard-Hassmann and Anthony Peter Lombardo, "Words Require Action: African Elite Opinion About Apologies from the West," in *The Age of Apology: Facing Up to the Past*, ed. Mark Gibney, Rhoda E. Howard-Hassmann, Jean-Mark Coicaud, and Niklaus Steiner (Philadelphia: University of Pennsylvania Press, 2007), 216–28.

2. Erving Goffman, *Relations in Public: Microstudies of the Social Order* (New York: Basic Books, 1971), 108, 113–14.

3. Janna Thompson, "Apology, Justice, and Respect: A Critical Defense of Political Apology," in *The Age of Apology: Facing Up to the Past*, ed. Mark Gibney, Rhoda E. Howard-Hassmann, Jean-Marc Coicaud, and Niklaus Steiner (Philadelphia: University of Pennsylvania Press, 2007), 32.

4. W. I. Thomas and D. S. Thomas, *The Child in America: Behavior Problems and Programs* (New York: Johnson Reprint Corporation, 1970 [1928]), 572.

5. Trudy Govier and Wilhelm Verwoerd, "The Practice of Public Apologies: A Qualified Defence," Unpublished manuscript, n.d., p. 1. Italics in original.

6. Elazar Barkan, "Restitution and Amending Historical Injustices in International Morality," in *Politics and the Past: On Repairing Historical Injustices*, ed. John Torpey (Lanham, Md.: Rowman and Littlefield, 2003), 98.

7. Michael Cunningham, "Saying Sorry: The Politics of Apology," *Political Quarterly* 70, no. 3 (1999): 291.

8. Nicholas Tavuchis, *Mea Culpa: A Sociology of Apology and Reconciliation* (Stanford, Calif.: Stanford University Press, 1991), 22.

9. Martha Minow, *Between Vengeance and Forgiveness: Facing History After Genocide and Mass Violence* (Boston: Beacon Press, 1998), 116.

10. Elazar Barkan, *The Guilt of Nations: Restitution and Negotiating Historical Injustices* (New York: W. W. Norton, 2000), 323.

11. Tavuchis, *Mea Culpa*, 48.

12. Andrew Rigby, *Justice and Reconciliation: After the Violence* (Boulder, Colo.: Lynne Rienner, 2001), 188.

13. BBC News, "Queen's Regret over Boer War," November 10, 1999.

14. Ibid.

15. BBC News, "Xhosa Demand Apology from Queen," November 8, 1999.

16. Paul Coslett, "Liverpool's Slavery Apology," BBC News, February 15, 2007.

17. Associated Press, "Mayor Apologizes for London's Role in Slave Trade," March 21, 2007.

18. Amelia Hill, "City Agonises over Slavery Apology," *The Observer*, May 7, 2006.

19. Kim Sengupta, "Mandela Boycotts Bristol's Slavery Commemoration," *The Independent* (London), March 25, 2007.

20. Tony Blair, "Prime Minister's Article for the New Nation Newspaper," 10 Downing Street, November 27, 2006, http://www.number10.gov.uk/output/Page10487.asp, accessed August 15, 2007.

21. BBC News, "Blair 'Sorrow' over Slave Trade," November 27, 2006.

22. Tony Blair, "PM Tony Blair's Bicentenary Speech for Elmina Castle, Ghana," 10 Downing Street, March 25, 2007, http://www.number-10.gov.uk/output/Page11342.asp, accessed August 15, 2007.

23. Deutsche Presse-Agentur, "European Church Leaders Ask for Forgiveness in Zimbabwe: Report," September 4, 2006.

24. Mavis Makuni, "Apology No Cure-All for Africa's Ills," *Financial Gazette* (Harare, Zimbabwe), September 13, 2006.

25. Church of England, General Synod, February 2006 Group of Sessions, "Bicentenary of the Act for the Abolition of the Slave Trade," Motion 801, February 8, 2006.
26. Stephen Bates, "Church Apologises for Benefiting from Slave Trade," *Guardian* (London), February 9, 2006.
27. Ibid.
28. Rowan Williams, "Archbishop's Sermon Given at the Service to Commemorate the 200th Anniversary of the Abolition of the Slave Trade," Archbishop of Canterbury, Westminster Abbey, March 27, 2007, http://www.archbishopofcanterbury.org/sermons_speeches/ 070327.htm, accessed August 15, 2007.
29. Bill Clinton, "Remarks by the President to the Community of Kisowera School Mukuno, Uganda," White House press release, March 24, 1998, http://clinton4.nara.gov/Africa/19980324-3374.html, accessed August 15, 2007.
30. George W. Bush, "President Bush Speaks at Gorée Island in Senegal," White House press release, July 8, 2003, http://www.whitehouse.gov/news/releases/2003/07/print/20030708-1.html, accessed August 15, 2007.
31. BBC News, "Gorée: The Slave Island," July 8, 2003.
32. Anthony Gifford, "Slavery: Legacy," *Hansard: Debate Initiated by Lord Gifford, QC, in the House of Lords of the British Parliament*, March 14, 1996, http://www.arm.arc.co.uk/LordsHansard.html, accessed August 12, 2007.
33. Alioune Ndiaye, "Intervention sur le quatrième et cinqième points de l'ordre du jour présentée par Alioune Ndiaye, magistrat, secrétaire permanent du comité sénégalais des droits de l'homme," World Conference Against Racism, Racial Discrimination, Xenophobia, and Related Intolerance, Durban, South Africa, September 5, 2001, http://www.un.org/WCAR/statements/sene_hrF.htm, accessed August 15, 2007.
34. Ralph A. Austen, "The Slave Trade and History and Memory: Confrontations of Slaving Voyage Documents and Communal Traditions," *William and Mary Quarterly* 58, no. 1 (2001).
35. Philip Curtin, "Gorée and the Slave Trade," *H-Net*, July 31, 1995, http://www.h-net.org/~africa/threads/goree.html, accessed August 15, 2007.
36. Emmanuel de Roux, "Le mythe de la Maison des esclaves qui résiste à la réalité," *Le Monde*, December 27, 1996, http://www.crdp.ac-martinique.fr/ressources/caraibe/histoiregeo/didactique/ali_shandora/mythe.htm, accessed August 15, 2007.
37. William B. Cohen, "The Sudden Memory of Torture: The Algerian War in French Discourse, 2000–2001," *French Politics, Culture & Society* 19, no. 3 (2001): 82–94.
38. BBC News, "Chirac Rejects 'Torture Apology,'" December 5, 2000.
39. Elaine Ganley, "French General Insists 'Everybody Knew' of Torture During Algerian War," Associated Press, May 7, 2001.
40. Associated Press, "French Government Sanctions Algerian War General for Torture Remarks," June 6, 2001.
41. Cohen, "The Sudden Memory of Torture," 90.
42. Robert Graham, "France Is Still Haunted by Its War in Algeria," *Financial Times* (London) November 3, 2004.
43. Adam Schatz, "The Torture of Algiers," *New York Review of Books* 49, no. 18 (2002): 53–57.
44. Hugh Schofield, "Colonial Abuses Haunt France," BBC News, May 16, 2005.
45. Ibid.

46. Agence France-Presse, "French Minister Pleads for an End to Dispute with Algeria over Past," November 13, 2006.
47. Ibid.
48. BBC News, "Belgian Apology to Rwanda," April 7, 2000.
49. BBC News, "Lumumba's Son Hails Belgian Apology," February 6, 2002.
50. Chambre de Représentants (Belgium), "Parliamentary Committee of Enquiry in Charge of Determining the Exact Circumstances of the Assassination of Patrice Lumumba and the Possible Involvement of Belgian Politicians: Summary of the Activities, Experts' Report and Full Conclusions," 2001.
51. BBC News, "Lumumba's Son Hails Belgian Apology."
52. Bill Clinton, "Remarks by the President to Genocide Survivors, Assistance Workers, and U.S. and Rwanda Government Officials," White House press release, March 25, 1998, http://clinton2.nara.gov/Africa/19980325-16872.html, accessed August 15, 2007.
53. Ibid.
54. Samantha Power, *"A Problem from Hell": America and the Age of Genocide* (New York: Basic Books, 2002), 329–89.
55. Warren Hoge, "Annan, at Rwanda Memorial, Admits U.N. Blame," *New York Times*, March 27, 2004.
56. Dudley Thompson, "The Debt Has Not Been Paid: The Accounts Have Not Been Settled," *African Studies Quarterly* 2, no. 4 (1999): 4.
57. Cunningham, "Saying Sorry: The Politics of Apology," 288.
58. Interview with Jacob Ade Ajayi, December 6, 2002.
59. Graham Dodds, "Political Apologies and Public Discourse: Conversation and Community in the Twenty-first Century," in *Public Discourse in America*, ed. Judith Rodin and Stephen P. Steinberg (Philadelphia: University of Pennsylvania Press, 2003), 141–43; Nava Löwenheim, "Asking Forgiveness for Wrongdoing in International Relations," working paper, website on Political Apologies and Reparations, Wilfrid Laurier University, Waterloo, Canada, 2007, http://political-apologies.wlu.ca/documents/working/Lowenheim_Nava, accessed August 7, 2007.
60. Randy Boyagoda, *Governor of the Northern Province: A Novel* (Toronto, Canada: Viking, 2006), 230.
61. Aaran Lazare, *On Apology* (New York: Oxford University Press, 2004), 203.
62. Ibid., 48.
63. Ibid.
64. Tavuchis, *Mea Culpa*, 31.
65. Marc Bossuyt and Stef Vandeginste, "The Issue of Reparation for Slavery and Colonialism and the Durban World Conference Against Racism," *Human Rights Law Journal* 22, no. 9–12 (2001): 349.
66. Christopher N. Camponovo, "Disaster in Durban: The United Nations World Conference Against Racism, Racial Discrimination, Xenophobia, and Related Intolerance," *George Washington International Law Review* 34, no. 4 (2003): 699.
67. World Conference Against Racism, Racial Discrimination, Xenophobia, and Related Intolerance, "Declaration," http://www.unhchr.ch/pdf/Durban.pdf, accessed August 7, 2007, pars. 100, 101.

Chapter 11. Remedies: A Truth Commission for Africa?

1. This chapter is a revised version of Rhoda E. Howard-Hassmann, "A Truth Commission for Africa?" *International Journal* 55, no. 4 (2005): 999–1016.

2. Priscilla B. Hayner, *Unspeakable Truths: Confronting State Terror and Atrocity* (New York: Routledge Press, 2001), 17.
3. Denis Sassou Nguesso, "Allocution de son excellénce monsieur Denis Sassou Nguesso, président de la République du Congo," World Conference Against Racism, Racial Discrimination, Xenophobia, and Related Intolerance, Durban, South Africa, September 1, 2001, http://www.un.org/WCAR/statements/congoF.htm, accessed August 15, 2007.
4. World Conference Against Racism, Racial Discrimination, Xenophobia, and Related Intolerance, "Declaration," 2001, http://www.unhchr.ch/pdf/Durban.pdf, accessed August 7, 2007, pars. 98, 106.
5. Human Rights Watch, "An Approach to Reparations," July 19, 2001, http://www.hrw.org/campaigns/race/reparations.pdf, accessed August 15, 2007.
6. United Nations Sub-Commission on the Promotion and Protection of Human Rights, "Recognition of Responsibility and Reparation for Massive and Flagrant Violations of Human Rights Which Constitute Crimes Against Humanity and Which Took Place During the Period of Slavery, of Colonialism and Wars of Conquest," United Nations High Commission for Human Rights, E/CN.4/Sub.2/2001/L/11, August 6, 2001.
7. Associated Press, "Four Men Convicted of Bombing U.S. Embassies in Africa," October 18, 2001.
8. Ali A. Mazrui, *Black Reparations in the Era of Globalization* (Binghamton, N.Y.: Institute of Global Cultural Studies, 2002), 124.
9. Mark Gibney, Katarina Tomasevski, and Jens Vedsted-Hansen, "Transnational State Responsibility for Violations of Human Rights," *Harvard Human Rights Journal* 12 (1999): 267–95.
10. African Union, "African (Banjul) Charter on Human and Peoples' Rights," adopted June 27, 1981, OAU Doc. CAB/LEG/67/3 rev. 5, 21 I.L.M. 58 (1982), entered into force October 21, 1986.
11. Mazrui, *Black Reparations in the Era of Globalization*, 62.
12. Advisory Council on International Affairs, "The World Conference Against Racism and the Right to Reparation," AIV report no. 22, 2001, http://www .aiv-advice.nl/ContentSuite/upload/aiv/doc/nr22eng(1).pdf, accessed August 15, 2007.
13. United Nations Department of Public Information, "Acknowledgment of Past, Compensation Urged by Many Leaders in Continuing Debate at Racism Conference," United Nations, September 2, 2001, http://www.un.org/WCAR/pressreleases/rd-d24.html, accessed August 7, 2007.
14. Anna Diamantopolou, "European Commissioner Responsible for Employment and Social Affairs Address to ACP Ambassadors," ACP Ambassadors' meeting, Brussels, June 21, 2001, http://europa.eu/rapid/pressReleasesAction.do?reference=SPEECH/01/339&format=HTML&aged=1&language=EN&guiLanguage=en, accessed August 15, 2007.
15. Alex Boraine, *A Country Unmasked* (New York: Oxford University Press, 2000), 288–91.
16. Audrey R. Chapman and Patrick Ball, "The Truth of Truth Commissions: Comparative Lessons from Haiti, South Africa, and Guatemala," *Human Rights Quarterly* 23, no. 1 (2001): 42.
17. "Truth and Reconciliation Commission of South Africa Report," 1999, 114, quoted in Chapman and Ball, "The Truth of Truth Commissions," 11.
18. Mazal Library: A Holocaust Resource, "Nuremberg Military Tribunal," http://www.mazal.org/archive/nmt/09/NMT09-C001.htm, accessed August 15, 2007.

19. Theodor van Boven, "United Nations Strategies to Combat Racism and Racial Discrimination: Past Experiences and Present Perspectives," United Nations Economic and Social Council, E/CN.4/1999/WG.1/BP.7, February 26, 1999.

20. Arthur Jay Klinghoffer and Judith Apter Klinghoffer, *International Citizens' Tribunals: Mobilizing Public Opinion to Advance Human Rights* (New York: Palgrave, 2002), 5.

21. Juan E. Mendez, "Review of *A Miracle, a Universe: Settling Accounts with Torturers* by Lawrence Weschler," *New York Law School Journal of Human Rights* 8, (1991): 583, quoting Professor Thomas Nagel of New York University.

22. Klinghoffer and Klinghoffer, *International Citizens' Tribunals*, 7–8, 103–62.

23. International Citizens' Tribunal for Sudan, "Indictment." Case Number ICT-1, The Prosecutor Against Omar Hasan Ahmad Al-Bashir, President of the Government of Sudan, 2006, http://www.judgmentongenocide.com/images/darfur_indictment.pdf, accessed August 15, 2007.

24. Jim Doyle, "Law Professor Has Leading Role in Mock Trial: She Will Prosecute Sudan's President for Genocide," *San Francisco Chronicle*, November 10, 2006.

25. International Citizens' Tribunal for Sudan, "Judgment," Case Number ICT-1, The Prosecutor Against Omar Hasan Ahmad Al-Bashir, President of the Government of Sudan, November 13, 2006, http:/www.judgmentongenocide.com/judgment.html, accessed August 15, 2007.

26. International Criminal Court, "Prosecutor Opening Remarks," ICC-OTP-20070227-208-En, February 27, 2007, http://www.icc-cpi.int/press/pressreleases/228.html, accessed August 15, 2007.

27. International Citizens' Tribunal for Sudan, "Judgment."

28. Rhoda E. Howard, *Human Rights in Commonwealth Africa* (Totowa, N.J.: Rowman and Littlefield, 1986), 172–77.

29. Hilary McDonald Beckles, "Slave Voyages: The Transatlantic Trade in Enslaved Africans," UNESCO, ED-2002/WS/37, 2002.

30. Jacob Ade Ajayi, "The Politics of Reparation in the Context of Globalisation," Distinguished Abiola Lecture, African Studies Association, Washington, D.C., December 7, 2002, 12–13. Printed in French as Jacob Ade Ajayi, "La politique de réparation dans le contexte de la mondialisation," *Cahiers d'études africaines* 173-74 (2004): 41–63.

31. Martha Minow, *Between Vengeance and Forgiveness: Facing History After Genocide and Mass Violence* (Boston: Beacon Press, 1998), 79.

32. Ajayi, "The Politics of Reparation in the Context of Globalisation," 4.

Chapter 12. Remedies: Economic Rights and Universal Obligations

1. United Nations Department of Public Information, "Opening Session of Conference General Debate Focuses on Addressing Legacy of Slavery, Colonialism," United Nations, Plenary RD/D/19, 2nd meeting (AM), September 1, 2001, http://www.un.org/WCAR/pressreleases/rdd19.htm, accessed August 11, 2007.

2. Rhoda E. Howard, "The 'Full-Belly' Thesis: Should Economic Rights Take Priority over Civil and Political Rights? Evidence from Sub-Saharan Africa," *Human Rights Quarterly* 5, no. 4 (1983): 467–90.

3. Trudy Govier, "Trust and Testimony: Nine Arguments on Testimonial Knowledge," *International Journal of Moral and Social Studies* 8, no. 1 (1993): 31. Italics in original.

4. Rhoda E. Howard, *Human Rights and the Search for Community* (Boulder, Colo.: Westview, 1995).
5. United Nations General Assembly, "Declaration on the Right to Development," Res. 41/128, December 4, 1986.
6. Thomas Pogge, *World Poverty and Human Rights: Cosmopolitan Responsibilities and Reforms* (Malden, Mass.: Blackwell Publishing, 2002), 24.
7. Daniel Jonah Goldhagen, *Hitler's Willing Executioners: Ordinary Germans and the Holocaust* (New York: Vintage Books, 1997).
8. Tony Blair, "Prime Minister's Remarks at the Launch of the Commission for Africa Report," 10 Downing Street, March 11, 2005, http://www.number-10.gov.uk/output/Page7314.asp, accessed August 15, 2007.
9. Kwasi Wiredu, *Cultural Universals and Particulars: An African Perspective* (Bloomington: Indiana University Press, 1996), 163–64.
10. Henry Shue, *Basic Rights: Subsistence, Affluence and U.S. Foreign Policy* (Princeton, N.J.: Princeton University Press, 1980), 52.
11. Edward O. Wilson, *On Human Nature* (New York: Bantam Books, 1978).
12. Charles Jones, *Global Justice: Defending Cosmopolitanism* (Oxford, UK: Oxford University Press, 1999), 112, passim.
13. Brian Orend, *Human Rights: Concept and Context* (Peterborough, Canada: Broadview Press, 2002), 123.
14. Rhoda E. Howard-Hassmann, *Compassionate Canadians: Civic Leaders Discuss Human Rights* (Toronto, Canada: University of Toronto Press, 2003), 200–214.
15. World Bank, "World Bank Development Indicators," 2007.
16. Karl Jaspers, cited in John Torpey, "Modes of Repair: Reparations and Citizenship at the Dawn of the New Millennium," in *Political Power and Social Theory*, vol. 18, ed. Diane E. Davis (Oxford, UK: Jai Press, 2007), 210.
17. Abdullahi Ahmed An-Na'im, *Toward an Islamic Reformation: Civil Liberties, Human Rights and International Law* (Syracuse, N.Y.: Syracuse University Press, 1990), 74.
18. Immanuel Kant, "Grounding for the Metaphysics of Morals," in *Moral Issues in Global Perspective*, ed. Christine Koggel (Peterborough, Canada: Broadview Press, 1999), 496.
19. Helen Fein, *Accounting for Genocide: National Responses and Jewish Victimization During the Holocaust* (Chicago: University of Chicago Press, 1979), 4.
20. Herbert Hirsch, *Genocide and the Politics of Memory: Studying Death to Preserve Life* (Chapel Hill: University of North Carolina Press, 1995), 151.
21. Mishna, "Pirkei Avot (Ethics of the Fathers)." Chapter 1, par. 14. I am grateful to Adele Reinhartz for this reference.
22. Pogge, *World Poverty and Human Rights*, 2.
23. Ibid., 205, 254, fn. 332.
24. Ibid., 176.
25. Richard Vernon, "Against Restitution," *Political Studies* 51, no. 3 (2003): 552.
26. Gloria Jacques, "Orphans of the AIDS Pandemic: The Sub-Saharan Africa Experience," in *AIDS and Development in Africa: A Social Science Perspective*, ed. Kempe Ronald Hope, Sr. (Binghamton, N.Y.: The Haworth Press, 1999) 93–108.
27. United Nations General Assembly, "International Covenant on Economic, Social and Cultural Rights," Resolution 2200A (XXI), December 16, 1966, Article 2(1).
28. Robert Calderisi, *The Trouble with Africa: Why Foreign Aid Isn't Working* (New York: Palgrave Macmillan, 2006), 218.

29. Kent Albert Jones, *Who's Afraid of the WTO?* (New York: Oxford University Press, 2004).
30. Jeffrey D. Sachs, *The End of Poverty: Economic Possibilities for Our Time* (New York: Penguin Press, 2005), 282.
31. Jagdish Natwarlal Bhagwati, *In Defense of Globalization* (New York: Oxford University Press, 2004), 53–55.
32. World Bank, "World Development Indicators," 2007.
33. Amartya Sen, *Development as Freedom* (New York: Alfred A. Knopf, 1999).
34. Bhagwati, *In Defense of Globalization*, 223.
35. Christopher Clapham, *Africa and the International System* (Cambridge, UK: Cambridge University Press, 1996), 142–50.

Bibliography

Abiola, Bashorun M. K. O. "Why Reparations?" *West Africa* (June 1–7, 1992): 910.

Abrahamsen, Rita. "A Breeding Ground for Terrorists? Africa & Britain's 'War on Terrorism.' " *Review of African Political Economy* 31, no. 102 (2004): 677–84.

"An Accurate Account of the Slave Trade." In *Slavers and Privateers: Liverpool Packet No. 5, Collections of Local History Materials*, ed. Fritz Spiegl. Liverpool, UK: Scouse Press, n.d.

Aceves, William J. "Affirming the Law of Nations in U.S. Courts: An Overview of Transnational Law Litigation." *The Federal Lawyer* 49, no. 5 (2002): 33–39.

Advisory Council on International Affairs. "The World Conference Against Racism and the Right to Reparation." AIV Report No. 22, 2001, http://www.aiv-advice.nl/ContentSuite/upload/aiv/doc/nr22eng(1).pdf, accessed August 15, 2007.

African American Policy Forum. "Oral Intervention at the Informal Consultation of the Preparatory Committee for the World Conference Against Racism, Racial Discrimination, Xenophobia, and Related Intolerance." Geneva, Switzerland, January 15–16, 2001. Website no longer available.

African Regional Preparatory Conference for the World Conference Against Racism, Racial Discrimination, Xenophobia, and Related Intolerance. "Draft Declaration of the African Regional Preparatory Conference for the World Conference Against Racism, Racial Discrimination, Xenophobia, and Related Intolerance." WCR/RCONF/DAKAR/2001/L.1 Rev. 3, January 24, 2001, http://www.africapolicy.org/docs01/wcar0101.htm, accessed August 7, 2007.

African Union. "Report of the First Conference of Intellectuals of Africa and the Diaspora." First Conference of Intellectuals of Africa and the Diaspora, Rapt/Rpt/CAID(I), Dakar, Senegal, October 6–9, 2004.

______. "African (Banjul) Charter on Human and Peoples' Rights." Adopted June 27, 1981, OAU Doc. CAB/LEG/67/3 rev. 5, 21 I.L.M. 58 (1982), entered into force October 21, 1986.

Agence France-Presse. "African Union Denounces EU 'Double Standards' over Zimbabwe." March 21, 2007.

______. "French Minister Pleads for an End to Dispute with Algeria over Past." November 13, 2006.

______. "Slavery Should Be Declared a 'Crime Against Humanity': OAU Head." September 1, 2001.

Ajayi, Jacob Ade. "La politique de réparations dans le contexte de la mondialisation." *Cahiers d'études africaines* 44, no. 1–2 (2004): 41–63.

———. "The Politics of Reparation in the Context of Globalisation." African Studies Association, Distinguished Abiola Lecture, Washington, D.C., December 7, 2002.

Ajayi-Soyinka, Omofolabo. "The Fashion of Democracy: September 11 and Africa." *Signs: Journal of Women in Culture and Society* 29, no. 2 (2003): 603–7.

Akwagyiram, Alexis. "Working in a Danger Zone." BBC News, January 20, 2006.

Allen, Chris. "Africa & the Drugs Trade." *Review of African Political Economy* 26, no. 79 (1999): 5–11.

Alpers, Edward A. "Slave Trade: Eastern Africa." In *Encyclopedia of Africa*, vol. 4, ed. John Middleton. New York: Charles Scribner's Sons, Vol. 4, 1997.

Alves, J. A. Lindgren. "The Durban Conference Against Racism and Everyone's Responsibility." *Netherlands Quarterly of Human Rights* 21, no. 3 (2003): 361–84.

Anderson, David. *Histories of the Hanged: The Dirty War in Kenya and the End of Empire*. New York: W. W. Norton, 2005.

Anglin, Douglas. "Rwanda Revisited: Search for the Truth." *International Journal* 56, no. 1 (2000-2001): 149–69.

An-Na'im, Abdullahi Ahmed, ed. *Human Rights Under African Constitutions: Realizing the Promise for Ourselves*. Philadelphia: University of Pennsylvania Press, 2003.

———. *Toward an Islamic Reformation: Civil Liberties, Human Rights and International Law*. Syracuse, N.Y.: Syracuse University Press, 1990.

Anstey, Roger T. "Capitalism and Slavery: A Critique." *Economic History Review* 21, no. 2 (1968): 307–20.

Appiah, Kwame Anthony. "Comprendre les réparations: une réflexion préliminaire." *Cahiers d'études africaines* 44, no. 1–2 (2004): 25–40.

———. "A Slow Emancipation." *New York Times Magazine*, March 18, 2007: 15–17.

Appiah-Kubi, Kojo. "State-Owned Enterprises and Privatization in Ghana." *Journal of Modern African Studies* 39, no. 2 (2001): 197–229.

Appleson, Gail. "Apartheid Victims Sue Citigroup, Other Banks." Reuters, June 19, 2002.

Arslanalp, Serkan, and Peter Henry Blair. "Policy Watch: Debt Relief." *Journal of Economic Perspectives* 20, no. 1 (2006): 207–20.

Associated Press. "African Union Chairman Calls Situation in Zimbabwe 'Embarrassing.' " March 15, 2007.

———. "Four Men Convicted of Bombing U.S. Embassies in Africa." October 18, 2001.

———. "French Government Sanctions Algerian War General for Torture Remarks." June 6, 2001.

———. "Lawyers for Kenyan Veterans Demand Apology from Britain for Alleged Atrocities." October 16, 2006.

———. "Mayor Apologizes for London's Role in Slave Trade." March 21, 2007.

Austen, Ralph A. "The Slave Trade and History and Memory: Confrontations of Slaving Voyage Documents and Communal Traditions." *William and Mary Quarterly* 58, no. 1 (2001).

Ayittey, George B. N. *Africa Unchained: The Blueprint for Africa's Future*. New York: Palgrave Macmillan, 2004.

Ba, Diadie. "Senegal's Wade Calls Slave Reparations Absurd." August 11, 2001, http://www.iol.co.za/general/news/newsprint.php?art_id=qw997554422285B252&sf=68, accessed August 11, 2007.

Bailey, Ronald. "The Slave(ry) Trade and the Development of Capitalism in the United States." In *The Atlantic Slave Trade: Effects on Economies, Societies and Peoples in Africa, the Americas, and Europe*, ed. Joseph E. Inikori and Stanley L. Engerman, 205–46. Durham, N.C.: Duke University Press, 1992.

Baker, Bruce. "Twilight of Impunity for Africa's Presidential Criminals." *Third World Quarterly* 25, no. 8 (2004): 1487–99.

Ball, Edward. *Slaves in the Family*. New York: Ballantine Books, 1998.

Banton, Michael. "Lessons from the 2001 World Conference Against Racism." *Journal of Ethnic and Migration Studies* 28, no. 2 (2002): 355–66.

Barkan, Elazar. *The Guilt of Nations: Restitution and Negotiating Historical Injustices*. New York: W. W. Norton, 2000.

______. "Restitution and Amending Historical Injustices in International Morality." In *Politics and the Past: On Repairing Historical Injustices*, ed. John Torpey, 91–102. Lanham, Md.: Rowman and Littlefield, 2003.

Barnes, Sandra T. "Global Flows: Terror, Oil & Strategic Philanthropy." *Review of African Political Economy* 32, no. 104–5 (2005): 235–52.

Bates, Stephen. "Church Apologises for Benefiting from Slave Trade," *Guardian* (UK), February 9, 2006.

Baumgartner, Frank R., and Bryan D. Jones. "Agenda Dynamics and Policy Subsystems." *Journal of Politics* 53, no. 4 (1991): 1044–74.

Bazyler, Michael J. *Holocaust Justice: The Battle for Restitution in America's Courts*. New York: New York University Press, 2003.

BBC News. "Africa Rejects Action on Zimbabwe." June 24, 2005.

______. "Belgian Apology to Rwanda." April 7, 2000.

______. "Blair 'Sorrow' over Slave Trade." November 27, 2006.

______. "Chirac Rejects 'Torture Apology'" December 5, 2000.

______. "France Gives Overseas Veterans More." November 21, 2002.

______. "France Remembers Slavery Victims." May 10, 2006.

______. "Gorée: The Slave Island." July 8, 2003.

______. "Lumumba's Son Hails Belgian Apology." February 6, 2002.

______. "Nigeria Hostages 'in Good Health.'" January 17, 2006.

______. "Queen's Regret over Boer War." November 10, 1999.

______. "Shell Told to Pay Nigeria's Ijaw." February 24, 2006.

______. "Xhosa Demand Apology from Queen." November 8, 1999.

______. "Zimbabwe Quits Commonwealth." December 8, 2003.

______. "Zimbabwe to Chair Major UN Body." May 12, 2007.

Beckles, Hilary McDonald. "Slave Voyages: The Transatlantic Trade in Enslaved Africans." UNESCO, ED-2002/WS/37, 2002.

Berger, Ronald J. *Fathoming the Holocaust: A Social Problems Approach*. New York: Aldine de Gruyter, 2002.

Besley, Timothy, and Robin Burgess. "Halving Global Poverty." *Journal of Economic Perspectives* 17, no. 3 (2003): 3–22.

Bhagwati, Jagdish Natwarlal. *In Defense of Globalization*. New York: Oxford University Press, 2004.

Black, Edwin. *IBM and the Holocaust: The Strategic Alliance Between Nazi Germany and America's Most Powerful Corporation*. New York: Crown Publishing, 2001.

Black, Henry Campbell. *Black's Law Dictionary*. 5th ed. St. Paul, Minn.: West Publishing, 1979.

Blair, Tony. "PM Tony Blair's Bicentenary Speech for Elmina Castle, Ghana." 10 Downing Street, March 25, 2007, http://www.number-10.gov.uk/output/Page11342.asp, accessed August 15, 2007.

______. "Prime Minister's Article for the New Nation Newspaper." 10 Downing Street, November 27, 2006, http://www.number-10.gov.uk/output/Page10487.asp, accessed August 15, 2007.

———. "Prime Minister's Remarks at the Launch of the Commission for Africa Report." 10 Downing Street, March 11, 2005, http://www.number-10.gov.uk/output/Page7314.asp, accessed August 15, 2007.

Boafo-Arthur, Kwame. "Ghana: Structural Adjustment, Democratization, and the Politics of Continuity." *African Studies Review* 42, no. 2 (1999): 41–72.

Boraine, Alex. *A Country Unmasked*. New York: Oxford University Press, 2000.

Bossuyt, Marc, and Stef Vandeginste. "The Issue of Reparation for Slavery and Colonialism and the Durban World Conference Against Racism." *Human Rights Law Journal* 22, no. 9–12 (2001): 341–50.

Bourdieu, Pierre. "The Forms of Capital." In *Handbook of Theory and Research for the Sociology of Education*, ed. John G. Richardson, 241–58. New York: Greenwood Press, 1986.

Boyagoda, Randy. *Governor of the Northern Province: A Novel*. Toronto, Canada: Viking, 2006.

Brooks, George E., and Bruce L. Mouser. "An 1804 Slaving Contract Signed in Arabic Script from the Upper Guinea Coast." *History in Africa* 14 (1987): 341–48.

Brooks, Roy L. *When Sorry Isn't Enough: The Controversy over Apologies and Reparations for Human Injustice*. New York: New York University Press, 1999.

Brysk, Alison. "'Hearts and Minds': Bringing Symbolic Politics Back In." *Polity* 27, no. 4 (1995): 559–85.

Buford, Warren, and Hugo van der Merwe. "Les réparations en Afrique Australe." *Cahiers d'études africaines* 44, no. 1–2 (2004): 263–322.

Bush, George W. "President Bush Speaks at Gorée Island in Senegal." The White House, July 8, 2003, http://www.whitehouse.gov/news/releases/2003/07/print/20030708-1.html, accessed August 15, 2007.

———. "Remarks by the President in Address to the United Nations General Assembly." U.S. Department of State, September 21, 2004, http://www.state.gov/p/io/rls/rm/2004/36350.htm, accessed August 12, 2007.

Buxton, Nick. "Debt Cancellation and Civil Society: A Case Study of Jubilee 2000." In *Fighting for Human Rights*, ed. Paul Gready, 54–77. New York: Routledge, 2004.

Calderisi, Robert. *The Trouble with Africa: Why Foreign Aid Isn't Working*. New York: Palgrave Macmillan, 2006.

Camponovo, Christopher N. "Disaster in Durban: The United Nations World Conference Against Racism, Racial Discrimination, Xenophobia, and Related Intolerance." *George Washington International Law Review* 34, no. 4 (2003): 659–710.

"Cancer Widows Sue US Petro-Giant." *Mail and Guardian* (South Africa), September 15, 2000.

Caplan, Gerald. "The Conspiracy Against Africa." *Walrus Magazine*, November 2006.

Centre for Human Rights. *Compendium of Key Human Rights Documents of the African Union*. Pretoria, South Africa: Pretoria University Law Press, 2005.

Chambre de Représentants (Belgium). "Parliamentary Committee of Enquiry in Charge of Determining the Exact Circumstances of the Assassination of Patrice Lumumba and the Possible Involvement of Belgian Politicians: Summary of the Activities, Experts' Report and Full Conclusions." 2001.

Chapman, Audrey R., and Patrick Ball. "The Truth of Truth Commissions: Comparative Lessons from Haiti, South Africa, and Guatemala." *Human Rights Quarterly* 23, no. 1 (2001): 1–43.

Chikoti, Georges. "Statement by Dr. Georges Chikoti, Angolan Deputy Minister of Foreign Affairs." World Conference Against Racism, Racial Discrimination, Xenophobia, and Related Intolerance, Durban, South Africa, September 2, 2001, http://www.un.org/WCAR/statements/angolaE.htm, accessed August 7, 2007.

Chinamasa, P. A. "Zimbabwe: Statement Delivered by the Hon. P. A. Chinamasa, M.P. Minister of Justice, Legal and Parliamentary Affairs and Head of the Zimbabwe Delegation to the World Conference Against Racism, Racial Discrimination, Xenophobia, and Related Intolerances." World Conference Against Racism, Racial Discrimination, Xenophobia, and Related Intolerance, September 3, 2001, Durban, South Africa, http://www.un.org/WCAR/statements/zimbE.htm, accessed August 7, 2007.

Church of England, General Synod, February 2006 Group of Sessions, "Bicentenary of the Act for the Abolition of the Slave Trade," Motion 801, February 8, 2006.

Cisse, Mariama. "République du Niger, communication de la commission nationale des droits de l'homme et des libertés fondamentales." World Conference Against Racism, Racial Discrimination, Xenophobia, and Related Intolerance, September 3, 2001, Durban, South Africa, http://www.un.org/WCAR/statements/niger_hrF.htm, accessed August 7, 2007.

Civil Liberties Organization. *Annual Report on Human Rights in Nigeria, 1990*. Lagos: Civil Liberties Organization, 1990.

Clapham, Christopher. *Africa and the International System*. Cambridge, UK: Cambridge University Press, 1996.

Clinton, Bill. "Remarks by the President to Genocide Survivors, Assistance Workers, and U.S. and Rwanda Government Officials," The White House, Office of the Press Secretary, March 25, 1998, http://clinton2.nara.gov/Africa/19980325-16872.html, accessed August 15, 2007.

______. "Remarks by the President to the Community of Kisowera School Mukuno, Uganda." The White House, Office of the Press Secretary, March 24, 1998, http://clinton4.nara.gov/Africa/19980324-3374.html, accessed August 15, 2007.

______. "Remarks in Apology to African-Americans on the Tuskegee Experiment." *Weekly Compilation of Presidential Documents* 33, no. 20 (1997): 695–724.

Cocker, Mark. *Rivers of Blood, Rivers of Gold: Europe's Conquest of Indigenous Peoples*. New York: Grove/Atlantic Inc., 1998.

Cohen, William B. "The Sudden Memory of Torture: The Algerian War in French Discourse, 2000–2001." *French Politics, Culture & Society* 19, no. 3 (2001): 82–94.

Coleman, James Samuel. *Foundations of Social Theory*. Cambridge, Mass.: Harvard University Press, 1990.

Commission of the African Union. "Strategic Plan of the Commission of the African Union, Volume 3: 2004–2007 Plan of Action." Addis Ababa: African Union, 2004.

Cooper, Frederick. "Islam and Cultural Hegemony: The Ideology of Slaveowners on the East African Coast." In *The Ideology of Slavery in Africa*, ed. Paul Lovejoy, 271–307. Beverly Hills, Calif.: Sage Publications, 1981.

Coslett, Paul. "Liverpool's Slavery Apology." BBC News, February 15, 2007.

Cowen, Tyler. "How Far Back Should We Go? Why Restitution Should Be Small." In *Retribution and Reparation in the Transition to Democracy*, ed. Jon Elster, 17–32. Cambridge, UK: Cambridge University Press, 2006.

"Critique of the HIPC Initiative." *Africa Action*, June 2002, http://www.africaaction.org/action/hipc0206.htm, accessed August 11, 2007.

Cunningham, Michael. "Saying Sorry: The Politics of Apology." *Political Quarterly* 70, no. 3 (1999): 285–93.

Curtin, Philip. "Gorée and the Slave Trade." H-Net, July 31, 1995, http://www.h-net.org/~africa/threads/goree.html, accessed August 15, 2007.

Dabor, Fode M. "Republic of Sierra Leone: Statement by President Fode M. Dabor." World Conference Against Racism, Racial Discrimination, Xenophobia, and Related Intolerance, September 4, 2001, Durban, South Africa, http://www.un.org/WCAR/statements/sierraE.htm, accessed August 7, 2007.

Dashwood, Havina S., and Cranford Pratt. "Leadership, Participation and Conflict Management: Zimbabwe and Tanzania." In *Civil Wars in Africa: Roots and Resolutions*, ed. Taisier M. Ali and Robert O. Matthews, 223–54. Montréal, Canada: McGill-Queen's University Press, 1999.

Davis, David Brion. *Slavery and Human Progress*. New York: Oxford University Press, 1984.

Day, Jim. "Lawsuit Launched Against Asbestos Companies." *Mail and Guardian* (South Africa), April 18, 1997.

de Roux, Emmanuel. "Le mythe de la Maison des esclaves qui résiste à la réalité." *Le Monde*, December 27, 1996, http://www.crdp.ac-martinique.fr/ressources/caraibe/histoiregeo/didactique/ali_shandora/mythe.htm, accessed August 15, 2007.

Deutsche Presse-Agentur. "European Church Leaders Ask for Forgiveness in Zimbabwe: Report." September 4, 2006.

———. "Zimbabwe Chair of UN Green Commission 'Destroyed Seized Farm.'" May 13, 2007.

Diamantopolou, Anna. "Anna Diamantopolou: European Commissioner Responsible for Employment and Social Affairs Address to ACP Ambassadors, ACP Ambassadors' Meeting, Brussels." SPEECH/01/339, June 21, 2001, http://europa.eu/rapid/pressReleasesAction.do?reference=SPEECH/01/339&format=HTML&aged=1&language=EN&guiLanguage=en, accessed August 15, 2007.

Dibie, Robert, and Johnston Njoku. "Cultural Perceptions of Africans in Diaspora and in Africa on Atlantic Slave Trade and Reparations." *African and Asian Studies* 4, no. 3 (2005): 403–26.

Dicklitch, Susan, and Rhoda E. Howard-Hassmann. "Public Policy and Economic Rights in Ghana and Uganda." In *Economic Rights: Conceptual, Measurement and Policy Issues*, ed. Shareen Hertel and Lanse Minkler, 325–44. New York: Cambridge University Press, 2007.

Dodds, Graham. "Political Apologies and Public Discourse: Conversation and Community in the Twenty-First Century." In *Public Discourse in America*, ed. Judith Rodin and Stephen P. Steinberg, 135–59. Philadelphia: University of Pennsylvania Press, 2003.

Donnelly, John. "Burdens of Oil Weigh on Nigerians." *Boston Globe*, October 3, 2005.

Dowden, Richard. "Zimbabwe's Commonwealth Suspension Extended." *The Independent* (London), December 8, 2003.

Doyle, Jim. "Law Professor Has Leading Role in Mock Trial: She Will Prosecute Sudan's President for Genocide." *San Francisco Chronicle*, November 10, 2006.

Du Plessis, Max. "The Creation of the ICC: Implications for Africa's Despots, Crackpots and Hotspots." *African Security Review* 12, no. 4 (2003): 5–15.

———. "Historical Injustice and International Law: An Exploratory Discussion of Reparation for Slavery." *Human Rights Quarterly* 25, no. 3 (2003): 624–59.

"ECOWAS Defense Commission." *West Africa*, February 11–17, 1991, 197.
Edwards, Paul, ed. *Equiano's Travels*. London: Heinemann Educational Books, 1967.
Eisenman, Joshua, and Joshua Kurlantzick. "China's Africa Strategy." *Current History* (May 2006): 219–24.
Elkins, Carol. *Imperial Reckoning: The Untold Story of Britain's Gulag in Kenya*. New York: Henry Holt and Company, 2005.
Energy Information Administration. "Crude Oil and Total Petroleum Imports: Top 15 Countries." *Energy Information Administration: Official Energy Statistics from the U.S. Government*, 2007, http://www.eia.doe.gov/pub/oil_gas/petroleum/data_publications/company_level_imports/current/import.html, accessed April 2007.
Engerman, Stanley L. "The Slave Trade and British Capital Formation in the Eighteenth Century: A Comment on the Williams Thesis." *Business History Review* 46, no. 4 (1972): 430–43.
Eveleth, Ann. "New Claim Against Chemical Giant Thor." *Mail and Guardian* (South Africa), February 20, 1998.
"Exploitation of Forced Labor." Dodd Archives (Nuremberg Trial), University of Connecticut, Box 288, Folder 7349, December 11–13, 1945.
Eyerman, Ron. *Cultural Trauma: Slavery and the Formation of African American Identity*. New York: Cambridge University Press, 2001.
Fanon, Frantz. *Black Skins, White Masks*. New York: Grove Press, 1967.
______. *The Wretched of the Earth*. New York: Grove Press, 1963.
Fein, Helen. *Accounting for Genocide: National Responses and Jewish Victimization During the Holocaust*. Chicago: University of Chicago Press, 1979.
Feinberg, Joel. "Collective Responsibility." *Journal of Philosophy* 65, no. 21 (1968): 674–88.
Ferree, Myra Marx, and Frederick D. Miller. "Mobilization and Meaning: Toward an Integration of Social Psychological and Resource Perspectives on Social Movements." *Sociological Inquiry* 55, no. 1 (1985): 39–61.
Finkelstein, Norman G. *The Holocaust Industry: Reflections on the Exploitation of Jewish Suffering*. 2nd ed. New York: Verso, 2001.
Finnemore, Martha. "International Organizations as Teachers of Norms: The United Nations Educational, Scientific, and Cultural Organization and Science Policy." *International Organization* 47, no. 4 (1993): 565–97.
"Forgiving Their Debtors." *Wall Street Journal*, October 12, 2000.
Forsythe, David P. *Human Rights in International Relations*. 2nd ed. Cambridge, UK: Cambridge University Press, 2006.
Fraser, Nancy. "From Redistribution to Recognition? Dilemmas of Justice in a 'Post-Socialist' Age." *New Left Review* 212 (1995): 68–93.
Free Zim-Youth. "We Need to Change Strategy to Oust Mugabe Says Zim-Youth." *Free Zim-Youth*, September 18, 2006, http://www.zimbabwejournalists.com/story.php?art_id=1000&cat=4, accessed August 7, 2007.
Freeman, Michael. *Human Rights: An Interdisciplinary Approach*. Cambridge, UK: Polity Press, 2002.
French, Howard W. "The Atlantic Slave Trade: On Both Sides, Reason for Remorse." *New York Times*, April 5, 1998.
Frynas, Jędrzej George. "Social and Environmental Litigation Against Transnational Firms in Africa." *Journal of Modern African Studies* 42, no. 3 (2004): 363–88.
Ganley, Elaine. "French General Insists 'Everybody Knew' of Torture During Algerian War." Associated Press, May 7, 2001.

Geo-Jaja, Macleans A., and Garth Magnum. "Structural Adjustment as an Inadvertent Enemy of Human Development in Africa." *Journal of Black Studies* 32, no. 1 (2001): 30–49.

Gewald, Jan-Bart. "More Than Red Rubber and Figures Alone: A Critical Appraisal of the Memory of the Congo Exhibition at the Royal Museum for Central Africa, Tervuven, Belgium." *International Journal of African Historical Studies* 39, no. 3 (2006): 471–86.

Gibney, Mark. *Five Uneasy Pieces: American Ethics in a Globalized World*. New York: Rowman and Littlefield, 2005.

Gibney, Mark, Katarina Tomasevski, and Jens Vedsted-Hansen. "Transnational State Responsibility for Violations of Human Rights." *Harvard Human Rights Journal* 12 (1999): 267–95.

Gifford, Anthony. "The Legal Basis of the Claim for Reparations." *First Pan-African Congress on Reparations*, Abuja, April 27–29, 1993, http://www.arm.arc.co.uk/legalBasis.html, accessed August 7, 2007.

Gifford, Anthony, "Slavery: Legacy," *Hansard: Debate Initiated by Lord Gifford, QC, in the House of Lords of the British Parliament*, March 14, 1996, http://www.arm.arc.co.uk/LordsHansard.html, accessed August 12, 2007.

Gilbert, Margaret. "Group Wrongs and Guilt Feelings." *Journal of Ethics* 1, no. 1 (1997): 65–84.

Giraud, Michel. "Le passé comme blessure et le passé comme masque: la réparation de la traite négrière et de l'esclavage pour les peuples des départements français d'Outre-Mer." *Cahiers d'études africaines* 44, no. 1–2 (2004): 65–79.

Global Afrikan Congress. News release, Toronto, Canada, n.d.

———. "Background to the GAC." 2003, http://www.globalafrikancongress.com/aboutus.html, accessed August 7, 2007.

Global Witness. "The Kimberley Process at Risk." *Global Witness*, November 2006: 1–4.

Goffman, Erving. *Relations in Public: Microstudies of the Social Order*. New York: Basic Books, 1971.

Goldhagen, Daniel Jonah. *Hitler's Willing Executioners: Ordinary Germans and the Holocaust*. New York: Vintage Books, 1997.

Gordimer, Nadine. "Purge This Evil." *Sunday Observer* (London), September 23, 2001.

Govier, Trudy. "An Epistemology of Trust." *International Journal of Moral and Social Studies* 8, no. 2 (1993): 155–74.

———. *Social Trust and Human Communities*. Montréal, Québec: McGill-Queen's University Press, 1997.

———. "Trust and Testimony: Nine Arguments on Testimonial Knowledge." *International Journal of Moral and Social Sciences* 8, no. 1 (1993): 21–39.

Govier, Trudy, and Wilhelm Verwoerd. "The Practice of Public Apologies: A Qualified Defense." Unpublished manuscript, n.d.

Graham, Robert. "France Is Still Haunted by Its War in Algeria." *Financial Times* (London), November 3, 2004.

Grono, Nick. "Briefing Darfur: The International Community's Failure to Protect." *African Affairs* 105, no. 421 (2006): 621–31.

Gyimah-Boadi, E. "A Peaceful Turnover in Ghana." *Journal of Democracy* 12, no. 2 (2001): 103–17.

Gyimah-Boadi, E., and Kwabena Amoah Awuah Mensah. "Afrobarometer Paper No. 28: The Growth of Democracy in Ghana Despite Economic Dissatisfaction: A Power Alternation Bonus?" *Afrobarometer* (April 2003): 1–46.

Haas, Peter M. "Introduction: Epistemic Communities and International Policy Coordination." *International Organization* 46, no. 1 (1992): 1–35.

Hamata, Max. "Germany Apologizes for Colonial-Era Genocide of Namibia's Herero People." Associated Press, August 14, 2004.

Harring, Sidney L. "German Reparations to the Herero Nation: An Assertion of Herero Nationhood in the Path of Namibian Development?" *West Virginia Law Review* 104 (2001–2002): 393–417.

Hayner, Priscilla B. *Unspeakable Truths: Confronting State Terror and Atrocity*. New York: Routledge Press, 2001.

Henkin, Louis, Gerald L. Neuman, David W. Leebron, and Diane F. Orentlicher, eds. *Human Rights*. New York: Foundation Press, 1999.

Hill, Amelia. "City Agonises over Slavery Apology." *The Observer* (London), May 7, 2006.

Hirsch, Herbert. *Genocide and the Politics of Memory: Studying Death to Preserve Life*. Chapel Hill: University of North Carolina Press, 1995.

Hochschild, Adam. *King Leopold's Ghost: A Story of Greed, Terror, and Heroism in Colonial Africa*. New York: Houghton Mifflin, 1999.

Hoge, Warren. "Annan, at Rwanda Memorial, Admits U.N. Blame." *New York Times*, March 27, 2004.

Howard, Rhoda E. *Colonialism and Underdevelopment in Ghana*. London: Croom Helm, 1978.

______. "The 'Full-Belly' Thesis: Should Economic Rights Take Priority over Civil and Political Rights? Evidence from Sub-Saharan Africa." *Human Rights Quarterly* 5, no. 4 (1983): 467–90.

______. *Human Rights in Commonwealth Africa*. Totowa, N.J.: Rowman and Littlefield, 1986.

______. *Human Rights and the Search for Community*. Boulder, Colo.: Westview, 1995.

Howard-Hassmann, Rhoda E. "An Airborne Disease: Globalization Through African Eyes." In *Autonomy, Democracy and Legitimacy in an Era of Globalization*, ed. Steven Berstein and William Coleman. Under review.

______. *Compassionate Canadians: Civic Leaders Discuss Human Rights*. Toronto, Canada: University of Toronto Press, 2003.

______. "Genocide and State-Induced Famine: Global Ethics and Western Responsibility for Mass Atrocities in Africa." In *Globalization and Political Ethics*, ed. Richard B. Day and Joe Masciulli, 237–66. Leiden-Boston: Brill, 2007.

______. "A Truth Commission for Africa?" *International Journal* 55, no. 4 (2005): 999–1016.

Howard-Hassmann, Rhoda E., and Anthony Peter Lombardo. "Framing Reparations Claims: Differences Between the African and Jewish Social Movements for Reparations." *African Studies Review* 50, no. 1 (2007): 27–48.

______. "Words Require Action: African Elite Opinion About Apologies from the West." In *The Age of Apology: Facing Up to the Past*, ed. Mark Gibney, Rhoda E. Howard-Hassmann, Jean-Mark Coicaud, and Niklaus Steiner, 216–28. Philadelphia: University of Pennsylvania Press, 2007.

Hughes, Tim. "Ghana: Tarnished Past, Golden Future." In *South African Yearbook of International Affairs 2002/03*. Johannesburg, South Africa: Jan Smuts House, 2003: 323–31.

Human Rights Watch. "An Approach to Reparations." Human Rights Watch, July 19, 2001, http://www.hrw.org/campaigns/race/reparations.pdf, accessed August 15, 2007.

______. "The Pinochet Precedent: How Victims Can Pursue Human Rights Criminals Abroad." New York: Human Rights Watch, 2000.

———. "Zimbabwe: Food Used as Political Weapon." Human Rights Watch, October 24, 2003, http://www.hrw.org/press/2003/10/zimbabwe102403.htm, accessed August 13, 2007.

———. "Zimbabwe: Not Eligible: The Politicization of Food in Zimbabwe." *Human Rights Watch* 15, no. 17(A) (2003).

Huntington, Samuel. *The Clash of Civilizations and the Remaking of World Order*. New York: Simon & Schuster, 1996.

Hyden, Goran. *African Politics in Comparative Perspective*. New York: Cambridge University Press, 2006.

———. *No Shortcuts to Progress: African Development Management in Perspective*. Berkeley: University of California Press, 1983.

Ibhawoh, Bonny. "Structural Adjustment, Authoritarianism and Human Rights in Africa." *Comparative Studies of South Asia, Africa and the Middle East* 19, no. 1 (1999): 158–67.

Idowu, Amos Adeoye. "Human Rights, Environmental Degradation and Oil Multinational Companies in Nigeria: The Ogoniland Episode." *Netherlands Quarterly of Human Rights* 17, no. 2 (1999): 161–84.

Idris, Alhaji Mustapha. "Republic of Ghana: Statement by Alhaji Mustapha Idris." World Conference Against Racism, Racial Discrimination, Xenophobia, and Related Intolerance, September 3, 2001, Durban, South Africa, http://www.un.org/WCAR/statements/ghanaE.htm, accessed August 7, 2007.

Imperato, Pascal James. "Differing Perspectives on Mau Mau." *African Studies Review* 48, no. 3 (2005): 147–54.

Inikori, Joseph E. "Slave Trade: Western Africa." In *Encyclopedia of Africa*, ed. John Middleton, 88–94. New York: Charles Scribner's Sons, vol. 4, 1997.

———. "Slavery in Africa and the Transatlantic Slave Trade." In *The African Diaspora*, ed. Alusine Jalloh and Stephen E. Maizlish. Arlington.: Texas A&M University Press, 1996.

———. "Slavery and the Revolution in Cotton Textile Production in England." In *The Atlantic Slave Trade: Effects on Economies, Societies and Peoples in Africa, the Americas, and Europe*, ed. Joseph E. Inikori and Stanley L. Engerman, 145–81. Durham, N.C.: Duke University Press, 1992.

Interim Steering Committee of the Africans and African Descendants Caucus. "Proposal for a Permanent Organizational Structure of the African and African Descendants Caucus." n.d., http://www.geocities.com/i_makeda/permanentstructure.htm, accessed August 7, 2007.

International Citizens' Tribunal for Sudan. "Indictment." Case Number: ICT-1, The Prosecutor Against Omar Hasan Ahmad Al-Bashir, President of the Government of Sudan, 2006, http://www.judgmentongenocide.com/images/darfur_indictment.pdf, accessed August 15, 2007.

———. "Judgment." Case Number: ICT-1, The Prosecutor Against Omar Hasan Ahmad Al-Bashir, President of the Government of Sudan, November 13, 2006, http:/www.judgmentongenocide.com/judgment.html, accessed August 15, 2007.

International Conference on Popular Participation in the Recovery and Development Process in Africa. "African Charter for Popular Participation in Development and Transformation." United Nations, A/45/427, August 22, 1990.

International Criminal Court. "Pre-Trial Chamber I Commits Thomas Lubanga Dyilo for Trial." January 29, 2005, http://www.icc-cpi.int/pressrelease_details&id=220&l=en.html, accessed August 14, 2007.

———. "Prosecutor Opening Remarks." ICC-OTP-20070227-208-En, February 27, 2007, http://www.icc-cpi.int/press/pressreleases/228.html, accessed August 15, 2007.

———. "Rome Statute of the International Criminal Court." 1998, http://www.un.org/law/icc/statute/99_corr/cstatute.htm, accessed August 7, 2007.

———. "The States Parties to the Rome Statute: African States." 2007, http://www.icc-cpi.int/php/show.php?page=region&id=3, accessed August 14, 2007.

———. "Warrant of Arrest Unsealed Against Five LRA Commanders." October 14, 2005, http://www.icc-cpi.int/pressrelease_details&id=114&l=en.html, accessed August 14, 2007.

International Monetary Fund and World Bank Development Committee. "Notes on the G8 Debt Relief Proposal: Assessment of Costs, Implementation Issues, and Financing Options." *International Monetary Fund and the World Bank*, DC 2005-0023, September 21, 2005.

International Panel of Eminent Persons. "Rwanda: The Preventable Genocide." Organization for African Unity, July 7, 2000.

IRIN. "AU Suspends Report on Zimbabwe Rights Abuses." July 8, 2006.

Jacques, Gloria. "Orphans of the AIDS Pandemic: The Sub-Saharan Africa Experience." In *AIDS and Development in Africa: A Social Science Perspective*, ed. Kempe Ronald Hope, Sr., 93–108. Binghamton, N.Y.: The Haworth Press, 1999.

Jamaica Reparations Movement. "Reparations Document." *Jamaica Reparations Movement*, February 28, 2003, http://www.geocities.com/i_makeda/draftdocument.html, accessed August 7, 2007.

Jason, Pini. "S-East/S-South Professionals and the N-Delta Crisis." *Vanguard*, March 7, 2006, http://odili.net/news/source/2006/mar/7/331.html, accessed August 12, 2007.

Joint Statement by African and Other NGOs. "Oral Intervention at the Informal Consultation of the Preparatory Committee for the World Conference Against Racism, Racial Discrimination, Xenophobia, and Related Intolerance." January 15–16, 2001, Geneva.

Jones, Charles. *Global Justice: Defending Cosmopolitanism*. Oxford, UK: Oxford University Press, 1999.

Jones, Kent Albert. *Who's Afraid of the WTO?* New York: Oxford University Press, 2004.

Jongwe, Fanuel. "Pressure Mounts on Mugabe with Blair Sanctions Call." Agence France-Presse, March 21, 2007.

"Jubilee Still Active Two Years Later." Africa News Service, June 13, 2003. http://www.comtextnews.com

Jubilee 2000 South Africa. "Founding Declaration of the South African Jubilee 2000 Campaign." Cape Town, South Africa, November 5, 1998.

Judah, Tim. "The Stakes in Darfur." *New York Review of Books* 52, no. 1 (2005): 12–16.

Justice and Equality Movement. "Proposal by the Justice and Equality Movement (JEM) for Peace in Sudan in General and Darfur in Particular." *Justice and Equality Movement*, n.d.

Kant, Immanuel. "Grounding for the Metaphysics of Morals." In *Moral Issues in Global Perspective*, ed. Christine Koggel, 494–502. Peterborough, Canada: Broadview Press, 1999.

Keck, Margaret E., and Kathryn Sikkink. *Activists Beyond Borders: Advocacy Networks in International Politics*. Ithaca, N.Y.: Cornell University Press, 1998.

Kennedy, Paul M. *The Rise and Fall of British Naval Mastery*. London: Ashfield Press, 1986.

Kimenyi, Mwangi S. *Ethnic Diversity, Liberty and the State: The African Dilemma*. Cheltenham, UK: Edward Elgar, 1997.

Klein, A. Norman. "The Two Asantes: Competing Interpretations of 'Slavery' in Akan-Asante Culture and Society." In *The Ideology of Slavery in Africa*, ed. Paul Lovejoy, 149–67. Beverly Hills, Calif.: Sage Publications, 1981.

Klein, Martin. "The Impact of the Atlantic Slave Trade on the Societies of the Western Sudan." In *The Atlantic Slave Trade: Effects on Economies, Societies and Peoples in Africa, the Americas, and Europe*, ed. Joseph E. Inikori and Stanley L. Engerman, 25–47. Durham, N.C.: Duke University Press, 1992.

———. *Slavery and Colonial Rule in French West Africa*. New York: Cambridge University Press, 1998.

Klinghoffer, Arthur Jay, and Judith Apter Klinghoffer. *International Citizens' Tribunals: Mobilizing Public Opinion to Advance Human Rights*. New York: Palgrave, 2002.

Konings, Piet. "The Anglophone Cameroon-Nigeria Boundary: Opportunity and Conflicts." *African Affairs* 104, no. 415 (2005): 275–301.

Kopytoff, Igor, and Suzanne Miers, 3–81. "African 'Slavery' as an Institution of Marginality." In *Slavery in Africa: Historical and Anthropological Perspectives*, ed. Igor Kopytoff and Suzanne Miers. Madison: University of Wisconsin Press, 1977.

Kusta, Elizabeth. "Oil Prices Jump Nearly $1.50 after Militant Violence in Nigeria." Associated Press, February 20, 2006.

Landes, David S. *The Wealth and Poverty of Nations: Why Some Are So Rich and Some So Poor*. New York: W. W. Norton, 1998.

Laremont, Ricardo René. "Jewish and Japanese American Reparations: Political Lessons for the Africana Community." *Journal of Asian American Studies* 4, no. 3 (2001): 235–50.

———. "Political Versus Legal Strategies for the African Slavery Reparations Movement." *African Studies Quarterly: The Online Journal for African Studies* 2, no. 4 (1999).

Lazare, Aaron. *On Apology*. New York: Oxford University Press, 2004.

League of Nations. "Convention to Suppress the Slave Trade and Slavery." September 25, 1926.

Leblanc, Daniel. "Mandela Tells West to Pay Colonial Debt." *Globe and Mail* (Toronto), April 9, 2002.

Légifrance: Le service public de la diffusion du droit. "Loi no 2001-434 du 21 mai 2001 Tendant à la reconnaissance de la traite et de l'esclavage en tant que crime contre l'humanité." 2001, http://www.legifrance.gouv.fr/WAspad/UnTexteDeJorf?numjo=JUSX9903435L, accessed August 7, 2007.

Leigh Day and Co. Solicitors. "Mau Mau Claims." Clerkenwell, UK. Letter sent by surface mail. Cited with permission of Mikewa Ogada, Program Officer: Research, Mau Mau Reparations and Recognition Project, April 2, 2007.

Lewis, Rupert Charles. *Walter Rodney's Intellectual and Political Thought*. Detroit, Mich.: Wayne State University Press, 1998.

Lindsay, Hillary Bain. "Shell Shocked: People of the Niger Delta Fight Back Against Violence and Corruption." *The Dominion: News from the Grassroots*, March 20, 2006, http://dominionpaper.ca/environment/2006/03/20/shell_shoc.html, accessed August 11, 2007.

Lombardo, Anthony Peter. "Reparations to Africa: Examining the African Viewpoint." Master's thesis, McMaster University, 2004.

Lovejoy, Paul. "Slavery in the Context of Ideology." In *The Ideology of Slavery in Africa*, ed. Paul Lovejoy, 11-38. Beverly Hills, Calif.: Sage Publications, 1981.

———. *Transformations in Slavery: A History of Slavery in Africa*. 2nd ed. Cambridge, UK: Cambridge University Press, 2000.

Löwenheim, Nava. "Asking Forgiveness for Wrongdoing in International Relations." Working paper, website on Political Apologies and Reparations, Wilfrid Laurier University, Waterloo, Canada, 2007, http://political-apologies.wlu.ca/documents/working/Lowenheim_Nava, accessed August 7, 2007.

Lynch, Colum. "Sudan Rejects Request to Allow U.N. Troops." *Washington Post*, September 20, 2006.

Lyons, Michelle E. "World Conference Against Racism: New Avenues for Slavery Reparations?" *Vanderbilt Journal of Transnational Law* 35, no. 4 (2002): 1235–68.

MacIntryre, Alasdair. *After Virtue: A Study in Moral Theory*. 2nd ed. London: Duckworth, 1981.

Mahmoud, Fatima Babiker. *The Sudanese Bourgeoisie: Vanguard of Development?* London: Zed Books, 1984.

Makanjuola, Bola. "Cost of Suffering: Africans Demand Compensation for Slavery and Exploitation." *West Africa*, February 4–10, 1991, 143.

Makuni, Mavis. "Apology No Cure-All for Africa's Ills." *Financial Gazette* (Harare, Zimbabwe), September 13, 2006.

Manning, Patrick. "The Slave Trade: The Formal Demography of a Global System." In *The Atlantic Slave Trade: Effects on Economies, Societies and Peoples in Africa, the Americas, and Europe*, ed. Joseph E. Inikori and Stanley L. Engerman, 117–41. Durham, N.C.: Duke University Press, 1992.

Mathiason, Nick. "Barclays Admits Possible Link to Slavery After Reparation Call." *The Observer*, London, April 1, 2007.

Mazal Library: A Holocaust Resource. "Nuremberg Military Tribunal." http://www.mazal.org/archive/nmt/09/NMT09-C001.htm, accessed August 15, 2007.

Mazrui, Ali A. "From Slave Ship to Space Ship: Africa Between Marginalization and Globalization." *African Studies Quarterly* 2, no. 4 (1999).

Mazrui, Ali A., Albert Luthuli, and Andrew D. White. "The Campaign for Black Reparations: An African Initiative." Website no longer available. 2002.

Mazrui, Ali A., and Alamin M. Mazrui. *Black Reparations in the Era of Globalization*. Binghamton, N.Y.: Institute of Global Cultural Studies, 2002.

Mbachu, Dulue. "Shell Misses Nigeria Deadline for Payment." Associated Press, May 22, 2006.

Mbeki, Thabo. "Mbeki: Tabling of TRC Report: Statement by President Thabo Mbeki to the National Houses of Parliament and the Nation, on the Occasion of the Tabling of the Report of the Truth and Reconciliation Commission." Office of the Presidency of South Africa, Cape Town, South Africa, April 15, 2003.

McCarthy, John D. "Pro-Life and Pro-Choice Mobilization: Infrastructure Deficits and New Technologies." In *Social Movements in an Organizational Society: Collected Essays*, ed. Meyer N. Zald, and John D. McCarthy, 49–66. New Brunswick, N.J.: Transaction Books, 1987.

McGreal, Chris. "Darfur Violence Wrecks Sudan's Attempt to Take AU Leadership." *The Guardian*, January 30, 2007.

Mendez, Juan E. "Review of *A Miracle, a Universe: Settling Accounts with Torturers*, by Lawrence Weschler." *New York Law School Journal of Human Rights* 8 (1991): 577–96.

Meyer, David S., and Nancy Whittier. "Social Movement Spillover." *Social Problems* 41, no. 2 (1994): 277–98.

Miers, Suzanne. *Slavery in the Twentieth Century: The Evolution of a Global Problem*. New York: Rowman and Littlefield, 2003.

Minow, Martha. *Between Vengeance and Forgiveness: Facing History After Genocide and Mass Violence*. Boston: Beacon Press, 1998.

Mishna. "Pirkei Avot (Ethics of the Fathers)."

Mittelman, James H., and Robert Johnston. "The Globalization of Organized Crime, the Courtesan State, and the Corruption of Civil Society." *Global Governance* 5, no. 1 (1999): 103–26.

Monshipouri, Mahmoud, Claude E. Welch, Jr., and Evan T. Kennedy. "Multinational Corporations and the Ethics of Global Responsibility: Problems and Prospects." *Human Rights Quarterly* 25, no. 4 (2003): 965–89.

Moore Jr., Barrington. *Social Origins of Dictatorship and Democracy: Lord and Peasant in the Making of the Modern World*. Boston: Beacon Press, 1966.

Morsink, Johannes. *The Universal Declaration of Human Rights: Origins, Drafting and Intent*. Philadelphia: University of Pennsylvania Press, 1999.

Murray, Rachel. *Human Rights in Africa: From the OAU to the African Union*. Cambridge, UK: Cambridge University Press, 2004.

Mutua, Makau. *Human Rights: A Political and Cultural Critique*. Philadelphia: University of Pennsylvania Press, 2002.

Mwaba, Andrew. "Beyond HIPC: What Are the Prospects for Debt Sustainability?" *African Development Perspectives* 17, no. 3 (2007): 536–51.

Mwangi, George. "Kenya's Mau Mau Rebels Celebrate 50th Anniversary with Plea for Legalization." Associated Press, August 12, 2000.

Narveson, Jan. "Collective Responsibility." *Journal of Ethics* 6, no. 2 (2002): 179–98.

National Reconciliation Commission [Ghana]. "Report." October 2004.

N'Cobra. "Global Pan-African Reparations Conference." n.d., http://www.ncobra-intl-affairs.org/conference.html, accessed August 7, 2007.

Ndiaye, Alioune. "Intervention sur le quatrième et cinqième points de l'ordre du jour présentée par Alioune Ndiaye, magistrat, sécrétaire permanent du comité sénégalais des droits de l'homme." World Conference Against Racism, Racial Discrimination, Xenophobia, and Related Intolerance, Durban, South Africa, September 5, 2001, http://www.un.org/WCAR/statements/sene_hrF.htm, accessed August 15, 2007.

Ndumbe, J. Anyu, and Babalola Cole. "The Illicit Diamond Trade, Civil Conflicts, and Terrorism in Africa." *Mediterranean Quarterly* 16, no. 2 (2005): 52–65.

Nduru, Moyiga. "Sudan Loses AU Chair to Ghana." Inter Press Service, January 29, 2007.

Newitt, Malyn D. *Portugal in Africa: The Last Hundred Years*. London: C. Hurst & Co., 1981.

"A New Scramble: China's Business Links with Africa." *The Economist*, November 27, 2004.

Nguesso, Denis Sassou "Allocution de son excellence monsieur Denis Sassou Nguesso, président de la République du Congo." World Conference Against Racism, Racial Discrimination, Xenophobia, and Related Intolerance, Durban, South Africa, September 1, 2001, http://www.un.org/WCAR/statements/congoF.htm, accessed August 15, 2007.

"Nigerian Hostage Crisis Continues." *The Star* (South Africa). March 6, 2006.

"Nigeria's Debt: No Longer Unforgivable." *The Economist*, March 19, 2005.

Nyathi, Kitsepile. "Zimbabwe: Refugee Crisis as Citizens Rush to Leave Their Country." *The Nation* (Kenya), March 22, 2007.

Obasanjo, Olusegun. "Nigeria: Statement by President Olusegun Obasanjo." World Conference Against Racism, Racial Discrimination, Xenophobia, and Related Intolerance, Durban, South Africa, August 31, 2001, http://www.un.org/WCAR/statements/nigeriaE.htm, accessed August 7, 2007.

Ocheje, Paul. "Refocusing International Law on the Quest for Accountability in Africa: The Case Against the 'Other' Impunity." *Leiden Journal of International Law* 15, no. 4 (2002): 749–79.

Oelbaum, Jay. "Populist Reform Coalitions in Sub-Saharan Africa: Ghana's Triple Alliance." *Canadian Journal of African Studies* 36, no. 2 (2002): 281–328.

Office of the High Commissioner for Human Rights (OHCHR). *Basic Principles and Guidelines on the Right to a Remedy and Reparations for Victims of Gross Violations of International Human Rights Law and Serious Violations of International Humanitarian Law*, C.H.R. Res. 2005/35 U.N. Doc. E/Cn.4/2005/L.10/Add.11: Office of the High Commissioner for Human Rights (OHCHR), 2005.

Ogada, Mikewa. "NGOs/Organization in Partnership with the Kenya Human Rights Commission (KHRC)." November 24, 2006.

Ogot, Bethwell A. "Britain's Gulag." *Journal of African History* 46, no. 3 (2005): 493–505.

Ollivier, Christine. "France Boosts Pensions for Colonial Vets." Associated Press, September 28, 2006.

O'Malley, Padraig. "Zimbabwe: South Africa's Failure." *International Herald Tribune*, April 2, 2005.

O'Neill, Barry. *Honor, Symbols, and War*. Ann Arbor: University of Michigan Press, 1999.

Onwuchekwa, Okey. "N/Delta: Militants Threaten Attack on Mobil." *Daily Champion* (Nigeria), April 11, 2006.

Orend, Brian. *Human Rights: Concept and Context*. Peterborough, Ontario: Broadview Press, 2002.

Organization for Economic Cooperation and Development. "OECD Annual Estimates of Total External Debt." 2002, http://www.oecd.org/dataoecd/54/53/31604144.xls, accessed August 11, 2007.

Organization of African Unity. "African Charter on Human and Peoples' Rights." Organization of African Unity, June 27, 1981.

———. "Constitutive Act of the African Union." Organization of African Unity, July 11, 2000.

———. "Resolution on the Environment." Organization of African Unity, CM/Res. 281 (XIX), June 5–12, 1972.

Orogun, Paul S. "'Blood Diamonds' and Africa's Armed Conflicts in the Post-Cold War Era." *World Affairs* 166, no. 3 (2004): 151–61.

———. "Plunder, Predation and Profiteering: The Political Economy of Armed Conflicts and Economic Violence in Modern Africa." *Perspectives on Global Development and Technology* 2, no. 2 (2003): 283–313.

Patton, Michael Quinn. *Qualitative Evaluation and Research Methods*. 2nd ed. Newbury Park, Calif.: Sage Publications, 1990.

Pavlu, George. "The First Slavers." *New African* 379 (1999): 16–19.

Paxton, Robert O. "The Trial of Maurice Papon." *New York Review of Books* 46, no. 2 (1999): 32–37.

Phimister, Ian, and Brian Raftopoulos. "Mugabe, Mbeki and the Politics of Anti-Imperialism." *Review of African Political Economy* 101 (2004): 385–400.

Phiri, Gift. "Mugabe Faces Class Action Lawsuit over Massacres." *Zimbabwe Independent*, November 3, 2006, http://www.newzimbabwe.com/pages/gukgenocide.1111607.html, accessed August 12, 2007.

Pogge, Thomas. *World Poverty and Human Rights: Cosmopolitan Responsibilities and Reforms*. Malden, Mass.: Blackwell Publishing, 2002.

"Policing the Undergoverned Spaces: Africa and the 'War on Terror.'" *The Economist,* June 16, 2007.

Potts, Deborah. "Restoring Order: Operation Murambatsvina and the Urban Crisis in Zimbabwe." *Journal of Southern African Studies* 12, no. 2 (2006): 273–91.

Power, Samantha. "How to Kill a Country." *Atlantic Monthly* 292, no. 5 (2003).

———. *"A Problem From Hell:" America and the Age of Genocide*. New York: Basic Books, 2002.

Preparatory Committee. "Report of the Regional Conference for Africa (Dakar, January 22–24, 2001)." United Nations, A/CONF.189/PC.2/8, March 27, 2001.

Pross, Christian. *Paying for the Past: The Struggle over Reparations for Surviving Victims of Nazi Terror*. Baltimore, Md.: Johns Hopkins University Press, 1998.

Randall, Vernellia R. "The Vienna Declaration and Program of Action with Background Information." *Washington and Lee Race and Ethnic Ancestry Law Journal* 8 (2002).

Regional Bureau for Southern Africa. "Projected Food Needs for 2007." *World Food Programme*, 2006.

République du Niger. "Communication de la commission nationale des droits de l'homme et des libertés fondamentales, à la conférence mondiale contre le racisme, la discrimination raciale, la xénophobie, et l'intolérance qui y est associé." World Conference Against Racism, Racial Discrimination, Xenophobia, and Related Intolerance, Durban, South Africa, September 3, 2001, http://www.un.org/WCAR/statements/niger_hrF.htm, accessed August 7, 2007.

Reuters Business News. "UK Court Approves Cape Payment to S. African Miners." June 27, 2003.

Rigby, Andrew. *Justice and Reconciliation: After the Violence*. Boulder, Colo.: Lynne Rienner, 2001.

Robertson, Geoffrey. *Crimes Against Humanity: The Struggle for Global Justice*. New York: New Press, 1999.

Rodney, Walter. *How Europe Underdeveloped Africa*. London: Bogle-l'Ouverture Publications, 1972.

Rosenberg, Nathan, and L. E. Birdzell. *How the West Grew Rich: The Economic Transformation of the Industrial World*. New York: Basic Books, 1986.

Rotberg, Robert I. "Failed States, Collapsed States, Weak States: Causes and Indicators." In *State Failure and State Weakness in a Time of Terror*, ed. Robert I. Rotberg, 1–25. Cambridge, Mass., and Washington, D.C.: World Peace Foundation and Brookings Institute Press, 2003.

Rousso, Henry. "Justice, History and Memory in France: Reflections on the Papon Trial." In *Politics and the Past: On Repairing Historical Injustices*, ed. John Torpey, 277–93. New York: Rowman and Littlefield, 2003.

Ryle, John. "Disaster in Darfur." *New York Review of Books* 51, no. 13 (2004): 55–59.

Sachs, Jeffrey D. *The End of Poverty: Economic Possibilities for Our Time*. New York: Penguin Press, 2005.

Salem, Mona. "Darfur Mini-Summit Aims to Ward Off UN Sanctions with African Solution." Agence France-Presse, October 18, 2004.

Sandbrook, Richard. *Closing the Circle: Democratization and Development in Africa*. London: Zed Books, 2001.

Sarkin, Jeremy. "Reparations for Past Wrongs: Using Domestic Courts Around the World, Especially the United States, to Pursue African Human Rights Claims." *International Journal of Legal Information* 32, no. 2 (2004): 426–60.

Schachter, Oscar. "Human Dignity as a Normative Concept." *American Journal of International Law* 77, no. 4 (1983): 848–54.

Schatz, Adam. "The Torture of Algiers." *New York Review of Books* 49, no. 18 (2002): 53–57.

Schofield, Hugh. "Colonial Abuses Haunt France." BBC News, May 16, 2005.

Scholte, Jan Aart. *Globalization: An Introduction*. Basingstoke, UK: Palgrave, 2002.

Scroggins, Deborah. *Emma's War: Love, Betrayal and Death in the Sudan*. London: HarperCollins, 2003.

Sebok, Anthony J. "Slavery, Reparations and Potential Legal Liability: The Hidden Legal Issue Behind the U.N. Racism Conference." September 10, 2001, http://writ.findlaw.com/sebok/20010910.html, accessed August 7, 2007.

Segal, Ronald. *Islam's Black Slaves: The Other Black Diaspora*. New York: Farrar, Straus and Giroux, 2001.

Sen, Amartya. *Development as Freedom*. New York: Alfred A. Knopf, 1999.

Sengupta, Kim. "Mandela Boycotts Bristol's Slavery Commemoration." *The Independent* (London), March 25, 2007.

Shelton, Dinah. "Righting Wrongs: Reparations in the Articles on State Responsibility." *American Journal of International Law* 96, no. 4 (2002): 833–56.

______. "The World of Atonement: Reparations for Historical Injustices." *Miskolc Journal of International Law* 1, no. 2 (2004): 259–89.

Sher, George. "Transgenerational Compensation." *Philosophy and Public Affairs* 33, no. 2 (2005): 181–200.

Shirbon, Estelle. "Insecurity in Nigeria's Oil Delta Here to Stay." Reuters, March 23, 2006.

Shue, Henry. *Basic Rights: Subsistence, Affluence and U.S. Foreign Policy*. Princeton, N.J.: Princeton University Press, 1980.

Shulnitzer, Doron. "Human Dignity: Functions and Meanings." *Global Jurist Topics* 3, no. 3 (2003): 1–21.

Silverstein, Ken. "Official Pariah Sudan Valuable to America's War on Terrorism." *Los Angeles Times*, April 29, 2005.

Skogly, Sigrun I. "Complexities in Human Rights Protection: Actors and Rights Involved in the Ogoni Conflict in Nigeria." *Netherlands Quarterly of Human Rights* 15, no. 1 (1997): 47–60.

"The Slave Labour Program and the Special Responsibility of the Defendant Speer for the Planning and Execution of That Program." Dodd Archives (Nuremberg Trial), University of Connecticut, Box 288, Folder 7349, 1945.

"Slavers." In *Slavers and Privateers: Liverpool Packet No. 5, Collections of Local History Materials*, ed. Fritz Spiegl. Liverpool, UK: Scouse Press, n.d.

Smillie, Ian. "Getting to the Heart of the Matter: Sierra Leone, Diamonds, and Human Security." *Social Justice* 27, no. 4 (2000): 24–31.

Smith, S. D. *Slavery, Family and Gentry Capitalism in the British Atlantic: The World of the Lascelles, 1648–1834*. New York: Cambridge University Press, 2006.

Snow, David A., and Robert D. Benford. "Ideology, Frame Resonance, and Participant Mobilization." *International Social Movement Research* 1 (1988): 197–217.

Snow, David A., E. Burke Rochford, Jr., Steven K. Worden, and Robert D. Benford. "Frame Alignment Processes, Micromobilization, and Movement Participation." *American Sociological Review* 51, no. 4 (1986): 464–81.

Soni, Darshana. "The British and the Benin Bronzes (ARM Information Sheet 4)." African Reparations Movement (ARM), n.d., http://www.arm.arc.co.uk/CRBBinfo4.html, accessed August 7, 2007.

"South Africa Takes on the Giants." *Mail and Guardian* (South Africa), June 21, 2002.

Southern African Development Community. "2007 Extra-Ordinary SADC Summit of Heads of State and Government." Communiqué, Dar-es-Salaam, Tanzania, March 28-29, 2007.
Soyinka, Wole. *The Burden of Memory, the Muse of Forgiveness*. New York: Oxford University Press, 1999.
Spar, Deborah L. "The Spotlight and the Bottom Line: How Multinationals Export Human Rights." *Foreign Affairs* (March–April 1998): 7–12.
Spitzer, Ryan Michael. "The African Holocaust: Should Europe Pay Reparations to Africa for Colonialism and Slavery?" *Vanderbilt Journal of Transnational Law* 35, no. 4 (2002): 1313–47.
Steinhardt, Ralph G. "Corporate Responsibility and the International Law of Human Rights: The New *Lex Mercatoria*." In *Non-State Actors and Human Rights*, ed. Philip Alston, 177–226. New York: Oxford University Press, 2005.
Stiglitz, Joseph E. *Globalization and Its Discontents*. New York: W. W. Norton, 2002.
———. "Odious Rulers, Odious Debt." *Atlantic Monthly* 292, no. 4 (2003): 39–45.
Suberu, Rotimi T. *Federalism and Ethnic Conflict in Nigeria*. Washington, D.C.: United States Institute of Peace Press, 2001.
Sudan Liberation Movement and Sudan Liberation Army (SLM/SLA). "Political Declaration." March 13, 2003, http://www.sudan.net/news/press/postedr/214.shtml, accessed August 12, 2007.
Sullivan, John. "U.N. Security Council Approves Joint Force of Up to 26,000 Peacekeepers for Darfur." *New York Times*, August 1, 2007.
Sullivan, Rory. "NGO Influence on the Human Rights Performance of Companies." *Netherlands Quarterly of Human Rights* 24, no. 3 (2006): 405–31.
Sunder, Katawala. "Zimbabwe and the Commonwealth." *Guardian Unlimited*, March 20, 2002, http://www.guardian.co.uk/theissues/article/0,6512,631253,00.html, accessed August 14, 2007.
"Supplementary Convention on the Abolition of Slavery, the Slave Trade, and Institutions and Practices Similar to Slavery." September 7, 1956, 266 United Nations Treaty Series 3.
Swan, Jon. "The Final Solution in South West Africa." *MHQ: The Quarterly Journal of Military History* 3, no. 4 (1991): 36–55.
Tan, Kok-Chor. "Colonialism, Reparations and Global Justice." In *Reparations: Interdisciplinary Inquiries*, ed. Jon Miller and Rahul Kumar. Oxford, UK: Oxford University Press, 2007.
Tavuchis, Nicholas. *Mea Culpa: A Sociology of Apology and Reconciliation*. Stanford, Calif.: Stanford University Press, 1991.
Taylor, Charles. "The Politics of Recognition." In *Multiculturalism*, ed. Amy Gutmann, 25–74. Princeton, N.J.: Princeton University Press, 1994.
Taylor, Ian. "Conflict in Central Africa: Clandestine Networks and Regional/Global Configurations." *Review of African Political Economy* 30, no. 95 (2003): 45–55.
Taylor, Ian, and Paul Williams. "The Limits of Engagement: British Foreign Policy and the Crisis in Zimbabwe." *International Affairs* 78, no. 3 (2002): 547–65.
Thipanyane, Tseliso. "Current Claims, Regional Experiences, Pressing Problems: Identification of the Salient Issues and Pressing Problems in an African Post-colonial Perspective." In *Human Rights in Development Yearbook 2001: Reparations: Redressing Past Wrongs*, ed. George Ulrich and Louise Krabbe Boserup, 33–56. The Hague, Netherlands: Kluwer Law International, 2003.
Thomas, Neil H. "Land Reform in Zimbabwe." *Third World Quarterly* 24, no. 4 (2003): 691–712.

Thomas, W. I., and D. S. Thomas. *The Child in America: Behavior Problems and Programs*. New York: Johnson Reprint Corporation, 1970 [1928].

Thompson, Dudley. "The Debt Has Not Been Paid, the Accounts Have Not Been Settled." *African Studies Quarterly* 2, no. 4 (1999).

Thompson, Janna. "Apology, Justice, and Respect: A Critical Defense of Political Apology." In *The Age of Apology: The West Faces Its Past,* ed. Mark Gibney, Rhoda E. Howard-Hassmann, Jean-Marc Coicaud, and Niklaus Steiner, 31–44. Philadelphia: University of Pennsylvania Press, 2007.

———. "Reparative Justice and International Relations." Unpublished manuscript, 2007.

———. *Taking Responsibility for the Past: Reparation and Historical Justice*. Cambridge, UK: Polity Press, 2002.

Torpey, John. *Making Whole What Has Been Smashed: On Reparations Politics*. Cambridge, Mass.: Harvard University Press, 2006.

———. "Making Whole What Has Been Smashed: Reflections on Reparations." *Journal of Modern History* 73, no. 2 (2001): 333–58.

———. "Modes of Repair: Reparations and Citizenship at the Dawn of the New Millennium." In *Political Power and Social Theory*, Vol. 18, ed. Diane E. Davis, 207–26. Oxford, UK: Jai Press, 2007.

Transparency International. "Corruption Perceptions Index 2006." Berlin, Germany, 2006.

Uchendu, Victor. "Slaves and Slavery in Igboland, Nigeria." In *Slavery in Africa: Historical and Anthropological Perspectives*, ed. Igor Kopytoff and Suzanne Miers, 121–32. Madison: University of Wisconsin Press, 1977.

United Kingdom Parliament. "Zimbabwe." Column 825W, House of Commons Hansard, written answers, March 2, 2004.

United Nations. "Charter of the United Nations." June 26, 1945.

———. "Sub-Commission Continues Debate on Situation of Human Rights Around the World." United Nations Sub-Commission on the Promotion and Protection of Human Rights, 53rd Session, August 1, 2001.

United Nations Department of Public Information. "Acknowledgement of Past, Compensation Urged by Many Leaders in Continuing Debate at Racism Conference." United Nations, September 2, 2001, http://www.un.org/WCAR/pressreleases/rd-d24.html, accessed August 7, 2007.

———. "General Assembly Seeks to End 15-Year Stalemate over Security Council Reform." United Nations General Assembly, GA/10552, December 11, 2006.

———. "Opening Session of Conference General Debate Focuses on Addressing Legacy of Slavery, Colonialism." United Nations, Plenary RD/D/19, 2nd meeting (AM), September 1, 2001, http://www.un.org/WCAR/pressreleases/rdd19.htm, accessed August 11, 2007.

United Nations Development Programme. *Human Development Report 2006: Beyond Scarcity: Power, Poverty and the Global Water Crisis*. New York: Palgrave Macmillan, 2006.

United Nations General Assembly. "Basic Principles and Guidelines on the Right to a Remedy and Reparations for Victims of Gross Violations of International Human Rights Law and Serious Violations of International Humanitarian Law." A/Res/60/147, December 21, 2005.

———. "Commemoration of the Two-Hundredth Anniversary of the Abolition of the Trans-Atlantic Slave Trade." United Nations General Assembly, 59th Plenary Meeting, Draft Resolution A/61/L.28, November 28, 2006.

———. "Convention on the Prevention and Punishment of the Crime of Genocide." Resolution 260 A (III), December 12, 1948, Entry into force January 12, 1951.

———. "Declaration of the Granting of Independence to Colonial Countries and Peoples." General Assembly Resolution 1514 (XV), December 14, 1960.

———. "Declaration on the Right to Development." Resolution 41/128, December 4, 1986.

———. "International Covenant on Economic, Social and Cultural Rights." Resolution 2200A (XXI), December 16, 1966, Entry into force January 3, 1976.

United Nations News Centre. "14 Elected to UN Human Rights Commission." United Nations News Centre, May 4, 2004, http://www.un.org/apps/news/story.asp?NewsID=10634&Cr=commission&Cr1=rights, accessed August 12, 2007.

United Nations Security Council. "Security Council Resolution 1556." United Nations Security Council, July 30, 2004, http://www.un.org/Docs/journal/asp/ws.asp?m=S/RES/1556(2004), accessed August 12, 2007.

———. "Security Council Resolution 1591." United Nations Security Council, March 29, 2005, http://www.un.org/Docs/journal/asp/ws.asp?m=S/RES/1591(2005), accessed August 12, 2007.

———. "Security Council Resolution 1593." United Nations Security Council, March 31, 2005, http://www.un.org/Docs/journal/asp/ws.asp?m=S/RES/1593(2005), accessed August 12, 2007.

United Nations Statistics Division. "United Nations Common Database." United Nations.

United Nations Sub-Commission on the Promotion and Protection of Human Rights. "Recognition of Responsibility and Reparation for Massive and Flagrant Violations of Human Rights Which Constitute Crimes Against Humanity and Which Took Place During the Period of Slavery of Colonialism and Wars of Conquest." United Nations High Commission for Human Rights, E/CN.4/Sub.2/2001/L/11, August 6, 2001.

U.S. Department of State. "2000 Country Reports on Human Rights Practices." 2000, http://www.state.gov/g/drl/rls/hrrpt/2000/, accessed August 7, 2007.

———. "2005 County Reports on Human Rights Practices." 2005, http://www.state.gov/g/drl/rls/hrrpt/2005/, accessed August 11, 2007.

Van Boven, Theodor. "Study Concerning the Right to Restitution, Compensation and Rehabilitation for Victims of Gross Violations of Human Rights and Fundamental Freedoms." Sub-Commission on Prevention of Discrimination and Protection of Minorities, United Nations Document E.CN.4/sub.2/1993/8, July 2, 1993.

———. "United Nations Strategies to Combat Racism and Racial Discrimination: Past Experiences and Present Perspectives." United Nations Economic and Social Council, E/CN.4/1999/WG.1/BP.7, February 26, 1999.

van den Beld, Ton. "Can Collective Responsibility for Perpetrated Evil Persist over Generations?" *Ethical Theory and Moral Practice* 5, no. 2 (2002): 181–200.

Vernon, Richard. "Against Restitution." *Political Studies* 51, no. 3 (2003): 542–57.

Veseley, Milan. "Cocaine Kings Target Kenya." *African Business*, February 1, 2005: 24–25.

———. "Shadow of the Gun: Who Funds Africa's Wars?" *African Business*, December 1999: 8–11.

Vesperini, Helen. "Kidnappings in Nigeria's Oil Region More Frequent, Bolder." Agence France-Presse, January 25, 2007.

Wade, Abdoulaye. "Sénégal: conférence mondiale contre le racisme, la discrimination raciale, la xénophobie, et l'intolérance qui y est associé, intervention de maître Abdoulaye Wade, président de la République du Sénégal." World Conference Against Racism, Racial Discrimination, Xenophobia, and Related Intolerance, September 1, 2001, Durban, South Africa, http://www.un.org/WCAR/ statements/senegalF.htm, accessed August 7, 2007.

Waldron, Jeremy. "Superseding Historic Injustice." *Ethics* 103, no. 1 (1992): 4–28.

Walvin, James. Public Lecture, Wilfrid Laurier University, Waterloo, Canada, February 8, 2006.

______. "The Colonial Origins of English Wealth: The Harewoods of Yorkshire." *Journal of Caribbean History* 39, no. 1 (2005): 38–53.

"War in Sudan: Don't Forget It." *The Economist*, May 15, 2004.

Warah, Rasna. "Illicit Diamonds: Africa's Curse." *UN Chronicle*, September 2004: 20–21.

Warburg, Gabriel R. "Ideological and Practical Considerations Regarding Slavery in the Mahdist State and the Anglo-Egyptian Sudan: 1881–1918." In *The Ideology of Slavery in Africa*, ed. Paul Lovejoy, 245–69. Beverly Hills, Calif.: Sage Publications, 1981.

Wareham, Roger. "The Popularization of the International Demand for Reparations for African People." In *Should America Pay? Slavery and the Raging Debate in Reparations*, ed. Raymond A. Winbush, 226–36. New York: HarperCollins, 2003.

WCAR NGO Forum. "WCAR NGO Forum Declaration." September 3, 2001, http://www.liberationafrique.org/IMG/article_PDF/article_384.pdf, accessed August 7, 2007.

Weber, Max. *The Protestant Ethic and the Spirit of Capitalism*. New York: Charles Scribner's Sons, 1958.

Weidlich, Brigitte. "Germany Admits 'Genocide' in Namibia, But Says No to Reparations." Agence France-Presse, August 14, 2004.

Welch, Claude E., Jr., *Protecting Human Rights in Africa: Strategies and Roles of Non-Governmental Organizations*. Philadelphia: University of Pennsylvania Press, 1995.

White, Richard Alan. *Breaking the Silence: The Case That Changed the Face of Human Rights*. Washington, D.C.: Georgetown University Press, 2004.

Wieczorek-Zeul, Heidemarie. "Speech at the Commemorations of the 100th Anniversary of the Suppression of the Herero Uprising." Okakarara, Namibia, August 14, 2004, http://www.windhuk.diplo.de/Vertretung/windhuk/en/seite_rede_bmz_engl_okakahandja.html, accessed August 11, 2007.

Williams, Eric. *Capitalism and Slavery*. New York: Capricorn Books, 1966.

Williams, Rowan. "Archbishop's Sermon Given at the Service to Commemorate the 200th Anniversary of the Abolition of the Slave Trade." Archbishop of Canterbury, Westminster Abbey, March 27, 2007, http://www.archbishopofcanterbury.org/sermons_speeches/070327.htm, accessed August 15, 2007.

Wilson, Edward O. *On Human Nature*. New York: Bantam Books, 1978.

Wines, Michael. "In Zimbabwe, Homeless Belie Leader's Claims." *New York Times*, November 13, 2005.

Wiredu, Kwasi. *Cultural Universals and Particulars: An African Perspective*. Bloomington: Indiana University Press, 1996.

World Bank. "Debt Relief." http://web.worldbank.org/WBSITE/EXTERNAL/NEWS/0,,contentMDK:20040942~menuPK:34480~pagePK:34370~theSitePK:4607,00.html, accessed August 11, 2007.

———. "The Enhanced Heavily Indebted Poor Countries Initiative." http://www.worldbank.org/hipc/about/hipcbr/hipcbr.htm, accessed August 11, 2007.

———. *Global Development Finance: The Development Potential of Surging Capital Flows*. Washington, D.C.: World Bank, 2006.

———. "The HIPC Debt Initiative." World Bank, 2007, http://www.worldbank.org/hipc/about/hipcbr/hipcbr.htm, accessed August 11, 2007.

———. "World Bank Development Indicators." World Bank, 2007.

———. "World Bank Implements Multilateral Debt Relief Initiative." Press Release No. 2006/504/WB, June 29, 2006.

World Conference Against Racism, Racial Discrimination, Xenophobia, and Related Intolerance. "Declaration." 2001, http://www.unhchr.ch/pdf/Durban.pdf, accessed August 7, 2007.

World Conference Against Racism, Racial Discrimination, Xenophobia, and Related Intolerance Preparatory Committee. "Report of the Regional Conference for Africa." United Nations, January 22–24, 2001, A/CONF.189/PC.2/8, http://www.unhchr.ch/Huridocda/Huridoca.nsf/(Symbol)/A.CONF.89.PC.2.8.En?Opendocument, accessed August 7, 2007.

World Public Opinion: Global Public Opinion on International Affairs. "Poll of 8 African Nations." 2003–2004, http://www.worldpublicopinion.org/incl/printable_version.php?pnt=138, accessed August 11, 2007.

World Trade Organization. "Times Series Statistical Database." 2007.

York, Geoffrey. "China Keeps Bad Company." *Globe and Mail* (Canada), March 4, 2006.

Zuma, Jacob. "Statement to the Plenary by Deputy President Jacob Zuma." World Conference Against Racism, Racial Discrimination, Xenophobia, and Related Intolerance, Durban, South Africa, September 2, 2001, http://www.un.org/WCAR/ statements/sthafricaE.htm, accessed August 11, 2007.

Zwanenburg, Marten. "The Van Boven/Bassiouni Principles: An Appraisal." *Netherlands Quarterly of Human Rights* 24, no. 4 (2006): 641–68.

Index

Acknowledgments

Although I am the senior researcher for this book and wrote it alone, I was ably assisted en route by Anthony Lombardo. I first encountered Anthony when he was registered in an undergraduate course on comparative genocide studies that I was teaching at McMaster University in Hamilton, Ontario, Canada. In early 2001, Anthony became my research assistant and worked for me until the end of August 2004. He assisted in drafting the interview questionnaire, he organized the interviews, and he conducted fourteen interviews on his own in addition to accompanying me to many more. He wrote his master's thesis on this topic.[1] Parts of his thesis are merged, with his permission, into this book. In addition, he was sequentially senior author, equal coauthor, and junior author of three journal articles and book chapters we published on our research.[2] I am very grateful to Anthony for his efficiency and organizational skills, for his interest in and intellectual input to this topic, and for his companionship, especially on research trips. He turned an arduous task into an enjoyable one.

Anthony Lombardo and I were also very ably assisted by two other students. Kristina Bergeron, then a doctoral candidate in political science at McMaster University, conducted fourteen of the twenty-three interviews in French. Dan Milisavjlevic, then an undergraduate student at McMaster,

[1]Anthony Peter Lombardo, "Reparations to Africa: Examining the African Viewpoint," master's thesis, McMaster University, August 2004.

[2]Anthony P. Lombardo and Rhoda E. Howard-Hassmann, "Africans on Reparations: An Analysis of Elite and Activist Opinion," *Canadian Journal of African Studies* 39, no. 3, 2005, 517–48; Rhoda E. Howard-Hassmann and Anthony P. Lombardo, "Words Require Action: African Elite Opinion About Apologies from the West," in *The Age of Apology: Facing Up to the Past*, ed. Mark Gibney, Rhoda E. Howard-Hassmann, Jean-Mark Coicaud, and Niklaus Steiner, 216–28 (Philadelphia: University of Pennsylvania Press, 2007); Rhoda E. Howard-Hassmann and Anthony P. Lombardo, "Framing Reparations Claims: Differences Between the African and Jewish Social Movements for Reparations," *African Studies Review* 50, no. 1 (2007): 27–48.

conducted library and Internet research for us from September 2002 to September 2004.

At Wilfrid Laurier University in Waterloo, Ontario, I was assisted at various stages by Keith Calow, Gregory Eady, James Gaede, Michael Lisetto-Smith, and Leslie Tallyn. I am most grateful to all of them for their hard work, their patience, and their sense of humor. I am especially grateful to Michael, who provided much technical assistance, as well as patiently dealing with my many requests for references. I am also very grateful to Keith, Gregory, and Leslie for critiquing entire drafts of the manuscript. Keith provided both historical and legal insight, as well as a rigorous eye for grammatical errors. Gregory doubted and argued with almost everything I wrote, yet was completely dedicated to this project, especially to all the detail that many academics would prefer to ignore. He had the arduous task of checking for the accuracy of every footnote, reference, and quotation in this book. Melany Banks also read parts of the manuscript and provided very provocative comments.

In 2000 I mentioned to Cees Flinterman, then director of the Netherlands Institute of Human Rights, that I was developing an interest in reparations to Africa. At his recommendation, George Ulrich invited me to attend a seminar on reparations in Copenhagen in 2001. I am grateful to both Cees and George for their encouragement. John Torpey's interest in the paper I wrote for the Copenhagen seminar encouraged me to go on to write the book. In 2001 Professor Laura Dickinson of the University of Connecticut Law School permitted me to audit her course on human rights and retrospective justice, where I obtained some grounding in the international law of reparations. Abdullahi An-Na'im's early skepticism about reparations, conveyed to me in a café in Amsterdam in 2000, encouraged me to decide whether I agreed with him. At later stages of this project, comments on draft chapters from Ugo Nwokegi, Paul Lovejoy, John Leband, and Bonny Ibhawoh, all historians of Africa, were very helpful. Useful also were the comments from audience members at various professional venues.

My beloved friend, Grace Stewart, read the entire draft, making suggestions from her dual perspective as an interested citizen and a teacher of English.

Research funds for this book were supplied by the Social Sciences and Humanities Research Council of Canada, through an individual grant and a grant to the Major Collaborative Research Initiative (MCRI) on Globalization and Autonomy based at McMaster University; I am very grateful for the assistance and support of William Coleman, director of the MCRI project. I am also grateful to Wilfrid Laurier University, which nominated me for the Canada Research Chair I presently hold and which afforded me much time to devote to this project. Wendy Webb, assistant to the chair, kept budgets, paychecks, conference travel, and much else under control during the last four years of this project, always with great efficiency, warmth, and sincere interest in the book's progress. My research assistants and I are all very grateful to her.

I thank Barry Riddell, Editor of the *Canadian Journal of African Studies*, for permission to reprint in this book an article in the CJAS.[3] I am also most grateful to Bert Lockwood, Peter Agree, and the staff at the University of Pennsylvania Press for their interest in and dedication to this book.

As always, my husband, Peter McCabe, has suffered through this project with me, patiently putting up with my many absences from home, as well as with many dinner conversations he might well have preferred not to have.

Finally, I thank all those Africans who so kindly gave us their time and discussed the questions of reparations to Africa with us. I will always remember them for their openness, their warmth, and their trust in this project. To hear the stories of so many people was a moving and humbling experience.

As is customary, I must note that all errors and misinterpretations in this volume are my responsibility, and no one else's.

Rhoda E. Howard-Hassmann

[3]Rhoda E. Howard-Hassmann, "Reparations for the Slave Trade: Rhetoric, Law, History and Political Realities," *Canadian Journal of African Studies* 41, no 3, 2007.